SUBVERSIVE
Scriptures

::

revolutionary
readings of the
christian bible
in latin america

edited and translated by
Leif E. Vaage

TRINITY PRESS INTERNATIONAL
Valley Forge, Pennsylvania

Trinity Press International, P.O. Box 851, Valley Forge, PA 19482-0851

Trinity Press International is a division of
the Morehouse Publishing Group

Library of Congress Cataloging-in-Publication Data

Subversive scriptures : revolutionary readings of the Christian Bible
in Latin America / edited by Leif E. Vaage.
    p. cm.
    Essays in this volume originally appeared in various issues of
"Revista de interpretación bíblica latinoamericana".
    Includes bibliographical references and index.
    ISBN 1-56338-200-8 (pbk. : alk. paper)
    1. Bible – Criticism, interpretation, etc. 2. Sociology,
Christian – Latin America. 3. Poor – Biblical teaching.
4. Liberation theology. I. Vaage, Leif E.
BS517.S83 1997
220.6 – dc21   96-54056
                                          CIP

Printed in the United States of America

97 98 99 00 01 02   10 9 8 7 6 5 4 3 2 1

SUBVERSIVE
Scriptures

....

Contents

....

v

Preface

....

The preface to a book is typically the last chance the author has to name the work s/he meant to write, if only the words and evidence at hand had turned out differently. In the present instance, however, the author of the preface did not write the book as such. Nonetheless, as editor and translator, I am responsible for its final design and the specific wording in English (plus the introductory essay). All inadequacies in these regards should, therefore, be ascribed to myself.

It is, moreover, as editor and translator I who have characterized the essays in this book as revolutionary readings of the Christian Bible in Latin America. The category of "revolutionary reading" is explained in the introduction. But, perhaps, it is also important to clarify why the essays are explicitly identified on the title page as readings of the Christian Bible.

At one level, of course, such a reference is simply a way of acknowledging that the authors of the essays in this book are all active members of specific Christian communities in Latin America and, therefore, read biblical texts from a Christian perspective. That they do so, however, is not because they have somehow been unable to achieve the "higher" level of a more "disinterested" or "objective" or "otherworldly" (e.g., ancient Near Eastern or Mediterranean) exposition that would thereby be "properly" historical.

For the authors of the essays in this book to read biblical texts from a Christian perspective is, in one sense, merely to be honest about the fact that the larger context of interest and concern to which their specific labor of textual interpretation belongs happens to be one that is pervasively — and, perhaps, from a North Atlantic point of view one should add: still — Christian in its basic symbolic texture. In other words, the reading of biblical texts in this book from a Christian perspective makes thereby no exclusive claims about how these texts must universally be understood beyond exemplifying the right and need of (biblical) scholars to practice the scientific work of textual description and discursive formation as part of a particular people's ongoing effort to have as satisfying a life together as possible. In the case of contemporary Latin America, it is the ongoing struggle to survive and to have a future by the routinely Christian poor majorities under the press of a dominant social order that is otherwise also (still) often characterized as representing Christian civilization that first makes the reading of biblical texts from a Christian perspective in this book a historically meaningful endeavor.

There is, moreover, at least one other reason for describing the essays in this book as readings of the Christian Bible. Because they are all plainly written within the social framework of Latin American Christian communities, the essays in this book do not pretend to interpret the textual memory of other related religious traditions, e.g., the Jewish "Bible" or Tanach, in this region. It would be very interesting to be able to compare revolutionary readings of the Christian Bible with similar contemporary interpretations of the Tanach in Latin America. The present book, however, precisely as a collection of readings of the Christian Bible, cannot and does not pretend to know what such a "cross-cultural" conversation would finally entail. At the same time, the present book seeks to invite, precisely through its self-conscious partiality, this very sort of wider interested conversation.

As stated in the introduction to the book, a primary reason for translating the essays assembled here into English has been to make a representative selection of the work of the Latin American biblical scholars associated with the *Journal of Latin American Biblical Interpretation (Revista de Interpretación Bíblica Latinoamericana)* available to those who otherwise might not be able to read the essays in their original Spanish or Portuguese. To edit and translate these writings into English has furthermore been a way for me personally to reciprocate in some measure for the generous *acogida* and *compañerismo* I have enjoyed over the past decade as an otherwise perhaps unlikely member of the same group. My thanks especially to Milton Schwantes for facilitating this possibility on more than one occasion.

It is also important to acknowledge the support I received, at a crucial point in the production of the manuscript, from the Centre for the Study of Religion in Canada (Prof. Roger Hutchinson, director) at Emmanuel College of Victoria University in the University of Toronto. The indicated support made it possible for me to be aided by Ms. Susan Campbell, who, among other things, has made sure that all the biblical references in the essays correspond to reality. Thanks are also due to Ms. Susanne Abbuhl who did what she could to compensate for my ignorance in Akkadian and Sumerian. Finally, Jorge Pixley responded promptly to a last-minute call for aid: *te agradezco, compa'*.

LEIF E. VAAGE

5 April 1997
Oslo, Norway

Contributors

Marcelo de Barros Souza is a Brazilian Benedictine monk: Caixa Postal 5, 76600-970 Goiás-GO, Brazil.

Carlos Bravo Gallardo is a Mexican Jesuit priest: Centro de Reflexión Teológica, Apdo. Postal 21-272, 04100 Coyoacán, México D.F., Mexico.

José Cárdenas Pallares is a Catholic parish priest: Capilla del Rosario, Lázaro Cárdenas 140, 28869 Salahua, Colima, Mexico.

José Severino Croatto is a former Catholic priest of the order of St. Vincent of Paul and now teaches at the major Protestant "union" theological seminary in Buenos Aires: Instituto Superior Evangélico de Estudios Teológicos, Camacuá 252, 1406 Buenos Aires, Argentina.

Carlos A. Dreher is a Brazilian Lutheran pastor working in support of popular biblical interpretation in the south of Brazil: Caixa Postal 1051 Scharlau 93.121-970 São Leopoldo-RS, Brazil.

Sandro Gallazzi is an Italian-born Catholic biblical scholar living and working among the poor in the northern Brazilian city of Macapá: Caixa Postal 12, 68906-970 Macapá-AP, Brazil.

Raúl Humberto Lugo Rodríguez is a Catholic parish priest: Casa Cural, 97820 Tecoh, Yucatán, Mexico.

Dagoberto Ramírez Fernández is a Chilean Methodist minister and former dean of the Evangelical Theological Community (Comunidad Teológica Evangélica) in Santiago: Argomedo 40, Casilla Correos 386-V, Santiago 21, Chile.

Milton Schwantes is a Brazilian Lutheran parish pastor and director of graduate studies in religion at the Methodist University in São Paulo: rua Faria de Lemos 84, Picanço, Guarulhos 07094-200-SP, Brazil.

Leif E. Vaage is a Lutheran pastor teaching at Emmanuel College of the Toronto School of Theology and Victoria University in the University of Toronto as well as the Biblical-Theological Community (Comunidad Bíblico-Teológica) in Lima, Peru: 75 Queen's Park Crescent East, Toronto, Ontario M5S 1K7 Canada.

Alicia Winters is a Presbyterian minister and former rector of the Presbyterian seminary in Barranquilla: Seminario Presbiteriano Reformado, Apartado Aereo 6078, Barranquilla, Colombia.

Introduction

LEIF E. VAAGE

....

I

In 1492, Christopher Columbus was still confused. He could not be sure what exactly the land mass was that had finally emerged in the open sea thirty-three days sailing due west of the Canary Islands.[1] A decade later, however, when the major portion of the extant form of the exegetical work *Libro de las profecías* was being compiled by Columbus, a much clearer vision of the precise significance of his now three voyages of "discovery" had been achieved — at least, in Columbus's eyes.[2]

In the *Libro de las profecías,* Columbus makes clear, principally on the basis of the biblical evidence assembled in this work, the reasons for his continuing conviction that the colonial project and concomitant search for readily exploitable wealth inaugurated by his enterprise of the Indies was, in short, divinely ordained. Indeed, Columbus believed that the entire undertaking, including Columbus himself, belonged to and fulfilled the eschatological events prefigured in the Christian Bible and needing to occur before the world soon came to its inevitable end.[3]

The exegetical elaboration of this enhanced self-understanding

---

1. See Cristóbal Colón, *Diario de a bordo,* ed. Luis Arranz (Madrid: Historia 16, 1985), 88ff.; also Consuelo Varela, "Introducción," in idem, ed., *Cristóbal Colón: Los cuatro viajes. Testamento* (Madrid: Alianza, 1986), 13.

2. See *The Libro de las profecías of Christopher Columbus,* trans. and commentary by Delno C. West and August Kling (Gainesville: University of Florida Press, 1991); also Juan Fernández Valverde, ed., *Cristóbal Colón: Libro de las Profecías* (Madrid: Alianza, 1992).

3. For the "messianic" character of Columbus's self-understanding, see Juan Gil, "Colón y la Casa Santa," *Historiografía y Bibliografía Americanistas* 21 (1977): 125–35; Alain Milhou, *Colón y su mentalidad mesiánica en el ambiente franciscanista español* (Valladolid: Museo de Colón, 1983); Pauline Moffitt Watts, "Prophecy and Discovery: On the Spiritual Origins of Christopher Columbus' 'Enterprise of the Indies,' " *American Historical Review* 90 (1985): 73–102.

in the *Libro de las profecías* was undoubtedly aided and abetted by the fact that at the end of his third voyage, when Columbus was compelled to return to Spain in chains, and before the mariner's fourth and final departure for the new world, his reputation and accomplishments were being severely attacked. Nevertheless, as Hector Avalos writes:

> Years before he sailed to the New World [for the first time], Columbus had begun to link biblical prophecy with a voyage to the Orient. In particular, Columbus' notes to Aeneas Sylvius Piccolomini's (Pope Pius II) *Historia rerum ubique gestarum* reveal that he had already begun to think systematically about biblical prophecy around 1481.[4]

The link, in other words, between a certain reading of the Christian Bible and the "venture capital" maritime expedition proposed and conducted by Columbus was not due merely to the fabled sea captain's advancing age, growing infirmity, or a side-effect of later successive disappointments. Nor should the interest shown by Columbus in the Christian Bible's witness to his personal destiny be construed as simply an aberrant feature of an otherwise exemplary modern scientific sensibility. Rather, the Christian Bible was plainly and profoundly one of the primary sources whence the inspiration and specific instructions for the execution of Columbus's thoroughly commercial and equally religious enterprise of the Indies was originally derived.

Spanish colonization of the new world began with Columbus's "discovery" of it.[5] So did the court intrigue and imperial account-

---

4. See Hector Avalos, "Columbus as Biblical Exegete: A Study of the *Libro de las profecías*," in Bryan F. Le Beau and Menachem Mor, eds., *Religion in the Age of Exploration: The Case of Spain and New Spain* (Omaha, Neb.: Creighton University Press, 1996), 59–80, esp. 59. See also idem, "The Biblical Sources of Columbus' *Libro de las Profecías*," *Traditio* 49 (1994): 331–35.

5. See the entry in Las Casas's abstract of Columbus's log-book during the first voyage for Thursday, 11 October 1492, which also treats the following day when Columbus initially disembarked on (as most scholars believe) Watlings Island: "Immediately they saw naked people, and the admiral went ashore in the armed boat, and Martín Alonso Pinzón and Vicente Yañez, his brother, who was captain of the *Niña*. The admiral brought out the royal standard, and the captains went with two banners of the Green Cross, which the admiral flew on all the ships as a flag, with an F and a Y, and over each letter their crown.... The admiral called the two captains and the others who had landed, and Rodrigo de Escobedo, secretary of the whole fleet, and Rodrigo Sánchez de Segovia, and said that they should bear wit-

ing that now endeavored to maneuver for profit the ever more westward tilting Spanish ship of state. As part of the early waves of crown-appointed governors, fortune-seekers and settlers, book-keepers and servants, *conquistadores* and *encomenderos,* among whom could be counted one initially quite undistinguished Bartolomé de Las Casas,[6] there also arrived members of the Christian clergy and of different religious communities.[7] From virtually the beginning, therefore, the institutions and traditions of European Christianity, including the Christian Bible, served to undergird

ness and testimony how he, before them all, took possession of the island, as in fact he did, for the King and Queen, his Sovereigns, making the declarations which are required.... What follows are the actual words of the admiral, in his book of his first voyage and discovery of these Indies. 'I,' he says, 'in order that they might feel great amity toward us, because I knew that they were a people to be delivered and converted to our holy faith rather by love than by force, gave to some among them some red caps and some glass beads, which they hung round their necks, and many other things of little value.... They should be good servants [*servidores*] and of quick intelligence, since I see that they very soon say all that is said to them, and I believe that they would easily be made Christians, for it appeared to me that they had no creed. Our Lord willing, at the time of my departure I will bring back six of them to Your Highnesses, that they may learn to talk. I saw no beast of any kind in this island, except parrots.' All these are the words of the admiral." See Cecil Jane, trans., *The Journal of Christopher Columbus,* with an appendix by R. A. Skelton (New York: Bonanza, 1989; orig. pub. 1960), 23–24; also Varela, *Los cuatro viajes,* 61–63.

6. See Pedro Borges, *Quién era Bartolomé de Las Casas* (Madrid: Rialp, 1990), 21–51; also Manuel Giménez Fernández, "Fray Bartolomé de Las Casas: A Biographical Sketch," in Juan Friede and Benjamin Keen, eds., *Bartolomé de Las Casas in History: Toward an Understanding of the Man and His Work* (DeKalb, Ill.: Northern Illinois University Press, 1971), 70–73; Henry Raup Wagner with the collaboration of Helen Rand Parish, *The Life and Writings of Bartolomé de las Casas* (Albuquerque: University of New Mexico Press, 1967), 4–7. More recently, Parish suggests that there is essential continuity in character between the early and the later Las Casas: see her "Introduction: Las Casas' Spirituality — The Three Crises," in idem, ed., *Bartolomé de las Casas: The Only Way,* trans. Francis Patrick Sullivan, S.J. (New York and Mahwah, N.J.: Paulist, 1992), 11–19. Reference is regularly made to new evidence collected in a forthcoming work by Parish: *Las Casas: The Untold Story* (Berkeley: University of California Press).

7. On Columbus's first voyage, there were neither religious nor women. See Varela, *Los cuatro viajes,* 12; Alicia B. Gould, *Nueva lista documentada de los tripulantes de Colón en 1492* (Madrid: Real Academia de la Historia, 1984). As part of Columbus's second voyage, however, which began 25 September 1493, and in response to the papal bull (4 May 1493) by Alexander VI granting the Spanish Catholic monarchs both jurisdiction over the newly discovered lands and responsibility for their proper Christian indoctrination, a number of different religious are known to have accompanied the still buoyant mariner. See Bartolomé de Las Casas, *Historia de las Indias,* bk. 1, chap. 81, in *Obras completas* (Madrid: Alianza, 1994), 4:842–44; also Varela, *Los cuatro viajes,* 20–21. For the two clerics on Columbus's third voyage, see Juan Gil, "El rol del tercer viaje colombino," *Historiografía y Bibliografía Americanista* 29 (1985): 83–110.

the reigning economic interests of material exploitation and the palliative needs of the colonizers and their sometimes troubled consciences.

At the same time, the Christian Bible, together with other official representations of the Christian Truth, began to be read in a critical and counter-colonial fashion by some of the same Christian clergy and religious. In his recent magnum opus on the theological legacy of Las Casas, Gustavo Gutiérrez has highlighted the little group of Dominican friars, headed by Pedro de Córdoba, who arrived in Hispaniola (modern-day Haiti/Dominican Republic) in 1510.[8] Also extremely important, of course, is the figure of Las Casas himself. Soon after his conversion — or "prophetic call" — in 1514 to the cause of the "indios," Las Casas too became a Dominican friar.[9] And throughout his long ensuing life (1481–1566), Las Casas remained an outspoken critic of the economic, political, and ecclesiastical culture of the developing "new" world.

Although, like all late mediaeval Catholic theologians and jurists, Las Casas used other sources of authority and argument besides the Christian Bible in his many memorials, disputations, and historical writings,[10] the Christian Bible minimally became, in Las Casas's hands, a further means of active resistance to the prevailing new world disorder and a promising instrument of its proposed subversion.[11] Las Casas's alternate reading of the Chris-

---

8. See Gustavo Gutiérrez, *Las Casas: In Search of the Poor of Jesus Christ,* trans. Robert R. Barr (Maryknoll, N.Y.: Orbis, 1993), 27–44; further, Parish, *The Only Way,* 196–200; *Fray Pedro de Córdoba, O.P.: Tercer Seminario "Grandes figuras de la evangelización de América"* (Santo Domingo: Universidad Católica, 1992); also Wagner, *Life and Writings of Casas,* 7–11.

9. Las Casas was already ordained a priest in Rome at the end of February 1507, but did not celebrate his first mass until 1510 when finally back again on Hispaniola. See Parish, "Introduction," 15–16; Gutiérrez, *Las Casas,* 482 n. 2. The precise nature of Las Casas's "change of heart" in 1514 has been predictably debated: see Gutiérrez, *Las Casas,* 45–48, esp. 48; 482 n. 1 and 483 n. 8. Las Casas was subsequently named bishop of Chiapas (after refusing to be appointed bishop of Cuzco), but was then unable to exercise his episcopal office due to local opposition.

10. See Bruno Rech, "Las Casas und die Autoritäten seiner Geschichtsschreibung," *Jahrbuch für Geschichte von Staat, Wirtschaft und Gesellschaft Lateinamerikas* 16 (1979): 13–52; idem, "Las Casas und die Kirchenväter," *Jahrbuch für Geschichte von Staat, Wirtschaft und Gesellschaft Lateinamerikas* 17 (1980): 1–47; idem, "Bartolomé de Las Casas und Aristoteles," *Jahrbuch für Geschichte von Staat, Wirtschaft und Gesellschaft Lateinamerikas* 22 (1985): 39–68.

11. For Las Casas, such subversion meant a new evangelization. To my knowl-

tian Bible testifies, therefore, to the always multivalent meaning of the book in Latin America; and, more importantly, to the coeval tradition of a resisting reading of the Christian Bible in these lands from the beginning of the *conquista*.[12] The Christian Bible has thus always been, in Latin America, a site of partisan debate about the legitimacy of prevailing cultural practices and, most importantly, a locus of enduring utopian demand for the proper — better — construction of a new world order.[13] The essays published in this book represent a contemporary instance of the same insistence, on the basis of biblical reasoning, that a more satisfying social arrangement be developed in this place.

II

The following texts speak for themselves. The main reason for translating them into English has been to make a representative selection of the work of the Latin American biblical scholars associated with the *Journal of Latin American Biblical Interpretation* (*Revista de Interpretación Bíblica Latinoamericana: RIBLA*) available to everyone who might have an interest in such writings, but is unable to read Spanish or Portuguese. It is especially hoped that those who share this group of Christian scholars' explicit commitment to the ongoing struggle for a more abundant life by socially oppressed and marginalized persons, especially in the "two-thirds" world, might thereby be enabled to encounter one another more easily and profoundly.

---

edge — and surprise — a full study of Las Casas's particular approach to biblical interpretation has yet to be undertaken or published. See Bruno Rech, "Las Casas und das Alten Testament," *Jahrbuch für Geschichte von Staat, Wirtschaft und Gesellschaft Lateinamerikas* 18 (1981): 1–30. I have not yet been able to see an article by A. Esponera, "El punto de partida de la hermenéutica bíblica de Bartolomé de Las Casas (1559–1564)," *Actas del VI Simposio de Teología Histórica* (1990): 379–98.

12. By "resisting reading," I do not mean primarily the individual reader's ability to interpret a text "against the grain" of authorial intention or of the final editorial arrangement of the text, but rather the practice of reading in order to resist concurrent uses of the text that diminish one's own life and that of others.

13. For another instance of a resisting reading of biblical tradition in Latin America, see Rudy V. Busto, " 'It Really Resembled an Earthly Paradise': Reading Motolinía's Account of the *Caída de nuestros primeros padres*," *Biblical Interpretation* 2 (1994): 111–37.

The essays in this book develop the modern practice of scientific "historical-critical" exegesis of the Bible in terms of the current "critical-historical" situation of the exegete and his or her particular people. The work of biblical interpretation is thus understood and conducted as one of the many social activities that either help to construct or serve to diminish the local life of particular human communities. In the case of the authors of the essays in this book, the indicated communities would be especially those of the postmodern neoliberal Latin American poor. The rigor of properly scientific exegesis is thereby made a function of the rigors of contemporary social struggle.

This is not just or even especially a matter of ideology.[14] Rather, at stake is principally the vocational question of what it means to be a biblical scholar or, more broadly, an intellectual and, more specifically, a "humanist" in the context of contemporary transnational — "globalized" — late capitalist culture. As Edward W. Said has written so aptly regarding North America:

> So pervasive has the professionalization of intellectual life [including academic biblical scholarship] become that the sense of vocation, as Julien Benda described it for the intellectual, has been almost swallowed up. . . . As for intellectuals whose charge includes values and principles — literary, philosophical, historical [biblical] specialists — the American [and Canadian] university, with its munificence, utopian sanctuary, and remarkable diversity, has defanged them. Jargons of an almost unimaginable rebarbativeness dominate their styles. Cults like postmodernism, discourse analysis, New Historicism, deconstruction, neopragmatism transport them into the country of the blue; an astonishing sense of weightlessness with regard to the gravity of history and individual responsibility fritters away attention to public matters, and to public discourse. The result is a kind of floundering about that is most dispiriting to witness, even as the society as a whole drifts without direction or coherence.[15]

---

14. The following writings are obviously not innocent of specific ideological commitments. But these commitments are by no means uniform nor have they been purposefully systematized.

15. See Edward W. Said, *Culture and Imperialism* (New York: Vintage Books, 1994; orig. pub. 1993), 303.

Said refers to:

...a steadily more powerful cult of professional expertise, whose main ideological burden stipulates that social, political, and class-based commitments should be subsumed under the professional disciplines, so that if you are a professional scholar of [biblical] literature or critic of culture, all your affiliations with the real world are subordinate to your professing in those fields. Similarly, you are responsible not so much to an audience in your community or society, as to and for your corporate guild of fellow experts, your department of specialization, your discipline.[16]

It is over against such highly specialized — in Said's terms, narrowly "professional" — models of the proper practice of North Atlantic academic biblical scholarship that the approach to reading the Christian book exemplified by the following essays is offered as a "revolutionary" alternative. I use the word "revolutionary," if only because the authors of these writings have chosen to perform their traditionally elite form of scribal service explicitly and concretely in alliance with specific projects of popular community-based social construction.[17]

The scholars whose work is published here interpret the Christian Bible as a mode of participation in their impoverished peoples' ongoing sociopolitical resistance to the many forms of contemporary cultural and economic domination accompanying the state of postcolonialism. At the same time and through the same activity, the same scholars seek to contribute to the same peoples' concomitant efforts to enjoy a life together in the time remaining.[18]

---

16. See Said, *Culture and Imperialism*, 321. This is not the place to elaborate such insights by undertaking, for example, a critical analysis of the corporate life and current management of professional organizations like the burgeoning Society of Biblical Literature or the American Academy of Religion, though it is certain that numerous aspects of the intellectual labor of the membership of both groups would easily fall within the governing strictures identified by Said. One need only review the published program of the annual meetings of the same scholarly conglomerates and witness their orchestrated rituals of "career" advancement, bearing these paragraphs by Said in mind, in order to recognize their lamentable truth.

17. "Popular" is used here and throughout the book with the meaning "of the *populus*" or *pueblo* or common people.

18. For a critical discussion of "Death and the Time That Is Left" as an adequate framework for understanding life together with the Other, viz., others, see Edith

In the words of Milton Schwantes, a member and coordinator of this merry band of *biblistas,* the work of *RIBLA:*

> locates itself within the experiences of faith and struggle of different local communities and churches. The Bible is being recovered by the people. The pain, utopian vision, and poetry of the poor have become, through the life of the communities, decisive hermeneutical mediations for the reading of the Bible in Latin America and the Caribbean. This journal [*RIBLA*] has as its context of origin the afflicted life of our peoples and their tenacious resistance for the sake of an existence characterized by dignity and justice.[19]

This approach to biblical scholarship may be compared to the theory of "organic" intellectuals developed by Antonio Gramsci. As Gramsci wrote to his sister-in-law Tatiana Schucht from prison in 1931, "I greatly extend the notion of intellectuals and I do not restrict myself to the current notion which refers [only] to great intellectuals."[20] More specifically, Gramsci sought to include other social and technical forms of critical analysis and creative invention within the sacred precinct of human intellection.[21]

At the same time, Gramsci distinguished between what he calls "traditional" versus "organic" intellectuals. Roughly speaking, the "traditional" intellectual in Gramsci's analysis would be equivalent to Said's "professional" academic, while Gramsci's "organic"

Wyschogrod, *Saints and Postmodernism: Revisioning Moral Philosophy* (Chicago and London: University of Chicago Press, 1990), 64–65.

19. This statement is found on the back cover of the journal: *RIBLA* "se sitúa dentro de las experiencias de fe y de lucha de las comunidades y de las iglesias. La Biblia está siendo rescatada por el pueblo. Los dolores, utopías y poesías de los pobres se tornaron, a través de las comunidades, mediaciones hermenéuticas decisivas para la lectura bíblica en América Latina y en el Caribe. Esta Revista [de Interpretación Bíblica Latinoamericana] tiene como cuna, la vida sufrida de nuestros pueblos y su tenaz resistencia en dirección de una existencia digna y justa."

20. See Antonio Gramsci, *Lettere dal carcere,* ed. Sergio Caprioglio and Elsa Fubini (Turin: Einaudi, 1965), 481. The translation is taken from David Forgacs, ed., *An Antonio Gramsci Reader: Selected Writings, 1916–1935* (New York: Schocken, 1988), 300.

21. See, e.g., Gramsci, "La formazione degli intellettuali," in Carlo Salinari and Mario Spinella, eds. *Il pensiero di Gramsci,* 2d ed. (Rome: Riuniti, 1972), 84–85; Forgacs, *Gramsci Reader,* 321: "There is no human activity from which every form of intellectual participation can be excluded: *homo faber* cannot be separated from *homo sapiens.*"

intellectual is defined precisely and properly by paying "attention to public matters, and to public discourse."

In the case of Gramsci, however, as is true for the scholars associated with *RIBLA,* the work of an "organic" intellectual is public precisely and only because it is partial or bound up with very particular and thus also politically defined processes of social struggle and transformation. In other words, an "organic" intellectual necessarily aids, through whatever form of muscular-nervous-cerebral labor that defines his or her daily toil, in the organization and construction or articulation of an actual social movement, viz., class.

This is what it means to say above that the "pain, utopian vision, and poetry of the poor have become, through the life of the communities, decisive hermeneutical mediations for the reading of the Bible in Latin America and the Caribbean." The scholarly work appearing through *RIBLA* is self-consciously produced in concert with the recurring bodily agonies and forced creative search for a better life, in every sense of the word, of the impoverished under-classes in Latin America. Such a reading of the Christian Bible seeks thereby to promote a more effective self-understanding and greater sense of the possibilities for social transformation on the part of these same people.

The purpose is not to "popularize" or to "apply" the results of a less colloquial, nontheological, more "purely scientific," or thoroughly historical approach to biblical research. No, the task of organic biblical scholarship, as practiced by the scholars associated with *RIBLA,* is to enact the intellectual labor of "searching the Scriptures" in accordance with the needs and aspirations of the concrete social groups for whose particular benefit such work exists, and whose larger life — in the case of the poor in Latin America, a life predominantly marked by the struggle for survival, dignity, and justice — is otherwise the encompassing matrix of the scholar's own mediated existence.

Thus, the practice itself of scholarly research, including the definition of appropriate problems and the determination or rules of acceptable evidence and persuasive argument, is put in question. It seems, therefore, not inappropriate once again to speak of the essays in this book as representing a "revolutionary" style of biblical scholarship.

III

Some hermeneutical observations about the status of the biblical text reflected in the following essays may help to clarify further what is meant here by revolutionary reading. I hasten to remark that these observations do not rehearse any methodological formula or theoretical creed self-consciously adopted by the group in question. Rather, the indicated observations are merely an effort on my part to articulate what I perceive to be some of the underlying and collective assumptions shaping the approach to reading the Christian Bible registered in these essays, as well as an attempt to render more explicit a few of the possible methodological implications of these same assumptions.[22]

Like the different lands in which the various scholars associated with *RIBLA* live and work, the biblical text is read first as yet another instance of occupied territory. The text is not viewed as in any way the neutral site of a transcendent meaning or a privileged zone reserved for the more or less free play of indeterminate signifiers. Rather, the text is seen as one of a number of contextually defined cultural spaces within contemporary Latin American civilization, where the self-understanding of specific subjects, including their will to hope and power to create, is shaped through the contestatory process of negotiation known as reading.

This self-understanding and the practices of interpretation that inform it thereby either serve to support and elaborate existing mechanisms of social control and subjugation, or they help to encourage and develop counter-cultural projects of liberation and the enjoyment of a more abundant life here and now. At stake in biblical interpretation is thus how best or properly to draw the map of social-historical reality that the text as a site for specifying self-understanding and corporate identity appears to articulate.

The text as literary legacy constitutes a landscape of worked remains, whose significance the reader must ascribe and in which

---

22. See, further, José Severino Croatto, *Biblical Hermeneutics: Toward a Theory of Reading as the Production of Meaning* (Maryknoll, N.Y.: Orbis, 1987); Carlos Mesters, *Defenseless Flower: A New Reading of the Bible* (Maryknoll, N.Y.: Orbis, 1989); Kjell Nordstokke, *Ordet Tar Bolig: Om folkelig bibellesning* (Oslo: Verbum, 1994); Christopher Rowland and Mark Corner, *Liberating Exegesis: The Challenge of Liberation Theology to Biblical Studies* (London: SPCK, 1990); Thomas Schmeller, *Befreiungstheologische Lektüre des Neuen Testaments in Lateinamerika* (Münster: Aschendorff, 1994).

ascription a particular stance or orientation to the same social-historical reality is defined. Interpretation of the Bible becomes revolutionary reading when the positions taken by the readers vis-à-vis the text stand self-consciously in a different place from the prevailing official or hegemonic interpretations of this reality.[23] Revolutionary reading requires the biblical interpreter both to appropriate the text and to resist it. This relationship to the text might seem to be just another version of the standard modern hermeneutical dialectic described, for example, by Paul Ricoeur as the enduring tension between a hermeneutics of suspicion or distanciation and one of identification or second naïveté.[24] Undoubtedly, there will be many points of shared perception and concern here. And if it should prove to be the case that the theoretical framework implicit in the reading practice of the scholars associated with *RIBLA* were, for all intents and purposes, the same as someone else's already published point of view, so much the better. Allies are always welcome! For revolutionary reading, at least as practiced in this book, is not primarily a matter of procedural or categorical novelty, but rather of discursive adequacy and insistence on the primacy of life-enhancing knowledge in the face of hostile social realities that surround and continue to threaten the well-being of the biblical interpreter and his or her particular people.

Methodologically, therefore, the key consideration is always to

---

23. We might compare this process to the not dissimilar problem of assessing the significance of the modern land of Israel. The soil itself shows signs of human habitation by many different groups of people over multiple millennia. But how the stratified archeological record of this history, literally embedded in the ground, should now be read is, of course, liable to various competing interpretations, all of which are furthermore immediately part of larger, ever more strident discourses about to whom this land — as a whole or in parts — should presently belong. Without pretending here to adjudicate these different claims, interpretation of the Bible in Latin America presents a similar scenario. It is the conviction of the scholars whose work is represented in this book that, like the soil of Palestine, the text of the Bible contains still-legible traces of specific liberating projects pertinent to the contemporary struggle for existence and thriving by the many marginalized and oppressed peoples of Latin America. These traces, however, are preserved and perceptible, both in the antecedent composition-history of the Bible and in its subsequent reception-history, always together with other signs of suppression and the domination of particular interests.

24. See, e.g., Paul Ricoeur, *Hermeneutics and the Human Sciences: Essays on Language, Action and Interpretation,* ed., trans., and introduced by John B. Thompson (Cambridge: Cambridge University Press; Paris: Maison des Sciences de l'Homme, 1981), esp. 131–44 ("The Hermeneutical Function of Distanciation") and 145–64 ("What Is a Text? Explanation and Understanding").

bear in mind the social context — both past and present — in which the biblical text is read, if only because the text has no meaning per se apart from the specific social context in which the practice of reading alone makes the text mean something. There is no way to interpret just the text itself or even somehow to begin the process of interpretation first with the text without thereby overtly or implicitly suppressing debate about the context — both original and contemporary — in which the discerned meaning-effect of the text will be deemed to realize itself.

Revolutionary reading thus starts self-consciously with the life situation of the reader, whence the problems and questions to which the biblical text should help to formulate a response. Likewise, historical interpretation of the text is first of all attentive to the concrete setting in which the text was originally written and read as a specific form of cultural intervention. Both writing and reading are thereby understood as modes of social action.

Jorge Pixley, commenting on an analysis of the uses of the Christian Bible in the theology of Gustavo Gutiérrez,[25] speaks of a "militant biblical scholarship." Pixley writes:

> Militant biblical scholarship means (1) the work of a scholar who puts his or her research after her or his life of Christian discipleship. This seems self-evident when one takes the Bible as the Word of God addressed to the poor; i.e., not in the first place to the scholar. If the scholar is to understand the Word, he or she must listen to the reception it has among the poor to whom it is addressed.
>
> (2) It also means scholarship which includes an analysis of the structural causes of the poverty which the interpreter struggles to eradicate. Bartolomé [de Las Casas] knew that the cause of the destruction of the Indies which he denounced was the "*encomienda*," the institution which allowed Christians to use the labor of the native peoples in "exchange" for giving them the Christian gospel. It was not enough to call *encomenderos* to conversion; the institution which was causing the death of whole peoples had to be abolished. To this Bartolomé devoted more than half of his long life. Poverty

---

25. See Jeffrey S. Siker, "Uses of the Bible in the Theology of Gustavo Gutiérrez: Liberating Scriptures of the Poor," *Biblical Interpretation* 4 (1996): 40–71.

today also has its roots in the structure of modern capitalism and cannot be fought without confronting these institutions. The scholar is bound as a Christian disciple to show love for his or her neighbor by joining this struggle. (3) This scholarship is exercised in the context of a community of faith. Gustavo [Gutiérrez] understands that the Word of God is addressed to communities first and foremost. A scholar who is disengaged from believing communities loses sensitivity to that Word. And (4) this scholarship will always be at the service of the political cause of the organized poor in their struggle to overthrow the structures that generate poverty. The scholar cannot be indifferent to the fact that his or her teaching has one or another effect on the struggle. His or her scholarship has been placed at the service of the poor, along with the rest of the life of the scholar.[26]

It is plain that, for Pixley as for the other scholars in this book, there are properly Christian reasons why a Christian biblical scholar would want to read the Christian Bible in this militant manner. For Christian readers of this book, these reasons may suffice.

At the same time, such reasons admit representation and merit reflection on other registers as well. One need not share Christian convictions in order to appreciate the theoretical import of Pixley's initial insistence that scholarly research always follows social life, and that the particular life of the individual researcher is always bound up directly with a very specific set of contextual conflicts and cultural concerns. As summarized broadly by Pixley, these conflicts and concerns would currently (still) be those of endemic poverty and the structures of late capitalism.

There is no such thing, in other words, as "free" inquiry, if, by such an expression, one were to suggest a disinterested or, more pointedly, apolitical approach to biblical study. Revolutionary reading begins with the acknowledgment and, indeed, embraces the fact that every reader of any text first belongs profoundly to the life-world that holds both together; hence also Pixley's

---

26. Jorge Pixley, "Toward a Militant Biblical Scholarship," *Biblical Interpretation* 4 (1996): 74.

third characterization of a militant Christian biblical scholarship as "exercised in the context of a community of faith." What makes for revolutionary reading is, next, the reading subject's self-conscious placement within the popular process. By popular process is meant precisely those different persons, practices, and cultural projects that remain unrecognized and often are opposed by existing official, viz., hegemonic regimes. In the case of Latin America, these persons, practices, and cultural projects are also plainly those of the majority of the population (hence their description as "popular"). And because, in Latin America, the same persons, practices, and cultural projects have been so pervasively conditioned by a politics of aristocratic domination and an economics of opportunistic exploitation, they may not incorrectly be characterized in terms of the problem of poverty.[27]

Again, there are specifically Christian reasons why a Christian biblical scholar would choose to read the Christian Bible from such a position; there may be other reasons as well. Though plainly important, such motivations are nevertheless *not* what principally distinguishes the practice of revolutionary reading and a militant biblical scholarship from other forms of interpretation. Rather, revolutionary reading may be identified most properly by its overtly pragmatic goals: by its fruits, in other words, it will be known. By pragmatic, I mean, specifically, the programmatic endeavor *through an explicit reconfiguration of the textual memory of a people* to bring about concrete and collective social change.

Thus, Pixley stresses as the final feature of such a reading practice: "scholarship...at the service of the political cause of the organized poor in their struggle to overthrow the structures that generate poverty." Flatly paraphrased, this would mean: biblical scholarship at the service of real-life social group construction, including the development of local and larger community structures,

---

27. Such a characterization is ultimately insufficient, however, if and when it leads one to imagine and to treat the poor person as somehow just an instance of the "economic" problem of poverty. In fact, it only makes sense to speak of such a problem after acknowledging first all the ways in which the poor person is not simply defined by what he or she "lacks" in material possessions. It is precisely because the poor person is first of all equally and wholly human in every emotive and artistic and relational sense of this word that it then becomes plainly impossible to justify his or her a priori or a fortiori exclusion from any of the basic material benefits of contemporary social life.

pointed political commentary, concrete proposals for specific acts of decision-making as well as the broader realignment of power relations and their related mechanisms.

This is biblical scholarship, not just with a social conscience but as part of the struggle to construct a consciousness capable of challenging and conquering the multiple forces arrayed against the perduring and thriving of its historical subjects. Such an approach to reading, refusing to be contained within the magisterial walls of the professional university or absorbed by the institutional interests of conventional social structures, thus becomes, in Latin America and conceivably elsewhere, one of the resources specifically made available to those social sectors whose life is otherwise presently and increasingly defined precisely by the scarcity, if not the total absence, of all such life-support systems.[28]

IV

The present book is not supposed to be merely a collection of different articles on diverse texts by various Latin American biblical scholars. The correlation between the essays suggested by the book's table of contents is intentional. There is a particular logic that links together here scholarly interest in the political economy of ancient Israel and early Christianity, the critique of institutionalized (sacralized) social violence, and the pastoral nurturing of a spirituality of resistance.

This self-conscious combination of the elements of a critical-historical analysis of material culture, emancipatory ethical concern, and traditional religious life in the reading of biblical texts is not, in my experience, a usual or sometimes even conceivable occurrence any longer in the current standardized academic arrangement of North Atlantic theoretical reflection and research in religion. Far from assuming, however, that such a situation some-

---

28. Manifest in this approach to biblical scholarship is thus self-conscious participation, from the same specific realm of intellectual and social endeavor, in larger efforts to provide endangered peoples with sufficient "nourishment" for survival and their flourishing. In the present instance, the preferred "food" is a certain form of knowledge, produced not principally for the sake of deeper theoretical insight or ever more brilliant states of enlightenment, but in order to maintain the requisite level of *ánimo* or will to live of persons otherwise routinely facing steady loss and humiliation.

how signifies the more fully developed rigor or clarity of "our" properly scientific and/or theological procedures, I would suggest that, at least in the case of biblical scholarship, the diminished discursive range of such normalized thinking about religion registers, instead, merely a profound impoverishment and restriction of the subject's proper social relevance.

At least, part of the wager that informs my presentation of the essays in this book as exemplary of a revolutionary reading of the Christian Bible is my sense that their authors' evident desire to engage directly and integrally the full range of chthonic social life surrounding such study may provide a model for reimagining how professional academic biblical scholars in North America and Europe might also choose to do their own regional work.

At the beginning of this essay, I briefly invoked the biblical interpretation of both Christopher Columbus and Bartolomé de Las Casas essentially as symbols of the exegetical territory mapped out and still traversed by scholarly and other readings of the Christian Bible in Latin America. A more detailed cultural history of the Christian Bible in Latin America — one exceeding the level of suggestive anecdote and promising probe — yet remains to be written.[29] Such a history is required in order to provide the comprehensive cultural framework within which the specific discourse of the essays in this book might hope to be adequately situated.

In the absence of such a history and beyond the broad patterns of reading represented by Columbus and Las Casas, there are at least two additional factors, undoubtedly obvious but important to recall, that further help to in form the immediate cultural context out of which the following essays have been written. The first

---

29. Indeed, the very components of such a narrative must still be gathered in a comprehensive fashion. Though devoted primarily to "books of fiction," the virtual absence of any discussion of the Bible is nonetheless telling, it seems to me, in Irving A. Leonard, *Books of the Brave: Being an Account of Books and of Men in the Spanish Conquest and Settlement of the Sixteenth-Century New World* (New York: Gordian, 1964; orig. pub. 1949). For my own first foray into this field, see Leif E. Vaage, "Text, Context, Conquest, Quest: The Bible and Social Struggle in Latin America," *Society of Biblical Literature 1991 Seminar Papers,* vol. 30, ed. Eugene H. Lovering, Jr. (Atlanta: Scholars Press, 1991), 357–65. What I am calling a "cultural history" of the Christian Bible in Latin America, Heikki Räisänen has described, in similarly undone terms, as the "effective history" of the book. See Heikki Räisänen, "The 'Effective' History of the Bible: A Challenge to Biblical Scholarship," *Scottish Journal of Theology* 45 (1992): 303–24.

of these factors is the eventual arrival and increasing presence of Protestantism in Latin America, especially after the wars of independence at the beginning of the nineteenth century and, even more so, in the twentieth century after World War II. The other factor is the Second Vatican Council (1963–65) and its ensuing regional (episcopal) interpretations, which allowed and promoted within the bounds of the Roman Catholic Church a variety of pastoral innovations and experiments. In Latin America, one effect of this process was to allow for a much greater degree of lay and popular participation in the task of interpreting the contemporary contextual significance of the Christian tradition.

Though by no means ubiquitous or uniform, the character of Latin American biblical scholarship produced in the light of these developments and reflected in the following essays has been to manifest both a certain ecumenical vision of the textual terrain under its gaze and explicit contact especially with the life of particular "base Christian communities." By "ecumenical vision," I mean a certain loosening of the classic confessional lenses through which the Christian Bible has been made to have specific theological meanings in North America and Europe since the Protestant Reformation. The same expression also describes the concomitant desire to make the shared social situation of an otherwise diverse readership in Latin America the fundamental frame of reference for energetic debate about the particular history (or histories) that the Christian Bible might be held to recall and the import of this recollection.

"Base Christian communities" is the term for a great variety of well-known — or, at least, well-publicized and often sensationalized — grassroots efforts throughout Latin America to construct, for economic and other reasons, informal or alternate modes of engaging in Christian worship, Bible study and parish and neighborhood ministry.[30] To differing degrees, reflecting distinct

---

30. For a famous example of biblical interpretation in such a context, see Ernesto Cardenal, *The Gospel in Solentiname,* trans. Donald D. Walsh, 4 vols. (Maryknoll, N.Y.: Orbis, 1976–82); also Carlos Mesters, "The Use of the Bible in Christian Communities of the Common People," in Norman K. Gottwald, ed., *The Bible and Liberation: Political and Social Hermeneutics,* 2d ed. (Maryknoll, N.Y.: Orbis, 1983), 119–33.

circumstances, the same efforts have also entailed participation in the defense of human rights, the promotion of programs of social change, and sometimes direct political engagement.[31]

V

The essays in this book plainly reflect the diverse and evolving tradition of critical social thought and ecclesial praxis known in Latin America as liberation theology. At the same time, the same essays represent an effort to extend the textual basis on which Latin American liberation theology has typically laid claim to biblical testimony in the hope that Latin American liberation theology and, more importantly, the pastoral and political practices aligned with it might thereby be enriched, refined, and continually "reformed."

The first set of essays in the book deals with the problem of debt, specifically, the foreign debt and, by extension, the fact of money itself as a source of social ill. Why these issues would be of interest and importance to persons living and working in Latin America presumably requires no further explanation. Together the first set of essays suggests both the general possibility of and some of the particular insights to be gained by rewriting the history of Israel in terms of the problem of chronic indebtedness and recurring economic exploitation.

The first essay, "Solomon and the Workers," by Carlos A. Dreher discusses the human cost of developing the Israelite empire associated with the figure of Solomon. An attentive reading of the canonical narratives of ancient Israel's monarchical period discloses both the accelerating tributary process whereby the fledgling kingdom's foreign debt load was increased and the ever more constrictive mechanisms employed to extract the labor and goods that alone could serve as payment from the limited material resources of the land and common people. The eventual separation of the northern tribes from Judah and Jerusalem in the south after the death of Solomon as recounted in 1 Kings 12 finally appears to be

---

31. See, e.g., Sergio Torres and John Eagleson, eds., *The Challenge of Basic Christian Communities: Papers from the International Ecumenical Congress of Theology, February 20–March 2, 1980, São Paulo, Brazil,* trans. John Drury (Maryknoll, N.Y.: Orbis, 1981); Kjell Nordstokke, *De Fattiges Kirke* (Oslo: Kirkelig Kulturverksted, 1987), esp. 85–105; Margaret Hebblethwaite, *Base Communities: An Introduction* (Mahwah, N.J.: Paulist, 1994).

not an act of infidelity or the result of rival ambition, but the sign of an unheeded plea for relief from the harsh servitude and heavy yoke imposed by Solomon's imperial pretensions.

In the next essay, "The Debt in Nehemiah's Social Reform: A Study of Nehemiah 5:1–19," we consider a text from the post-exilic period when Israel's erstwhile efforts at empire had long since proven in vain. José Severino Croatto reviews the description in Neh 5:1–19 of the attempt by Nehemiah, the governor of Judah, to intervene constructively in the deteriorated social situation of the land due to excessive debt loads. Croatto seeks to show, through a specific type of structural analysis, how this seldom-read text — at first glance "not very promising, perhaps because of where it is located (in a little used work) or because its content appears to be exhausted in a specific event of the past" — nonetheless provides, in the end, not a little food for thought, including the prospect of an already proven solution to current problems of impossible debt repayment.[32]

The third essay, "The Kingdom of God or the Kingdom of Money," by José Cárdenas Pallares rehearses the critique by Jesus and the early Christian communities that came after him of contemporary economic practices and their dehumanizing consequences under Roman rule in the name of God's reign. At stake in this reading, however, is primarily the meaning of Christian faith in present-day Latin America, marked as the continent is "by savage *exploitation* and its child, extreme poverty." It is especially the vision of Luke and of one of his sources: the "Greek-speaking community before Matthew and Luke," or Q, that Cárdenas Pallares investigates. His conclusions, both exegetical and herme-neutical, are challengingly, perhaps even prophetically, unnuanced. For example: "Question: Who, then, should pay the foreign debt? Answer: Those who caused it and have taken advantage of it."

The fourth and final essay in this section is an examination of the economic perspective of the book of Revelation, especially chapter 18. In "The Judgment of God on the Multinationals: Revelation 18," Dagoberto Ramírez Fernández first contextualizes his analysis, both at the level of the current situation of the eccle-

---

32. An appendix, "Debt and Justice in Texts of the Ancient Near East," helps further to contextualize historically Croatto's proposed reading of Neh 5:1–19.

sial reader and at the level of the literary structure of the book of Revelation itself. Then, in an extended discussion of the three successive theophanies recorded in chapter 18, Ramírez Fernández underscores how the fall of Babylon depicted here consistently betrays an economic factor. Most noteworthy, perhaps, and discussed at some length by Ramírez Fernández is the list of products and merchandise enumerated in Rev 18:11–13. In the end, the book of Revelation appears to critique not only the (Roman) imperial project of political domination, but also the economic project of production, exploitation, and commercialization that sustains and helps to consolidate such a rule.

The book's second group of essays addresses the problem of sacrifice: specifically, the unacceptable social costs — especially so because they are unacceptable to God — of a sacrificial theology. Behind this concern is, first of all, outrage and chagrin at the willingness and insistence of modern governments and other powerful political-economic institutions like the International Monetary Fund and the World Bank that the cost of so-called "necessary structural adjustments" to support the current new world order be paid for especially by the poor and un(der)privileged. The continuing production of wealth or "steady growth" for certain sectors of the global economy is kept viable only by making everyone else — i.e., those without a choice — "tighten up their belts" another notch or two.

The result is routinely higher rates of infant and premature mortality, arrested childhood and adolescent development, and certainly dramatic reductions in whatever precarious level of personal and social well-being might previously have been enjoyed. Political strategies of greater efficiency and flexibility or a more effective "squeezing" of the juice out of the orange amount, in practice, to programmatic social strangulation. The logic is eminently sacrificial: It is deemed better for the nation (of the wealthy and their beneficiaries) that one (ever larger underclass) suffer and die than that the whole nation (of late capitalist culture) should perish.

The first essay in this section, " 'Do Not Extend Your Hand against the Child,' " by Milton Schwantes discusses the well-known story in Genesis 22 of Abraham's required — then interrupted — sacrifice of Isaac, Abraham's son of promise. But Schwantes considers the story not as if this were an isolated incident, not as if such a horrifying test ever occurred, whether in life or in the narrative world of the Bible, apart from an enveloping system of literary connections and social-group oppositions. Most notably, the divinely frustrated sacrifice of Isaac — by Abraham — is read by Schwantes together with the preceding description in Genesis 21 of the divinely frustrated condemnation of Hagar and Ishmael — by Abraham — to certain death in the desert.

According to Schwantes, in these discrete but related traditions — multigenerational in their ongoing formation, most likely postexilic in their final formulation — God (Yahweh) is revealed to be, first and foremost, a protector of threatened life. From the very beginning of his accompaniment of the particular people whose history is recounted here, God (Yahweh) does not want and therefore intervenes directly to prevent the death of even the most minor of victims. "This Yahweh of the poor," writes Schwantes in conclusion, "is the God that deserves to be 'feared' and 'obeyed.' "

The other article in the middle group of essays, " 'Worthless Is the Fat of Whole Burnt Offerings': A Critique of the Sacrifice of the Second Temple," by Sandro Gallazzi initially summarizes the social system created by the second temple cult of sacrifice. Gallazzi then provides a reading of the story of Judith (8–16) as a further instance — beyond the writings of Job, Jonah, Ruth, Song of Songs, and Ecclesiastes — of critical and effective resistance to the cultural logic or habits of heart and mind established through the same prescribed practices.

Furthermore, Gallazzi stresses the fact that in the book of Judith it is notably a woman who resists the oppressor most valiantly and effectively. Moreover, this resistance is achieved precisely through those aspects of Judith's person that are most "womanly." In other words, Israel's liberation from the oppressor Holofernes is achieved in the book of Judith through what were otherwise the quintessential signs of a (putatively) greater state of (potential) alienation from the sacred center of postexilic Israel. Thus Gallazzi seeks to link the critique of sacrificial thinking and its related social practices with the gender-specific consequences of such a system.[33]

---

33. In this regard, the article by Gallazzi anticipates the immediately subsequent essay by Alicia Winters, in which the courageous resistance of another woman, Rizpah, to the Davidic monarchy's sacrificial politics of ethnic cleansing — the surviving line of Saul — is similarly highlighted.

The third and final series of essays in the book discusses the spirituality of resistance that the authors find manifest throughout the Christian Bible.

The first of these essays, "The Subversive Memory of a Woman: 2 Samuel 21:1–14," by Alicia Winters discusses the frequently overlooked and otherwise regularly misconstrued action of Rizpah, the erstwhile concubine of Saul, keeping watch in the desert beside the corpses of her and Saul's last two surviving sons, whom David had just handed over to be executed by the Gibeonites.

Winters seeks to show how Rizpah's vigil on behalf of the memory of her sons — not unlike the well-known and extended protest on behalf of their own "disappeared" children by the mothers of the Plaza de Mayo in Buenos Aires during Argentina's recent "dirty [civil] war" — is more than just the act of a mother's pained heart. In, with, and under the tears and lamentation of maternal loss may be seen a more broadly based social determination not to allow the brutality of official political expediency and genocidal cleansing to rule unimpeded.

The second article, by Marcelo de Barros Souza, "The Powerful Prayer of Lament and the Resistance of the People of God: A Particular Approach to the Book of Psalms," treats the psalms of lament as instances of "powerful prayer" or "strong words." With such utterances the poor and the oppressed, both in ancient Israel and in contemporary Brazil, give voice to their conviction that their current plight is neither deserved nor insoluble.

Specifically revealed in the psalms' unflagging practice of steady lamentation — not unlike what shines forth in the constant and insistent complaining of children to their parents — is the underlying assurance that the one to whom they cry is both capable of and committed to restoring their well-being, viz., salvation. In his discussion of the psalms, de Barros Souza reflects and, indeed, self-consciously reads the psalms out of the experience, both ritual and political, of the numerous "base Christian communities" that have developed and continue to evolve in Brazil. The article by de Barros Souza thus explores and demonstrates how the biblical text, like the human heart, often has "reasons that reason does not know."

The third article, by Carlos Bravo Gallardo, "Matthew: Good News for the Persecuted Poor," endeavors to provide "a comprehensive key to the interpretation of the gospel of Matthew," specifically as "a gospel of consolation, of christological revelation regarding the identity of Jesus, of ecclesiological revelation about the true Israel, and of ethical revelation about what constitutes the true justice granting access to the kingdom." The beatitudes at the beginning of the Sermon on the Mount are read as "a hermeneutical key for discovering the internal structure and central thread of the gospel." It was the "restructuring process" that challenged the identity of both synagogue and church alike after the destruction of Jerusalem which, according to Bravo Gallardo, the gospel of Matthew works to resolve through the construction of a new self-understanding: "In this way, the gospel of Matthew seeks to reground their hope and their ability to resist in this situation."

Finally, the fourth article, by Raúl Humberto Lugo Rodríguez, "'Wait for the Day of God's Coming and Do What You Can to Hasten It....' (2 Pet 3:12): The Non-Pauline Letters as Resistance Literature," attempts to reread a series of texts (in detail: 1 Pet 2:13–17 and 2 Peter 3) that otherwise have usually been seen to be more exemplary of cultural "accommodation" than as counter-cultural writings. Part of the argument entails a proper understanding of the literary genre of paraenesis, which Lugo Rodríguez eventually describes as the early Christian community's "practical creed" or effort to specify and underscore the importance of orthopraxis. Thus, it is by no means a step-down or misstep on the ladder of early Christian theology, according to Lugo Rodríguez, to find in these letters a principal focus on mundane problems, such as how to achieve a sustainable relationship — or, at least, not to provoke fruitless antagonism — with the governing authorities, and the development of a utopian vision or representation of eschatological hope that does not require instant gratification in order to be valid. Indeed, it is precisely in the successful management of these and similar everyday "small accomplishments," especially in the face of liberal capitalism's rejuvenated worldwide rampage, that Lugo Rodríguez finally comes to identify the spirituality of resistance in Latin American popular communities most worthy of our esteem.

1

Solomon and the Workers

CARLOS A. DREHER

The Israelite Tributary Monarchy

The Israelite monarchy had already developed under Saul within the framework of the tributary mode of production. Under the pretext of an efficient defense against the Philistines, the need was created for a small full-time army. The first "state" was probably never really more than this: a king and a small group of mercenaries.

The surplus production required to guarantee the maintenance of this emergent state was achieved through the technological revolution represented by the introduction of the ox as a plough animal in Israelite agriculture. This new technology supplied the kingdom with its economic support. Conditions thereby existed for a level of production exceeding the needs of the community and permitting the development of a nonproductive elite that could take up the service of war. A contract between the king and the people determined the "right of the king" (see 1 Sam 8:11–17, despite discussion about its actual historical context), according to which, in exchange for defending the people (see 1 Sam 8:20), the monarch acquired the right to exact tribute in the form of products or a levy.

The extraction of tribute, however, does not appear to have been imposed very heavily on the Israelite population at the beginning. Rather, the impoverished peasants (see 1 Sam 22:2; 25:10) probably became poor originally as a result of the internal economic imbalance caused by the enrichment of those who owned oxen and who succeeded in progressively marginalizing those in their debt. The still small apparatus of the state managed to

25

maintain itself through the looting of vanquished enemies, despite the restrictions established by cultic prescriptions (see 1 Samuel 13–15).

These conditions continued under David as well. His expansionist policies made it possible for him to maintain the royal court with the booty of war and with the tribute extracted from conquered peoples (2 Sam 8:1–14; 10:19; 12:26–31). Such a situation served to restrict the extraction of tribute from the Israelites themselves, at the same time that it justified the existence of the monarchy. The need for a king seemed plain and compelling, as long as the army was active. The service rendered by the monarch was not put in doubt.

Nevertheless, it would be naive to think that the extraction of tribute was not already imposed on the Israelites at this time as well. After all, among the functionaries of the Davidic court there was an administrator of forced labor (2 Sam 20:24). Thus, the practice of imposing levies already existed. At the same time, the census taken by David (2 Sam 24:1–9; 1 Chr 21:1–6) that was so strongly criticized must certainly have had the objective of extracting tribute from the population under his rule.

Still, nothing here was as severe and heavy as what would subsequently be imposed, especially on the northern tribes, during the reign of Solomon. The protest of these tribes against the heavy yoke and harsh servitude imposed on them (1 Kgs 12:4 and passim), which eventually led them to separate, is evidence of this. Such excessive extraction of tribute most certainly had its origin in the foreign debt created by Solomon through his intense building projects, including the construction of the temple and the promotion of international trade at the time.

The Reign of Solomon

As his own name seems to indicate, Solomon ascended to the throne during a period of peace. His father, David, put an end to whatever threat his neighbors might have represented to Israel and Judah. He subdued them all, annexing the territories of some, reducing others to vassalage, becoming occasionally their king as, for example, in the case of Ammon. He assumed sovereignty over all Syria-Palestine, the successor to the Egyptian empire in that region.

The absence of war put the tributary system in a state of crisis. The need for the development of the monarchy no longer existed. Without a specific service to render to the population, the king found himself in a situation where his right to tribute would appear questionable. What could be done in order to maintain power?

A new service, different from the previous one, reestablished the contractual relationship between the king and the people. In exchange for the right to tribute, Solomon would offer a set of public works involving religion. The temple in Jerusalem emerged as the ideological cover for the tributary system. The king would build a house for God; the people would guarantee the labor and the upkeep of the court.

In this way, the work of building the temple sustained the Solomonic monarchy. While he was building the house of God, Solomon would have time to strengthen his own royal army, an efficient mechanism of repression that guaranteed the exploitation of those under him.

It is interesting to note that the Deuteronomist, who otherwise, as a rule, is so eager to highlight the king's mistakes, himself falls into this trap. The temple obscures his critique. Only after the inauguration of the sanctuary does the Deuteronomist succeed in indicating Solomon's idolatry, the consequence of his multiple marriages to foreign women (see 1 Kgs 11:1–8). But only thus far. The biblical text does not curtail the praise of Solomon's wisdom and the greatness of his building activities, with the possible exception of the first two chapters of 1 Kings, where mention is made of the summary execution or exile of opponents to the new king.

Apart from this initial resistance, as well as some problems with the other peoples subdued by David (1 Kgs 11:14–25), Solomon seems to have been successful with his stratagems. He does not appear to have encountered popular opposition during his government, *pace* the frustrated attempt at revolt undertaken by Jeroboam (1 Kgs 11:26–28, 40). Although the text of 1 Kings 12 shows us that the tribute imposed on the people, mainly the tribes in the north, was seen as very harsh, the contractual relationship between the king and the people was respected during the reign of Solomon. The temple and the army guaranteed his throne. Only Solomon's death provided the occasion for a new contract to be proposed to his successor by the Israelites. Normally, the death of a king destabilizes the system.

Solomon the Builder

The building activities of Solomon were not restricted to the temple. The biblical text tells us about the construction of innumerable other works. For example, 1 Kgs 7:2–7 refers to the "Forest of Lebanon" house, which was considerably larger than the temple itself and furnished with a portico of columns (v. 6) and the throne room (v. 7). Moreover, the same chapter informs us of the construction of a royal dwelling and a house for the daughter of Pharaoh, one of the wives of Solomon (v. 8).

These buildings were made of stone, with the inside covered in cedar wood. Regarding the stones, we are told that they were cut, made to measure and joined together. The enormous stones used for the foundation measured between 8 and 10 cubits, that is, between 3.6 and 4.5 meters in length (v. 10).

To finish the work of the temple, seven years were needed (1 Kgs 6:38); for the palaces, thirteen years (1 Kgs 7:1). A total of twenty years to complete these buildings is also attested in 1 Kgs 9:10.

The work, however, did not stop there. According to 1 Kgs 9:15ff., Solomon also built terraces — this must be the meaning of the word *milo'*. He built the walls of Jerusalem. He restored and fortified different cities, modernizing their walls and gates. He also organized cities of provision, in order to keep there the goods received as tribute. Furthermore, with the introduction of war chariots into his army, he made provision for different cities, spread throughout his territory, to be equipped with horse stables and harnesses for the troops.

1 Kgs 9:26–28 informs us at the same time of the construction of a fleet of merchant ships in the Gulf of Acaba. Finally, 1 Kgs 11:7–8 gives an account of the construction of pagan sanctuaries, intended for the cults practiced by the women of the harem. But aside from the fact that such information is debatable regarding its historicity whenever its presence in the text is due to the Deuteronomist, it is not possible for us to establish if these were major sanctuaries or merely minor altars surrounded by a sacred perimeter.

The number of works, the length of time required for their construction, and the size of the stones all allow us to imagine the immense amount of human labor required to build such splendor. For the people, however, the large works meant sacrifice. Within the tributary system, such works put in play the practice of a levy: forced labor, imposed on underlings or their children, to which the king had a right by contract.

We cannot detail here the practice of a levy during the reign of Solomon. A reading of 1 Kgs 5:27–32 (the Hebrew text) is sufficient, in any case, to satisfy our curiosity. Possible doubts about whether or not such a levy was actually imposed on the Israelites themselves, possibly suggested by the information given in 1 Kgs 9:20–23 (where only foreigners are subject to forced labor, while the Israelites simply form part of the army), collapse in the face of the rebellion described in 1 Kings 12. The "heavy yoke" and "harsh servitude" referred to in this chapter (vv. 4, 9, 10, 11, 14) plainly reveal the facts. It was the severeness of the levy that led to the demand for its reduction and the subsequent division of the Davidic reign into two kingdoms.

Much more important, however, is something else. The building activities promoted by Solomon created a series of needs unable to be met solely through the work and production of the people of the land. The temple and other buildings required materials and skilled labor found only elsewhere. Here, then, is the beginning of the Israelite foreign debt.

Imports, Debts, and Extraction of Tribute

From the very beginning, Hiram of Tyre was a notable person in Solomon's building program. King of the important Phoenician port city of Tyre, Hiram held the monopoly on cedar wood. He also had the skilled labor needed for what Solomon planned to do (see 1 Kgs 5:32; 7:13f.; but also already 2 Sam 5:11!). In addition, Hiram was involved in international commerce, made possible by his knowledge of navigation. This knowledge would be transferred to the king of Israel (see 1 Kgs 9:26–28; 10:11, 22).

Once construction of the temple was projected, Hiram entered on the scene (1 Kgs 5:15ff.). It was to Hiram that Solomon sent messengers, letting him know firsthand about the undertaking. At the same time, Solomon solicited from Hiram the necessary raw material, namely, cedars of Lebanon (v. 20). Further on, we are informed that Hiram would also provide Solomon with cypress wood (vv. 22, 24) in the amount that Solomon wanted.

It is interesting that Solomon also asks for Sidonian workers, that is, Phoenicians, servants of Hiram, to cut the wood, because Solomon does not have the people who know how to do this (v. 6). Solomon's servants would accompany the task; nonetheless, it is clear that Phoenician specialists were necessary; their salary would be paid by the king of Israel.

The context seems to indicate that the wood was destined solely for construction of the temple. But subsequent texts inform us that more cedar wood became necessary for other buildings including the "Forest of Lebanon" house (1 Kgs 7:2ff.) and the throne room (1 Kgs 7:7), most likely an annex to the previous building. Besides these works, the other ones referred to in this chapter (1 Kings 7) would also have surely used the same material.

It is difficult to determine how much wood Solomon imported from Lebanon. But he certainly paid dearly for it and for the specialized Phoenician aid. 1 Kgs 5:23 indicates that the contract between the two monarchs anticipated that Solomon would make provision for the house of Hiram as the latter desired in exchange for these goods and technical knowledge. Such provision of products from the countryside was the only source of Israelite wealth. There was no other way to pay for the imports. From the peasants' land would be taken most of the tribute needed to pay the foreign debt.

The biblical text gives an account of the debt payments. According to 1 Kgs 5:25 [5:11], Hiram received 20,000 measures of wheat and 20 measures of ground olive oil every year. There is no information to indicate how many years the payment continued. It is debated how much a measure entailed. Interpretation varies between 350 and 450 liters. If we take the median value of 400 liters, we obtain a figure of 8,000,000 (!) liters of wheat and 8,000 liters of oil given annually to the king of Tyre.

The small amount of oil, in comparison with the 8,000,000 liters of wheat, is noteworthy. The Greek translations later make two types of effort to correct the Hebrew text, modifying the number in the one case to 20,000 measures, and changing the value of the term in the second case to a tenth of a measure, thus making the total only 800 liters. It seems, however, that the explanation for the smaller amount of oil may rest in the quality of the oil. In question is ground olive oil, that is, not pressed or crushed; it was therefore of the highest "grade-A" variety. Imagine, then, the number of olives needed to obtain 800 liters of ground olive oil! And how many more if, in fact, 8,000 liters were the amount!

In order to have a clearer idea of the significance of such amounts and the burden of this level of tribute on the peasant population, it is important to bear in mind another aspect of the situation: the supply of goods for the court of Solomon. Information about this supply is given to us in 1 Kgs 4:22–28. According to this text, the daily supply of Solomon's court consisted of 30 measures of the finest flour and 60 measures of ordinary flour (v. 22). We have here the equivalent of 12,000 liters of fine flour and 24,000 liters of ordinary flour. Taking as our basis the lunar year of 355 days, we would have, as the indicated quantities, 4,260,000 liters of the finest flour, plus 8,520,000 liters of ordinary flour, in other words, 12,780,000 liters of flour to be delivered annually to the court. On the basis of this calculation, the annual transfer of grain to Hiram would thus have amounted to a little less than two-thirds of the annual provision of Solomon's court.

It is clear that the court did not live on flour alone. The text also informs us about the daily consumption of meat — a luxury item in Israel — consisting of 10 fattened oxen, and 20 pasture-fed oxen, 100 sheep, as well as deer, gazelle, stags, and fattened birds, of which we have no number (v. 23). According to Neh 5:17f., 150 men were fed by Nehemiah every day with an ox, six ewes, and some birds. On the basis of this information, one could suppose that Solomon's court, if it really consumed all this, would have had between 3,000 and 4,500 persons, given that the numbers that refer to animals are between twenty and thirty times greater than those registered in Nehemiah. If we add to this the consumption of flour, the numbers in the court must have been much higher.

However big the court was, the Israelite peasantry found itself in the difficult situation of having to sustain the sizeable apparatus of *two* states. And without a doubt, given the current conditions of arable land, the sacrifice involved in paying such tribute together with the obligation to supply labor for the levy has to have been enormous: truly a heavy yoke and an extremely harsh servitude (see 1 Kings 12).

In order to collect such tribute, the state apparatus of Solomon had developed an efficient system of administration. A list, quite old, which certainly goes back to the time of Solomon himself, presents us with the body of functionaries at the royal court. The text in question is 1 Kgs 4:1–19. In the first part (vv. 1–6) we are introduced to Solomon's main overseers or ministers. Next, the text provides us with a list of twelve district officials or governors set by the king over all Israel. Their function was to ensure the maintenance of the monarch and his household. Each month, one of the district officials was responsible for supplying goods to the court. Thus, the number of these officials (twelve) guaranteed this royal service throughout the year (v. 7). The service consisted of the daily supply of the products indicated and already discussed in 1 Kgs 4:22–23.

Doubt remains as to whether or not the governors were also the persons responsible for the collection of the goods to be handed over to Hiram. Hypothetically, the foreign debt could have been paid with part of what was handed over to the court. However, it does not seem likely that the royal house would have given up nearly two-thirds of its benefits. On the other hand, 1 Kgs 4:28 informs us that the district officials also provided barley and straw for the horses and traction animals for the army, in the same way that they supplied goods for the court. It seems likely, therefore, that these officials also took care of the other collection requirements, as with the Phoenician king.

Each one of these governors was set over a district, whose jurisdiction is indicated in 1 Kgs 4:8–19. It is noteworthy that these geographical references cover only the territory of Israel, that is, the northern tribes. There is no reference to any area of the tribe of Judah.

There has been a lot of discussion about this among exegetes. Some think that there must have been a reference to the tribe of Judah, and that the corresponding part of the list has subsequently been lost (see similarly the note in the Jerusalem Bible on this passage). Nonetheless, the number 12 would seem to indicate that the list is, in fact, complete (see v. 7). Indeed, the text progressively presents us with twelve officials in charge of twelve districts. Apparently, then, the tribe of Judah — the tribe of the king! — was exempt from paying such tribute.

The story of the separation of the two kingdoms also confirms this fact. 1 Kgs 12:16 relates the decision of the Israelites to separate. There is no allusion to any dissatisfaction on the part of the people of Judah. These persons would seem to have accepted Rehoboam as their new king from the very beginning. It was, therefore, the northern tribes who carried the burden of keeping up the court of Solomon and who had to pay the foreign debt due the provider of wood and skilled labor, i.e., the Phoenician king Hiram of Tyre.

International Commerce by Sea

Contact with Hiram of Tyre opened up further prospects for King Solomon. Because the king of Tyre was knowledgeable about the sea and practiced navigation, he maintained full commercial contact with the other peoples of the Mediterranean. His ships reached northern Africa and all the way to Spain. Under his government, maritime expansion by the Phoenicians reached its greatest extension.

Apparently dazzled by the intense commercial activity in which his supplier of wood was engaged, Solomon decided to imitate him. According to 1 Kgs 9:26, Solomon built ships in Ezion-geber (a port city located on the Gulf of Acaba, which itself was built or at least restored by Solomon for this particular purpose). The following verse (v. 27) makes direct mention of Hiram's servants, who were acquainted with the sea and would have sailed with the servants of Solomon. It is certain that these Phoenician specialists were also responsible for the construction of the ships. As far as we know, this is also true for later periods. Israel never exercised control over the knowledge of navigation and the building of ships (see, e.g., 1 Kgs 22:48).

Archeological excavations confirm the existence of the port city of Ezion-geber and suggest that if the city proves not to have been founded by Solomon himself, it was at least expanded during his reign for this specific purpose. In view is a commercial enterprise at the edge of the sea, equipped with facilities for the storage of goods. Departing from Ezion-geber, ships that had been loaded here with more imported wood and were manned by servants of Solomon and Phoenician sailors launched an enterprise of intensive trading across the southern seas.

Despite the royal monopoly, the business depended entirely upon Phoenician specialists with regard to both ship construction and navigation. This alone already increased the debt payment due to Hiram. Furthermore, it certainly intensified the extraction of tribute from the peasantry. After all, Israel had no merchandise for commercial exchange other than agricultural products. Oil, wine, and grain were the barter materials used by Solomon to acquire the articles he desired.

The ships' goal was to reach Ophir. We are unable to locate this land with greater precision than to suppose that it probably was situated between India and the west-central coast of Africa. Its existence, nonetheless, is confirmed by a stele found at Tell-Qasile, near modern-day Tel Aviv, on which there is written the inscription: "gold of Ophir for Beth-Horon."

It is an important observation that gold was sought in Ophir, for gold did not exist in Palestine. The gold of Ophir is praised in other parts of the Old Testament (see Isa 13:12; Ps 45:10 [9]; Job 28:16) as an especially precious form of this metal. Moreover, the amount of this good gold brought by Solomon's fleet is truly amazing. 1 Kgs 9:28 records the sum of 420 talents. Using as a basis for comparison the approximate equivalency of 35 kilograms per talent, we arrive at a quantity of almost 15,000 kilograms! Although such an amount may well represent an exaggeration, the strong impression persists that a large amount of gold must have been imported.

This impression is confirmed by two other subsequent passages. 1 Kgs 10:11 takes up again the theme of gold brought from Ophir, and adds the importation of sandalwood and precious stones to the list. Further on, 1 Kgs 10:22 informs us that gold and silver, ivory, apes, and peacocks were brought from Tarshish! Although the mention of Tarshish (Spain) seems secondary, given that it is improbable that Solomon also sent his ships across the Phoenician-controlled Mediterranean, gold and luxury items are mentioned as part of the Solomonic period. Furthermore, it is not impossible that trade elsewhere in the Mediterranean may have occurred through Hiram of Tyre himself.

The mention of gold together with ivory and other metals is consistent with what is otherwise said about this period. There is much talk, for example, about gold in the construction and adornment of the temple (1 Kgs 6:20ff., 28, 35; 7:48ff.). The queen of Sheba is said to have brought gold to Solomon (10:10), and the weight of the gold that arrived each year for Solomon is claimed to have been 666 talents (10:14), from which different pieces of artisanal work were then fashioned (10:16–21).

It is clear that all this gold did not simply come from imports. As we shall soon see, part of it could have been obtained through the sale of other articles to neighboring peoples (see 1 Kgs 10:15, 29). Most of it, however, whatever the royal amount might be, came from commercial naval exchange.

War Chariots and Horses

Beyond gold and the other luxury items mentioned above, another piece of merchandise should be highlighted: military equipment, specifically, war chariots and horses. 1 Kgs 10:28f. reports that Solomon imported horses and war chariots. The first of these came from Cilicia (Asia Minor), the second from Egypt.

The notice itself, which has everything needed in order to be considered authentic and which goes back to the time of Solomon himself, describes import-export activity. The king's businessmen assumed responsibility for effecting the transfer of warfare merchandise to the Hittites and the Syrians. This accords with the fact that Palestine represented the emporium of commercial exchange in the ancient Near East. It is very possible that the better part of the gold attributed to Solomon was obtained in such transactions.

It is interesting, however, to observe that this merchandise was handed over to the Syrians and the Hittites for the same price that was paid for it. The passage, to be sure, is text-critically a difficult one. Taken as it is, it hardly allows one to assume that much wealth would have been acquired through the transaction.

In this case, there is no way to avoid the question of how Solomon and his businessmen would have gotten the silver needed in order to acquire equipment for the royal army itself. Every chariot cost the royal treasury 600 shekels of silver, and every horse 150 shekels. At an approximate weight of 11.4 grams per shekel, each chariot would have cost about 6.8 kilograms of silver, and every horse about 1.7 kilograms. The reference in 1 Kgs 10:26 to 1,400 chariots and 12,000 horses is rather doubtful. If the numbers seem exaggerated, however, there is also no clear correspondence between the number of chariots and number of horses. In any case, no doubt exists about the fact that Solomon significantly equipped the Israelite army with modern weaponry of this sort. In addition, he also necessarily had to acquire, doubtless through the extraction of tribute from those beneath him, other products in a sufficient quantity to be able to trade them for the silver needed to pay the price of these goods.

National Sovereignty Threatened

Cedar wood, skilled labor, horses and war chariots, gold and luxury items, including apes and peacocks, all certainly gave greater brilliance and splendor to Solomon's court and covered the king with praise. Thus he exceeded all the other kings of the earth in wealth and wisdom (1 Kgs 10:23).

However, the same brilliance and splendor also required an enormous sacrifice on the part of the workers. They all bore the burden of the court's extravagance: the laborers who built the public works, constructed the ships, and were employed in military and naval service; the peasants with their agricultural products that sustained the royal court, the army, and the levies of workers; as well as the peasants who produced the goods for a program of energetic foreign commerce.

For all this labor and sacrifice, the workers received no benefits. Even God, who before had moved around from tribe to tribe, was now firmly ensconced in Jerusalem in a house controlled by the king. All the workers had left was paying off both the internal and the foreign debt. They suffered a heavy yoke and harsh servitude.

By the end of his government, Solomon had raised Jerusalem to an enviable position. The rich city shone. On the other hand, only a few times prior to the later onset of foreign domination had Israel suffered such a profound level of poverty as during Solomon's reign. The foreign debt pushed the outer limits of what was possible. The people handed over much more of their surplus production in order to service the debt.

Even so, Solomon did not succeed in paying off what was owed. Thus the foreign debt ended up threatening national sovereignty! 1 Kgs 9:11 tells us that Solomon handed over to Hiram of Tyre nothing less than twenty cities of the region of Galilee — probably a series of cities located along the border near the Bay of Acho. The motive for this secession of territory is not made especially clear in the text. Verse 11 allows us to think that the cities were given to Hiram as payment for wood and gold. But according to v. 14, it seems that the cities were sold or offered as a guarantee for a loan in gold — 120 talents — which then could not be paid back.

Whatever the proper interpretation, there is no reason to doubt that the territory was seceded to Hiram. And this, obviously, reflects the chaotic economic situation in which the kingdom found itself. Its economic dependence vis-à-vis the Phoenicians is beyond question. Solomon's fascination with the Phoenicians' goods and culture had led Solomon to hand over to the Phoenicians oil, wheat, and even cities.

But Resistance Took Shape

All this oppression with the exploitation and expropriation caused by keeping up the court and the development of the foreign debt would not have gone unnoticed by the Israelite people. It certainly called forth resistance and a longing for liberation. I consider it certain that a number of biblical texts, which may go back to the period of Solomon, express the dissatisfaction of the general populace. I cannot treat them here in detail, but it is proper to mention them in conclusion.

Among these texts must be included 1 Sam 8:11-17 with its discussion of the so-called "right of the king," where the entire population finally becomes the monarch's slave. The texts attributed to the Yahwist in the thematic block of Exodus 1-14 would figure here as well. The oppression described in Ex 1:11; 2:11f.; 5 would certainly have identified, in a disguised manner, the oppression suffered under Solomon with the experience of slavery in Egypt. Finally, Deut 17:14-17, a text that seeks to limit the rights of the king by preventing the multiplication of horses (the army), wives (international agreements and commercial exchange), and much gold and silver likewise appears to stem from that first frightening experience.

Nonetheless, the resistance did not succeed in achieving clear popular definition while Solomon ruled. The only exception would be the frustrated coup attempt initiated by Jeroboam (1 Kgs 11:26–40). Together with the ideological cover provided by the construction of the temple for all these outrages, the strong and well-equipped army also functioned as a means of repression. Without these two elements — the temple and the army — neither the splendor of the court nor the foreign debt would have been able to reach such a point; perhaps they would never even have existed at all. In the end, however, while the court swam in luxury and wealth and also supported the Phoenician palace, the peasants became poorer and poorer, watching their products disappear at the table of the king and in foreign commercial transactions.

As a consequence, it is no accident that the northern tribes, the ones most seriously exploited during this period, broke with Jerusalem after the death of Solomon (1 Kings 12). The forced labor and exaggerated taxation of agricultural products had completely upset any harmony there might have been. Harsh was the servitude, heavy the yoke (12:4ff.). Either things had to change, or there could be no agreement between Israel and the royal house of Judah.

Presumptuously, Rehoboam did not take seriously the complaint of the north. He tried to be even more voracious than his father. He had to take care of himself. Israel refused to pay the debt contracted by the royal house in order to sustain its "good life." Lacking the same ability to get things done as his father, Rehoboam next saw his kingdom reduced to the state of Judah.[1]

---

1. Throughout this study I have allowed myself to be accompanied by different authors, having recourse to them in order to settle doubts and to clarify details, without, however, using bibliographical notes. I append here the bibliography. Still basic for the analysis of 1 Kings 3–11 is the commentary by Martin Noth, *Könige I,1–16*, Biblischer Kommentar, Altes Testament 9/1 (Neukirchen-Vluyn: Neukirchener, 1968). I have also used idem, *Historia de Israel* (Barcelona, 1966), with John Bright, *Historia de Israel* (São Paulo, 1978) and Jorge Pixley, *Historia sagrada, historia popular* (San José, Costa Rica: DEI-CIEETS, 1989). The sociological discussion is based primarily on François Houtart, *Religião e modos de produção pre-capitalistas;* also published as *Religion et modes de production précapitalistes* (Bruxelles: Éditions de l'Université de Bruxelles, 1980). Finally, I ought to mention that I have already treated this theme, but from another point of view, in Carlos Dreher, "O trabalhador e o trabalho sob o reino de Salomão," *Estudos Bíblicos* 11 (1986).

2

......

The Debt in
Nehemiah's Social Reform

A Study of Nehemiah 5:1–19

JOSÉ SEVERINO CROATTO

....

The text of Nehemiah 5, little used for kerygmatic purposes, is one of great theological wealth that derives from its sociopolitical and economic center. On the one hand, the action of the governor of Judah, Nehemiah, can be compared with the social reforms of Urukagina of Lagash, a Sumerian king of the twenty-fifth century B.C.E., or Ammisaduqa, the next to the last king of the great Babylonian dynasty (ca. 1830–1531 B.C.E.), whose maximum expression was Hammurabi.[1] On the other hand, we are reminded of the proclamations of the Mesopotamian kings regarding gestures of justice in favor of the people (Nebuchadrezzar I; see the titles and epithets that the kings gave themselves).[2] Third, the reader of the Bible cannot help but sense the opposition between Nehemiah 5 and 1 Samuel 8: in the latter instance, the oppressive practices of the kings are described (imitated by the governors and overseers of Judah in the Persian period); in the former instance, the *different* administration of the governor Nehemiah is emphasized. Besides these comparisons, however, if the text of Nehemiah 5 is looked at

---

1. See Appendix II, p. 53 below; F. R. Kraus, *Ein Edikt des Königs Ammisaduqa von Babylon* (Leiden: Brill, 1958).

2. See W. G. Lambert, "Nebuchadrezzar, King of Justice," *Iraq* 27 (1965): 1–11; A. Gamper, *Gott als Richter in Mesopotamien und im Alten Testament* (Innsbruck: Universitätsverlag Wagner, 1966); M. J. Seux, *Epithètes royales akkadiennes et sumériennes* (Paris: Letouzey et Ané, 1967), 22.

from the perspective of the current situation of the Third World, the theme of "debt" stands out in a way that it otherwise would not without this point of view. In fact, it is lacking in traditional biblical commentaries.

At first glance, it seems that the text is a set of diffuse themes. And, in fact, literary criticism does show us that vv. 14–18 are by a different hand (the Hebrew of v. 14a presupposes that another text preceded it). Furthermore, the presentation of the "case" in vv. 1–5 discusses different abuses within the Jewish community of the fifth century B.C.E. The text itself is nonetheless especially well placed in the economic sphere, with excursions made now and then into the political, social, and ideological realms, thereby constructing a chain-of-meaning that is more than abundantly clear. In the basic economic sphere, the plurality of figures and figurative fields (in the semiotic sense) may be condensed, we believe, in the semantic nucleus of "debt." At the same time, the grouping of themes related to an economic-social "project" becomes more visible through the manifest structure of the text.

We will proceed in the following manner. We will begin with a description of the text in order to highlight certain of its features. We will then see how the theme of debt emerges along with a project of reform, highlighting certain new themes. At that point it will be the moment to present the manifest structure of the entire text in order to visualize its internal relations. Finally, we will create a register of the lexemes according to the economic, social, political, and ideological instances where they are found. In conclusion, we will consider the question of our reinterpretation of the passage, namely, Nehemiah 5.

The Text and Its Content

Nehemiah 5 has been "redactionally" placed in its present location (at the level of the composition of the current book). Literarily, the passage "cuts off" the narration of the conflict with Sanballat begun in Neh 2:10, which (with certain other interruptions) extends from 4:7 to 6:1ff. The context of chapter 5 is indefinite. From the narrative point of view, one would expect it to be at some point in chapter 7. As far as one can discern, the redactor wished somehow to situate the reform of Nehemiah *before* the solemn reading of the law (Nehemiah 8–10) as well as the dedication of the city walls (postponed until 12:27ff.).

Verses 1–5 describe the crisis situation of the Jewish community (only in Jerusalem?). The complaint is not due to foreign domination (as in Neh 9:36f.) but "between brothers" (v. 1). Neither are the Samaritans part of the picture. Everything takes place within a community of "Jews" who, the text assumes, are divided socioeconomically.

The internal oppression is expressed by three speakers (spokespersons of the people and their women; see v. 1a).[3] Some indicate that their families are numerous[4] and do not have anything to eat; others, that they will have to pawn their primary means of production (fields and vineyards) as well as secondary holdings (houses) in order to get food. This is the first form of indebtedness. A third group says that they will have to borrow *money* "for the king's tax."[5] Introduced thereby — the only time that this occurs — is the element of foreign domination, implacable as is well known. The rich could pay such taxes, but the poor had to incur a new debt in order to pay the imperial tribute. It is possible that v. 4b (without agreement) wishes to clarify that the form of repayment was the handing over of fields and vineyards.

This state of poverty and indebtedness forced families into self-destruction. The debtors had to hand over their sons and daughters as slaves (v. 5a), a fact that occurred especially with women (see 1 Sam 8:13).[6] There was no way to avoid it. Finally, as if that were not enough, the family members that became slaves had to work in the fields and vineyards that were already mortgaged.

Noteworthy are both the similarities and differences between Nehemiah 5 and 1 Sam 8:11–17. On the one hand, the practices in the economic order are alike regarding agriculture and human

---

3. The reader can follow the diagrammed text, as printed below in Appendix I, p. 52.

4. Unless one should read 'ōrᵉbîm instead of *rabbim* (see v. 3a). The phrase would be better syntactically; nonetheless, the practice assumed by such a reading would be strange.

5. This is the only time that *middah* (tax/tribute) appears; cf. the Akkadian *mandattu>maddatu>*Hebrew: *midda*.

6. There is no reason to understand the feminine *nikbašot* as meaning "dishonored" (see the Jerusalem Bible), given that the same verb in v. 5a refers to sons and daughters. The oppression of women occurred more often than that of men, hence the specification of the text.

slavery. Nevertheless, they are different insofar as in 1 Samuel 8, versus the processes of indebtedness described in Nehemiah 5, rules are established for the "expropriation" of the means of production and the forced labor of underlings in the king's domains, as well as for the extraction of tribute in kind.

The situation of the postexilic Jewish community is, thus, one of differentiated penury. There are persons with large debts (internal and foreign). In order to repay these debts, they could only hand over their articles of production and their housing, and even had to go to the extreme of giving up their children as slaves to work for others. An infernal circle is the result that allows for no escape. The economic-political "system" becomes manifest that, juridically restrained, generates poverty and injustice and renders the social differences ever more profound.

Verse 6, where Nehemiah begins to speak in the first person, serves as a transition. Verse 7 identifies the actors in this social imbalance for the first time. They belong to the political and administrative level: the noble noteworthies (*ḥorim*) and the officials (*seganim;* cf. the Akkadian *sakun*). Further on, they will be the concrete targets of Nehemiah's discourse. Verse 8 establishes an interesting comparison that provides us with a piece of information unknown from other sources. Nehemiah reminds his interlocutors that their fellow Jews who had been "sold" to other countries were later "purchased" and therefore were now in Judah. If the expression is not rhetorical, it indicates that those who had returned to their native land from exile came back through both the edict of Cyrus and the effort of their fellow Jews who "bought" them with money.

Now, the governor's critique makes clear the inconsistency of the current practice of "selling" again those fellow Jews who otherwise had been "bought." Ironically, they would now be sold to Nehemiah himself and his collaborators who would again buy them back. The verse is interesting because the lexical term "purchase/sale" is the axis around which the entire comparison spins. From the ideological point of view, such attitudes are contrary to the fear of God (and his laws) and the good name that he deserves among the peoples (v. 9b).

The reform of Nehemiah, set forth more as a proposal than a final decision, is indicated in vv. 10–12a. We will return to it in the following section. The complementary vv. 14–18 return to the recent past to indicate two very different practices. These verses do not refer to oppression in the same way as the reference to abuses in vv. 1–5, but rather to Nehemiah's social sensibility in the face of the harshness of his predecessors in government. Nehemiah did not customarily exercise his right to "the governor's bread" (v. 14) while his predecessors demanded it, adding further conditions (v. 15) which had the result of being another type of oppression of the people. The example of Nehemiah himself is elaborated in v. 16 (he did not take over any fields) and in v. 17, where he recalls that all personnel costs went to his account and were not included in "the governor's bread." The chapter ends with an exclamatory prayer (v. 19; see Neh 3:36f.; 6:14; 13:14, 22b, 29, 31b).

The Debts and Project of Nehemiah

The accusation by Nehemiah of the noteworthy nobles and officials in v. 7 constitutes a special axis-of-meaning. First, it pulls together, at the literary and redactional level, the report of the social disorders indicated in vv. 1–5; and, second, by virtue of its content, it reduces the discussion to the theme of *debt:* "each one of you imposes a debt on his brother."

The Hebrew text twice uses the lexeme *nš'* (to lend — with interest) at both extremes of the phrase as though to emphasize the idea: *maššaʾ . . . nošʾim*. It is not necessary, as many commentators and translators in fact proceed to do, to change *nšʾ* (to lend) for *nśʾ* (to load), a metaphor that generalizes the situation of vv. 1–5 (see the Jerusalem Bible: "What a load each one of you imposes on his brother!"). There is no textual support for this change. Furthermore, in vv. 1–5 it is not a question of expropriation (see Isa 5:8) nor of forced labor for the king (1 Sam 8:11–17) but of mortgaging all goods (fields, vineyards, houses) in order to obtain food (v. 2) and to pay the debt to the Persian empire (v. 4). In other words, debt is incurred to eat and to pay off another debt.

To recover the goods that have been mortgaged requires paying off one's debts. But how can they be paid off in this vicious circle of "become indebted in order to pay off one's debts"? The extreme situation consists of payment through the handing over of one's children (the power of youthful labor) as slaves (v. 5b), whose unremunerated work is equivalent to money (Deut 15:18). Only the coming of a Sabbatical year (1b; vv. 12ff.) could bring the liberation of slaves.

The proposal of Nehemiah is expressed in vv. 10–12a, and developed in three parts:

a. Nehemiah recognizes that both he and his people lent money and cereals. Nevertheless, he anticipates his gesture of "letting this debt go" (v. 10b). The cohortative of the verb "to leave" indicates a decided will.

b. Nehemiah demands — an imperative reinforced with the particle -na' — that his interlocutors immediately ("today") return fields, vineyards, olive groves (this term is now added), and houses (v. 11a). This clause refers to v. 3. In view is an authentic cancellation of debts, for these were goods taken as surety for money lent. Nevertheless, as the poor had also borrowed money to pay the tribute to the Persian king (v. 4a), Nehemiah insists that the creditors forgive them (v. 11b).

The Hebrew text contains a detail that is generally overlooked, although it may be of great interest to us. What is the significance of (*hašibu*) *meʾat hakkesep* . . . ? The verb *meʾat* is the construct of *meʾah* (a hundred). The proposal to modify the text to *maššaʾt* (debt/loan of) makes sense, but has no basis. Worse yet is the suggestion based on the Septuagint (*apo tou argyriou*) to convert *meʾat* into *meʾet* (of/from among) in order to translate: "and part of the money." Nehemiah would thus ask for a partial cancellation, perhaps minimal. The same occurs with those who translate the current text as "a hundredth (part) of the money" (see the note in the Jerusalem Bible).

These "generous" interpretations presuppose that to pardon part of a debt is already a grand gesture. Why not understand the text as it is written: "return to them today their fields, their vineyards, their olive groves and their houses; and a hundred (for one) of the money . . . which you have lent"? There is no known case in which *meʾah* signifies "the hundredth (part)," although sometimes it is a multiple: 100 times (see Qoh 8:12; Prov 17:10).

Is a "hundred for one" in our passage just a rhetorical phrase (see Luke 8:8)? Or can it be understood as a maximum proposal, requiring the restoration of the persons affected by the poverty of indebtedness? To return "a hundred (for one)" is a way of inverting the terms of the previous means by which the creditors became wealthy. The text goes on to add to the mention of money the articles, "wheat, wine, and oil," all consumer goods appropriated by the creditors perhaps for a long while.

Does it not make sense, therefore, that Nehemiah asks them to return "a hundred (for one)" of the money and the consumer goods produced by the lands that were pawned (vv. 3–4)? In this way, the return is satisfactory and would cover the deterioration occurred since the time when the mortgages were made, at the same time allowing the debtors to begin their own productive process. The text would imply that the creditors had plainly become exceedingly wealthy and indicates with clarity that economically they *can* do what Nehemiah is insisting that they do.

c. The officials who are creditors reply: "we will return (*našib*: picking up the terms of the proposal in v. 11a)... and we will not seek back..." (v. 12a). Did they keep their word? Was it only a promise made by the rich in order to carry on as before? Nehemiah, in any case, ensures both juridically and religiously that the promise will be executed, committing the priests through an oath to make sure that what has been promised is done (v. 12b), if the oath was not in fact requested by the interested parties themselves.[7]

The context is the covenant (see Ezra 10:3–5, esp. v. 5: the phrase is the same as in our passage). Now when covenants were made, it was customary to include a symbolic rite to dissuade against any transgression (see Jer 34:18–20). In this case, the gesture consists of shaking out the pleats (the "pockets") of the mantle (cf. the symbol and its explanation in v. 13).

With all this, we must not forget that we are in full popular assembly (vv. 7b and 13b). An issue of interest to the people who bring the complaint (v. 1a) is not resolved in the privacy of the powerful. Nehemiah's critical discourse is developed in the assembly (vv. 8–11), as are the creditors' promise (v. 12a) and the taking

---

7. More than having the priests take an oath, the text seems to refer to the subjects themselves of the commitment: "I called the priests [as witnesses] and I made them [the creditors] swear that they would do in accordance with this word [or promise]." For a similar expression, also in the context of the covenant, see Ezra 10:5.

of the oath (v. 12b–13a). The mention of the assembly (vv. 7b and 13b) serves as an inclusio for this central part of the chapter.

What does the conclusion of v. 13b signify: "the people did in accordance with this word"? The expression seems to refer to the keeping of a promise (see v. 12b; Ezra 10:5b). The people were the ones who raised the complaint and not those accused. Or is the phrase a general one and says that the people "did the same thing," that is, the symbolic gesture of shaking out the pockets of the mantle? It would have been an impressive gesture, both visually and aurally.[8]

The seriousness of the whole issue stems from the fact that a community of *brothers* (and sisters) has been injured. We shall see below the relevance of the lexeme "brother." The situation indicated in vv. 1–5 is not one of mutual aid, of help by the rich for those in need, but rather one of the former taking advantage of the latter. Wealth creates more poverty in the form of debt. Against this perversion Lev 25:35–55 warns in an interesting series of laws that begins, "if your brother becomes poor...." Proscribed are interest, usury, and the treating of brothers as slaves, who have to work in order to pay off their debts. Nehemiah goes even farther, asking for a generous and restorative cancellation of all debts.

The Manifest Structure of Nehemiah 5

A text communicates not only through words and phrases, but also by the position of these within an enclosed whole. The following commentary refers to the schematic presentation of the text appended below (see Appendix I). The vocable "people" serves as an inclusio both between vv. 1–13 (as already observed) and between vv. 1–19 (thematically between vv. 1 and 18b). The center of the narrative is occupied by the creditors, despite the fact that the narrative's framework shows that the people are the principal referent, initially oppressed (the opening situation of the story) but ultimately benefitted by the decisions taken (the final situation).

The situational section (vv. 1–5+6) has various inclusios: the "cry" (vv. 1 and 6); the exploited "brothers" (v. 1b) are our

---

8. "Did the same thing/did in accordance with this word" are equivalent, given that *dabar* signifies both "word" and "thing."

"brothers" of the same flesh (v. 5a); our numerous and deprived "children" (v. 2) are the same as their "children" that nonetheless are enslaved (v. 5). The sequence is "brothers-children-brothers-children."

The result is "our sons and daughters are slaves of their brothers." This situation, which has its origin in the economic order, is heavily emphasized in these verses. At the level of structure, the reader must read three times the combination "our fields and our vineyards" (vv. 3a, 4b, 5b), which is related to the plight of hunger, the individual foreign debt (at the center) and the work of slaves. When the text is looked at closely in this way, a noteworthy rhetorical effect is produced. It is a text both compact and full.[9]

The situation expressed in A corresponds to the brief conclusion of A'. "Everything that I did for this people" presupposes that the procedure to reverse the situation has been carried out, something not narrated in the text. Hence the importance of this final correspondence.

We will consider B and B' together. B (v. 7) specifies for the first time those who have caused the social crisis. These are not the rich in general, but the political authorities who work with Nehemiah. In B', the officials of a former time are mentioned again,[10] officials who did not behave as those now do (B). B and B' are thus opposed to one another. This relationship of opposition is underscored by "you" in v. 7 versus "they/I" in vv. 17–18.

The reprimand by Nehemiah of the present officials becomes greater in C (v. 8), creating an opposition between "we" (buyers) and "you" (sellers). In C', the critique of the previous functionaries who also oppressed the people (v. 15a) is opposed by the example of Nehemiah himself in a fairly long period of administration (vv. 14, 15b–16). This play of suboppositions (in C') is expressed in the following manner:

---

9. This impression is reinforced when attention is paid to the redundancy (=frequency) of the first-person plural suffixes in the mouth of the speakers in vv. 2–5 (16 times without counting the three instances of "we" and the five verbal suffixes in Hebrew). In the case of the nominal suffixes, in question are "*our* children/fields," that is, the community which is speaking.

10. The text in v. 17 says "Jews and officials," which some exegetes correct to read "noteworthies (*ḥorim* instead of *yᵉhudim*) and officials," in accordance with the formula in v. 7. We believe that the reading of the Masoretic Text is better.

  a governor (Nehemiah): "I did not eat the governor's bread"
  (v. 14)

  b governors (previous): "they oppressed the people (in
  different ways)" (v. 15aa)

  b' his servants: "they also oppressed the people" (v. 15ab)

  a' I (Nehemiah): "I did not behave in this way" (v. 15b); "I did
  not acquire any field" (v. 16)

As a unit, B–C highlights opposed examples, the same as B'-C',
only that the second time the past is referred to as a testimony in
favor of Nehemiah.

The relationship between D and D' is primarily lexematic: the
equation "word = thing/you do" (v. 9a) is reflected chiastically
in "he did/this word" of v. 13b. In D' (vv. 12b–13) the vocable
haddabar hazzeh appears three times.

Verses 10–12a constitute the center of the chapter and, properly speaking, the program of reform. In E and E' two different
speakers come to speech: the "we" of Nehemiah and his co-
workers (E: v. 10) — who have also lent money and wheat but
no longer seek repayment — precedes and provides motivation for
the "we will return" of the current abusers of the people's needs
(E': v. 12a). That Nehemiah had made loans of money and food
(v. 10a) does not equate him with the others, who made themselves the owners especially of the means of production and of life
(fields...houses).

In any case, E and E' show two desires: the remission of normal debts (E) and the remission of goods and the debts that create
injustice and impoverishment. The entire chapter underscores this
difference (see the oppositions between the crisis provoked by the
"noteworthy nobles and officials" and the good example of Nehemiah and his administration) and especially the convergence of
E and E' at the center of the chapter and the reformist project
of Nehemiah (X: v. 11). In the first place, the abusing "brothers" (v. 1b) are commanded to give back the means of production
(fields, vineyards, *olive groves*,[11] housing, and, of course, money)

---

11. The "olive groves" are only indicated in this passage, precisely at the center,
perhaps to underscore the extent of the mortgages.

and the agricultural products (wheat, wine, oil) that correspond to the first triad of "fields/vineyards/olive groves."

This central verse (Neh 5:11) deserves further commentary. Here, the vocable "loan-debt" (*maššaʾ*) is not employed nor the expression "to cancel debts" or something similar. Nevertheless, the mortgaging of fields and other goods takes place in exchange for money or food in order to subsist (v. 3). In order to recover their fields, the poor must pay off their debts. Far from being able to do so, they have to sell their own children as slaves (v. 5). The debt that they indeed must pay is the imperial tribute; in order to do this they have to incur new debts (v. 4: as clear as day!). The internal debt becomes impossible to pay, generating a cycle of indebtedness.

Verse 11 indicates, in addition, a noteworthy irony. The creditors have lent the poor not only money, but also "wheat, wine, and oil," precisely the products that the peasants ought to be producing *for themselves*. But they produce them for their creditors (who own the fields either under mortgage or through expropriation), who then "lend" them back to the peasants. How could they be restored?

Thus, if v. 11 does not speak of "canceling debts," but rather of *paying back,* it is for a profound reason. It is the only way to rehabilitate the poor, so that they have their own means of production. If these are not already mortgaged, it means that there are no debts. Also v. 11b indicates more than the cancellation of debts. If it were only the latter, the debtors would not have to pay back money and food. Instead, it is *the creditors* who have to "pay back" these things that they themselves had lent! How can one pay back what one has lent? These goods were given as loans in exchange for guarantees, mortgages, or expropriations, in such a way that they were produced by the very persons who now receive them. They are theirs, and Nehemiah demands that they be "returned" with interest (a hundred for one, probably) for the damage caused and in order to give the peasants time to renew their own productive cycle. It is, therefore, not strange at all that this verse (11) lies at the center of the manifest structure of the chapter and Nehemiah's reform project.

The Four Sides of the Text[12]

The point is not to underscore all the vocables or phrases that refer to economic, social, political, and ideological instances. If we were to do so, we would observe the prevalence of the economic level (loan-debt, the king's tribute, the governor's bread, buy, sell, fields...pawn-mortgage, lend, money, shekel, etc.) with terms that recur within the text.

What is important to notice is the interrelationship woven in the text between the different levels. For example: the fact that the ruling class of Jerusalem (political level) lends money or consumer goods (economic level) with the mortgage of articles of production (economic-juridical level) creates slaves and the poor (social level) within a community explicitly called "brothers" (ideological level). In the opposite direction: the memory of being the same flesh and the fear of God (vv. 5, 9, 15b) works ideologically on Nehemiah (who hears the cry of the oppressed) and on those responsible for the crisis (who all belong to the political ruling class) so that they cancel debts and return the pawned goods (economic level) in order to undo the social differences.

In order to distinguish each of these instances, one must go through the entire text. This means that none is independent of the others, but rather that they crisscross one another in order to create the "sense" of the entire text. It is clear that the political level predominates, given that the reform is carried forward by Nehemiah in an instance of power, namely, that of governor. It would not have been possible to effect a social reform of the economic base in any other way, insofar as the oppressors — though "brothers" (v. 1b) — belong to a social class with political and economic power. The point is to speak about the "salvific" function of the power used to defend the oppressed, who are in this condition because another power subdues them.

In order to conclude this section, there is another significant fact to note, which the text "states" implicitly. The initiative of Nehemiah is only secondhand. The *primary actor,* who raises a complaint or protest, is the people (v. 1), including the women.

---

12. For other studies of Nehemiah 5, see L. Alonso Schökel, " 'Somos iguales que nuestros hermanos': Para una exégesis de Neh. 5, 1–13," *Salmanticensis* 23 (1976): 257–66.

This fact is sociologically relevant. Would it have occurred to Nehemiah to effect the reform without this cry of the people? According to v. 6, it appears *not*. Also in Ex 3:7, 9, the project of liberation by Yahweh *happens* at the cry of the oppressed. The political power of Nehemiah makes the reform possible and viable. Nevertheless, the initiative does not come from above, but rises from below. It is a noteworthy sociopolitical fact. Political power is a form of mediation which, in this case, serves the interests of the people.

Conclusion

At first glance, a biblical text like Nehemiah 5 does not look very promising, perhaps because of where it is located (in a little used work) or because its content appears to be exhausted in a specific event of the past. It is not a prophetic text nor a "law" or code. Nonetheless, as a historical fact, at least essentially, it is more suggestive and correlates those different levels or instances better than our commentary reveals. In regulations like those of Deuteronomy 15, for example, the popular action that pressured the political instances in favor of a social change is not reflected.

To us in Latin America today, a text like Nehemiah suggests many things: that the "cry" of an oppressed people can generate change; that the oppressors have power on their side, but that it is a conflicted, insecure, doddering power; that the poor of the earth are not afraid to insist on their rights; that there may be a political instance that uses its power for those who have none and therefore are oppressed; that the witness of good rulers is a necessary condition for asking others to change (remember the testimonial argument of Nehemiah in vv. 14ff.).

And there is yet another "point" in the text, namely, that the debt of the oppressed forms an endless chain of new debts, making it impossible to pay them back. Neh 5:11 proposes amputation for the sake of health (cancel the entire burden of debt) and something more: to rehabilitate the oppressed, "restoring" to them what seemed to have been "lent" to them. Is it not said now and then that the foreign debt of Latin America has already been more than repaid, and that the creditors ought to "pay back" richly what they have seemingly "lent"? Nehemiah 5 provides food for thought....

Appendix I: Nehemiah 5:1-19

[A] [1]Now there arose a great outcry of the people and of their wives against their Jewish brethren. [2]For there were those who said, "With our sons and our daughters, we are many; let us get grain, that we may eat and keep alive." [3]There were also those who said, "We are mortgaging our fields, our vineyards, and our houses to get grain because of the famine." [4]And there were those who said, "We have borrowed money for the king's tax upon our fields and our vineyards. [5]Now our flesh is as the flesh of our brethren, our children are as their children; yet we are forcing our sons and our daughters to be slaves, and some of our daughters have already been enslaved; but it is not in our power to help it, for other men have our fields and our vineyards."

[6]I was very angry when I heard their outcry and these words.

[B] [7]I took counsel with myself, and I brought charges against the nobles and the officials. I said to them, "You are exacting interest, each from his brother." And I held a great assembly against them,

[C] [8]and said to them, "We, as far as we are able, have bought back our Jewish brethren who have been sold to the nations; but you even sell your brethren that they may be sold to us!" They were silent, and could not find a word to say.

[D] [9]So I said, "The thing that you are doing is not good. Ought you not to walk in the fear of our God to prevent the taunts of the nations our enemies?"

[E] [10]Moreover I and my brethren and my servants are lending them money and grain. Let us leave off this interest.

[X] [11]Return to them this very day their fields, their vineyards, their olive orchards, and their houses, and the hundredth of money, grain, wine, and oil which you have been exacting of them."

[E'] [12]Then they said, "We will restore these and require nothing from them. We will do as you say."

And I called the priests, and took an oath of them to do as they had promised. [D'] [13]I also shook out my lap and said, "So may God shake out every man from his house and from his labor who does not perform this promise. So may he be shaken out and emptied."

And all the assembly said "Amen" and praised the Lord. And the people did as they had promised.

[a] [14]Moreover from the time that I was appointed to be their governor in the land of Judah, from the twentieth year to the thirty-second year of Artaxerxes the king, twelve years, neither I nor my brethren ate the food allowance of the governor.

[C'] [b] [15]The former governors who were before me laid heavy burdens upon the people, and took from them food and wine, besides forty shekels of silver.

[b'] Even their servants lorded it over the people.

[a'] But I did not do so, because of the fear of God. [16]I also held to the work on this wall, and acquired no land; and all my servants were gathered there for work.

[B'] [17]Moreover there were at my table 150 men, Jews and officials, besides those who came to us from the nations which were about us. [18]Now that which was prepared for one day was one ox and six choice sheep; fowls likewise were prepared for me, and every ten days skins of wine in abundance; yet with all this I did not demand the food allowance of the governor, because the servitude was heavy upon this people.

[A'] [19]Remember for my good, O my God, all that I have done for this people.

Appendix II: Debt and Justice in Texts of the Ancient Near East

1. The theme of debt appears in numerous documents of ancient Mesopotamia from texts that record contracts to codes of law. Loans in kind (barley, silver, etc.) or of money (not paper, but metal with interchangeable "value") are found. Loans *with interest* are also found even in the most ancient economic texts. Volume 8 of the *Archives royales de Mari,* published by George Boyer in 1958, brings together a long series of short texts concerning loans of silver (measured in shekels) with interest.[1] The laws of Eshnunna (ca. 1800 B.C.E.) and the code of Hammurabi (ca. 1700 B.C.E.) fix the terms of interest for loans of silver and grain, but do it only in a general way. The texts from Mari (eighteenth century B.C.E.), on the other hand, indicate every time precisely the type of interest. Let us look at an example:

> 3 sicles ⅓ d'argent affiné, poids de Mari.
> L'intéret pour 10 sicles d'un quart (de sicle)
> augmente.
> De Samas
> et (d')Ili-idinnam, l'orfèvre,
> Iar'ip-E(a)
> et dame Tàbuti-em[d]i
> au mois de Hibirtum, le 10eme jour
> accompli, ont pris l'argent.
> Au mois d'Abum,
> l'argent et son intéret
> il paiera.
> Cet argent, si un mois de prolongation
> est institué, ne sera pas "prolongé."
> Par devant Ili-tukulti,
> par devant Enlil-ublam, le négociant,
> par devant Akka, le charpentier,
> par devant Silli-Dagan,
> par devant Sin-ublam,
> par devant Puzur-Dagan,

---

1. See George Boyer, *Archives Royales de Mari. VIII. Textes juridiques* [hereafter ARM] (Paris: Imprimerie Nationale, 1958), nos. 22–61 (commentary on pp. 199–216).

> par devant Ili-Lim, le jardinier,
> par devant Ahu-aplia,
> par devant Habdu-Malik, le scribe.
> L'année où Zimri-Lim
> (la ville de) Dur-Iahdun-Lim
> a construit.[2]

The recipient of the silver, Iar'ip-Ea, must pay interest of 2.5 percent, which one assumes is monthly (30 percent annually). In Babylonia, it was usually 20 percent annually.[3] On other occasions in Mari, interest is raised to 33 percent and even to 50 percent.[4] More than monthly or annually, the terms of interest are virtually fixed, since the documents identify the month in which the loan must be repaid with interest. In the texts from Mari, there is no evidence of the cancellation of debts. This fact is probably due to the type of documents that we have, namely, records of loans before witnesses.

2. We should turn, then, to another class of witnesses. Among the sovereign powers of the kings of the ancient Near East, one should include that of "establishing justice." For this, the kings praise themselves in the titles that they give themselves;[5] their inscriptions of self-glorification proclaim it;[6] they bear witness to it in certain prologues and epilogues of "codes" of law as, e.g., that of Hammurabi.[7] Among the expressions that are typical and full of significance, the following are worth highlighting:

---

2. See Boyer, *ARM* VIII, no. 33 (pp. 56ff.).

3. See Boyer, *ARM* VIII, 204.

4. See Boyer, *ARM* VIII, no. 34 (33 percent) and nos. 38–39 (50 percent). There are also loans without interest, although one can charge interest when there is a delay in repayment (no. 49).

5. See M. J. Seux, *Epithètes royales akkadiennes et sumériennes* (Paris: Letouzey et Ané, 1967), 22 and passim.

6. See, e.g., the text published by W. G. Lambert, "Nebuchadnezzar King of Justice," *Iraq* 27 (1965): 1–11. In 2.22 and 26f., we read: "he was not negligent regarding judgments of truth and justice.... He established new regulations for the city, rebuilt the court, imposed regulations."

7. In the prologue: "I, Hammurabi, jealous prince who fears the Gods, who in order to make justice appear in the land, to eliminate the iniquitous and the evil, so that the strong does not oppress the weak...was called by my name by Anu and Enlil to provide well-being for the peoples." In the epilogue: "So that the strong does not oppress the weak, to make justice for the orphan and the widow..., to make justice for the oppressed."

- *misaram sakanum:* to "establish justice" (cf. *mišor* in Isa 11:4, in a similar context; *mešarim* in Ps 96:10; 98:9; 99:4, also in a framework of royalty and the exercise of power);

- *andurarum sakanum:* to "establish freedom-liberation" (the substantive has been maintained in the Bible as *dᵉror* in Lev 25:10 in the law of the Jubilee year; Jer 34:8 on the liberation of slaves; Isa 61:1 on the liberation of prisoners; and Ezek 46:17 with respect to the "liberation" of the goods of the future prince). The Sumerian equivalent is *ama.ar.gi,* which is already attested in the well-known social reform of the king of Lagash, Urukagina (twenty-fourth century B.C.E.)[8] and even a half century earlier when another king of Lagash, this time Entemena, "made her child to be restored to the mother, made its mother to be restored to the child, brought into effect liberation from interest."[9] Almost at the other extreme chronologically, Sargon II (end of the seventh century B.C.E.) boasts of having made gestures of *andurarum* (liberation) in his empire, and Esarhaddon states that "I freed them from cereal debts, rents, exploitation, embarkation tolls, and highway tolls in my country, and I *established their liberation* [*andurarsunu askun*]";[10]

- *tuppam hepum:* to "break the tablet," in the sense of annul the document (inscribed tablet) on which an obligation or debt has been recorded; to "write on a tablet" (*tuppam satarum*) means precisely to record a debt or other legal commitment.

The action of the kings for the sake of justice or liberation is also named *simdat sarrim,* or "decision of the king"; the verb *wussurum* (to "condone, free, allow"), on the other hand, is used in

---

8. For example: "[When Urukagina] received the crown from Girsu, he established liberation." See W. G. Lambert, "Les 'reformes' d'Urukagina," *Revue d'Assyriologie* 50 (1956): 169–84, esp. 182ff.

9. See W. G. Lambert, "L'expansion de Lagas au temps d'Entéména," *Rivista degli Studi Orientali* 47 (1972): 1–22.

10. See R. Borger, *Die Inschriften Asarhaddons Königs von Assyrien* (Graz, 1956), 3. For the history of the term *andurarum,* see N. P. Lemche, "*Andurarum* and *Misarum:* Comments on the Problem of Social Edicts and Their Application in the Ancient Near East," *Journal of Near Eastern Studies* 38 (1979): 11–22, esp. 15ff. Regarding the adoption of the term in biblical literature, see J. Lewy, "The Biblical Institutions of *Deror* in the Light of Akkadian Documents," *Eretz Israel* 5 (1958): 21.

many different senses, though also in one that interests us here, namely, to "free" or "condone" taxes, tributes, debts, etc. In one text from Mari, the theme is the liberation (from taxes) of a field,[11] while in another the cancellation of a debt of wheat with interest is established; the text runs as follows: "This is what I thought: now the wheat that they have taken at interest [*ana hubullim*] I will grant to them [*luwassar*]."[12] Such gestures of debt cancellation were thus possible, perhaps even usual.

3. But the most interesting cuneiform document on this theme is the so-called "edict of Ammisaduqa" promulgated at the beginning of the reign of this king of the first dynasty of Babylon, the sixth after Hammurabi and the next to last of the series (beginning of the sixteenth century B.C.E.). The text was published and discussed by F. R. Kraus in 1958[13] and reconstructed (and renumbered) by J. J. Finkelstein in 1969.[14] The first clause runs as follows: "Tablet [of the decree that the country had to] hear when [the king] instituted [the condonation] for the country." Already there appears the general and guiding phrase, *inuma sarrum misaram ana matim iskunu*, where the formula *misaram sakanum* alluded to before can be seen and reappears in this edict another six times in concrete cases of debt remission. Already it becomes apparent that the same formula not only means to "establish justice," but to "establish condonation-remission-amnesty."

The second clause establishes the condonation of the overdue debts of peasants, shepherds, provincial employees, and other subjects of the crown; the collector (*musaddinum*, "that one to whom [tribute] is given") cannot register a complaint against the property of any one who pays tribute. This decision is reaffirmed in the third clause.

Another case is contemplated in paragraph 4:

---

11. See *ARM* V, no. 28, ll. 28–40 (a peasant offers money to *liberate* his land from taxes; nonetheless, "his land was not liberated: *eqelsu ul wussur*" [l. 38]). See *ARM* II, no. 55, ll. 26–33; on the liberation from taxes of four destroyed cities.

12. See *ARM* IV, no. 16, ll. 5'–8'.

13. See F. R. Kraus, *Ein Edikt des Königs Ammisaduqa von Babylon* (Leiden: Brill, 1958). See also H. Petschow, "Gesetze," *Reallexikon der Assyriologie* 3 (1966): 272ff.

14. See J. J. Finkelstein, "The Edict of Ammisaduqa: A New Text," *Revue d'Assyriologie* 63 (1969): 45–64.

Whoever has granted barley or silver to an *acacho* or an *amorreo* as a *loan with interest* — and a document has been exchanged — given that the king has established remission for the country [*assum sarrum misaram ana matim iskunu*], the document is nullified (literally "his tablet is broken": *tuppasu hepi*); he cannot collect the barley or the silver on the basis of the document.

The creditor loses not only the interest, but also the capital. As a general rule, this measure would be unthinkable. In practice, it would suppress all lending. Nonetheless, it has rightly been said that the edict of Ammisaduqa, like other similar edicts, were *not* permanent codes or laws, but contextually specific acts of royal power to be explained on the basis of situations of economic crisis or social abuse. They are precisely so-called "acts of *misarum*" like the one that we are presently discussing (see paragraphs 1 and 4).

The third month (*Simann,* literally "the harvest") was the normal time for cancelling debts in Mesopotamia, given that the harvest gave the peasants and businessmen new income. Anticipating an act of debt remission at that time, some creditors might try to collect their debts *before* such a moment, which, on the other hand, was the most critical time of the year, insofar as people were using up their reserves of food or money in metal.

Against such a "scheme" by the creditors, paragraph 5 of the edict of Ammisaduqa establishes that "if...[someone] collected using compulsion, he must return everything he received through such a collection. Whoever does not make such a restoration in accordance with the order of the king will die." To compel repayment is all the more vexing, given that in question was the most critical moment of the year from an economic point of view, forcing the debtors to seek other resources to pay off their debts, whereby they became once again indebted (see Neh 5:2–5). It is against this vicious circle of debt that paragraph 5 of our edict takes precautions.[15]

Clause 7 is also striking, insofar as it is directed against fraud in the documentation of debts: someone *lends* barley or silver at interest, has the corresponding document prepared, but does not hand over a copy to the debtor or denies that at issue is a loan,

---

15. For this interpretation, see Finkelstein, "Edict of Ammisaduqa" 58ff.

making the transaction out to be a commercial one, probably in order deftly to avoid a possible "act of *misarum*" by the king. The debtor then presents witnesses regarding the content of the document who have to swear before God (see Neh 5:12b). The text then concludes:

> Insofar as (the creditor) unfavorably altered the document [*tupassu uwuu;* see Hebrew *'iwwa:* "pervert-distort"] and denied what was stipulated [literally "the word"] he must give [*inaddin;* to the debtor what was lent] six times (its value). If he cannot fulfill this obligation, he must die.

The death penalty is a threat; nonetheless, what is interesting about this clause is the fine the *creditor* must pay *to the debtor,* which is not only what was lent, but 500 percent more. Why? Probably because the creditor's fraud implies the realization of special gains. The anticipated punishment would be a just form of returning what was financially stolen. This clause reminds us of the proposal of Nehemiah to the governing class of Jerusalem to return "one hundred (for one)" (and not the hundredth part!) of what they themselves had lent (Neh 5:11).[16]

The particular cases that the edict of Ammisaduqa legislates later refer to obligations within the palace; nevertheless, what has been discussed is sufficient to give us an idea of its content. In 1965, Professor F. R. Kraus published a new text on the remission of debts, the "edict of Samsuiluna," one of the first kings of the first dynasty of Babylon (ca. 1700 B.C.E.). In its contents, it is similar to that of Ammisaduqa, here discussed in part.[17]

4. Conclusions: This summary presentation of the theme of debt in the ancient Near East is enough to make us think a number of things. Commercial and financial matters were regulated then as now. There were codes and individual contracts that established the conditions for repayment of debts. Nevertheless, there also existed "acts of *misarum*" (remission of debts) and "acts of *andurarum*" (liberation of persons or debts)[18] that made exceptions

---

16. See the commentary on this text (Neh 5:11) above, p. 45f.

17. See Petschow, "Gesetze," 275ff.

18. In the edict of Ammisaduqa (paragraph 21) the term *andurarum* appears (the only time that it does in this document) in connection with the manumission (denied: *andurarsu ul isakkan*) of slaves taken as surety. A foundational study

in favor of the debtors. These royal decisions were occasional and context-specific. The motive, it seems, was situations of economic crisis that made it impossible to repay debts.

Present-day countries of the Third World, and especially in Latin America, also have economic problems and cannot pay back their debts. But who would now be the power capable of choosing to decree an "act of *misarum*"? Will the people be capable of uniting to achieve it?

Another reflection: Clause 7 of the edict of Ammisaduqa and Neh 5:11 (which not only oblige the creditor to cancel the debt — what was lent and the interest due — but also to "return" much more than that to the debtor) indicate that it is possible to indemnify the impoverished debtor out of the wealth that the creditor has gained at the debtor's expense. Ancient peoples already had the "consciousness" that we now have (that the creditors of the foreign debt are really the "debtors"). They found a solution to the problem of unpayable or difficult debts. It is a good precedent.

---

of law and right in Mesopotamia has been B. Landsberger, "Die babylonischen Termini für Gesetz und Recht," in J. Friedrich, J. G. Lautner, and J. Miles, eds., *Symbolae ad iura orientis antigui pertinentes Paulo Koschaker dedicatae quas adiuvante Th. Folkers* (Leiden: Brill, 1939), 219–34. The relationship between the "acts-of-*misarum*" and the legal codes has been excellently analyzed by Finkelstein, "Ammisaduqa's Edict and the Babylonian 'Law Codes,'" *Journal of Cuneiform Studies* 15 (1961): 91–104.

3

....

The Kingdom of God
or the Kingdom of Money

JOSÉ CÁRDENAS PALLARES

....

I doubt that any important functionaries of the large world banks are going to read this essay. If by some chance they were to read it, they would most likely laugh at it, and in the best-case scenario judge me naive.

This essay is imagined as a conversation with Christians and non-Christians who take seriously the cause of Jesus. More than an academic exercise, it wishes to be a testimony of faith by someone who endeavors to love God with his whole mind and who, thanks to God, has not been able to extinguish or disguise his hunger and thirst for justice. I wish to share my vision of faith and hope in these lands of ours, marked as they are by savage *exploitation* and its child, extreme poverty.

I

The first episode in the public life of Jesus as told by Luke is Jesus' teaching in the synagogue at Nazareth (Luke 4:16–30). According to the other two synoptic gospels, this was not so. There were other events that took place prior to this one. And without leaving the confines of our gospel (namely, Luke), we can see in v. 23 of the same chapter (4) that Luke was aware that Jesus' ministry in Capernaum preceded his visit to Nazareth. Nevertheless, not only by virtue of its present position but also through the general statement made here about Jesus' mission "this scene becomes the primary illustration of what Jesus was saying when teaching in the synagogues, [and] it interprets his ministry as a whole."[1]

This type of teaching is what Jesus will continue to expound in the synagogues (Luke 4:43–44). For Luke, this is the center of Jesus' preaching. This passage (Luke 4:16–30) is probably due to the evangelist, given that the text cited by Jesus corresponds closely to the Septuagint at those points where the Septuagint differs from the Hebrew text, which only has a divine name and speaks of the blind who recover their sight. Furthermore, there is no discussion of the day of vengeance of the Lord; and instead of speaking of bandaging the broken-hearted, Isa 58:6 is cited where it speaks of freeing the oppressed. On the other hand, the first reading in the synagogue was from the Torah. Of this Luke says nothing nor of the function of the translator into Aramaic who regularly interrupted the reading of the Hebrew text.[2]

Likewise, it was not the custom to divide the sacred texts or to mix them for their public reading. "The type of homily attributed to Jesus is not the type that would be expected on such occasions," since there is no question here of discovering the sense of the text and encouraging one to put it into practice, but rather Jesus presents himself as the fulfillment of the prophetic word.[3] Therefore, these are not the *very* words and deeds of Jesus *himself,* but Luke's vision of Jesus.

·······

What the summary statement in Mark 1:14–15 with its call to conversion and the proclamation of the nearness of God's reign is for Mark, the interpretation of Isa 61:1 attributed to Jesus (in Luke 4:16–30) is for Luke. What the episode in the synagogue in Capernaum is for Mark, where Jesus' powerful teaching is demonstrated through the rescue of a man from demonic forces (Mark 1:21–28), the presentation of Jesus in Nazareth (Luke 4:16–30) is for Luke. It is a total program and vision of the entire work of Jesus.

---

1. See Robert C. Tannehill, *The Narrative Unity of Luke-Acts* (Philadelphia: Fortress, 1986), 1:61.

2. See Jacques Dupont, *Études sur les évangiles synoptiques* (Leuven: Leuven University Press/Peeters, 1985), 1:39.

3. See Charles Perrot, "Luc. 4, 16–30 et la lecture biblique dans l'ancienne synagogue," *Revue des Sciences Religieuses* 47 (1973): 324–40.

From an obscure corner of the empire — obscure also in the context of colonized Palestine (John 1:46) — Jesus delivers his first words in public. But they are not his; they rather recall those of an ancient prophet in order to indicate that Jesus understands his mission to be in line with this great stream that generates hope, and that what interests him is making the order of God happen for the welfare of his people.

On the Sabbath, Jesus announces liberty to the captives, gives sight to the blind, announces the liberation of the oppressed, and proclaims the year of the Lord. On the Sabbath, the day when the liberation from slavery that God called forth ought to be celebrated in a special way (Deut 5:15), Jesus characterizes his mission, fruit of the anointing of the Lord's Holy Spirit, as cause for the poor to be happy, because to release the poor from hunger and humiliation is the best way to give glory to God (Luke 6:1–5, 6–11).

Here begin the difficulties. Jesus, some say, announces good news to "the poor who are not poor," since being poor as such has no merit. On the contrary, it may be the consequence of vice, of ignorance, or of laziness. One could continue *usque ad nauseam* with this sort of rhetorical juggling.

Since for Luke the deaf person is one who cannot hear, and the lame person one who cannot walk well, and the leper one whose skin is spoiled, so also for Luke the poor person is the one who is half alive, the one who is defenseless in the face of arbitrary events, the person who has been exploited. The poor are those to whom Zacchaeus is disposed to distribute his goods — not spiritual goods, but those that he obtained through robbery and extortion (Luke 19:8). Poor are those with whom the ruler who wanted to possess eternal life did not wish to share his patrimony (18:18–23). Poor is Lazarus, who does not even get the crumbs from the table of the rich man and whose sores the dogs lick (16:19–21). Poor is the widow who, unlike the rich, can only throw a few small coins into the money-box of the temple (21:1–3). Poor are those at the same level as the disabled, the blind, and the lame, those unable to do business in ancient agrarian society (14:18–21). They are those who cannot even return a favor (14:12f.).

The poor person is socially worth what the blind, the lame, the lepers, and the deaf are worth (Luke 7:22). (Or were there spiritually lame and spiritual lepers in Luke's universe?) For this reason:

> the poor to whom the good news is announced cannot be separated from the other categories with which the mission of the *anointed* one is defined.... This is even more significant because Luke suppressed one of the categories mentioned in Isa 61:1, "heal those whose hearts are torn" and replaced it with another group: "free the oppressed."[4]

In this way, any possible confusion has been removed.

For the Jews at the time of Jesus, blindness, as with us, was greatly feared. For the Jews, there was no harsher punishment or more profound suffering than blindness (Midrash on Ps 146:5–8). The blind person was seen as a dead person (T. B. Nedarim 64b). For most blind people, begging was the only way to survive (Mark 10:46; Luke 14:13f., 21; John 9:8).

"In captivity" (*aichmalotos*): its sense is clear. It is enough to look at Luke 21:24 and Rev 13:10. Nonetheless, in question are not primarily common criminals or even prisoners of war. It is most likely that, before anything else, prisoners on economic grounds are meant.

The world described by Luke is a pyramidal society where the poor live bent over by many burdens and pressures. Life is spent in the midst of scarcity and surrounded by economic and fiscal obligations. The poor had to pay taxes to the emperor (Luke 20:20–26; 23:2) and were exposed to the arbitrary whims of the military (Matt 5:41). The poor had to send tithes of their meager harvests to the authorities in Jerusalem (Luke 11:42; 18:12; Matt 17:24–27). They had to pay large dividends to their patron (Luke 20:10) who often was exceedingly harsh with the worker (19:21). The poor suffered extortion at the hands of the public functionaries (Luke 3:12–14; 18:11; 19:18). The religious leaders commonly took advantage of the people, especially those who were weaker (Luke 11:39; 20:47). Furthermore, the poor ran the risk that thieves would leave them with nothing in the field or on the road (Luke 6:29; 10:30; 11:21–22).

---

4. See Dupont, *Études*, 95.

"Poverty was a basic fact of life in Galilee" (Mark 10:46; 12:41–44; John 9:1).[5] For this reason, it is not surprising that Luke frequently refers to people with hunger (1:53; 3:11; 4:25; 6:3, 21; 9:13; 12:29; 14:13f.; 15:17; 16:21) or notable needs (8:34; 11:5). Unemployment was high (Matt 20:1–7). Much land belonged to owners who did not even live in the vicinity (Luke 20:9ff.) and who were interested only in increasing their capital without working (Matt 25:14ff.). For this reason, debt was frequent in such a society (Luke 6:34; 7:41–42; 16:1–9) and given the impossibility of paying it off, debtors ended up in jail (Luke 12:58–59; Matt 18:28–30).

For people who suffered such a situation of pain and extreme poverty, salvation meant, more than anything else, the end of their suffering. Jesus proclaims that he has been anointed by the Spirit who is now upon him (Luke 4:18a), who directs him (4:1, 14), who has descended upon him (3:22), in order to send Jesus to proclaim rejoicing to the poor, liberty to the prisoner, that is, to the victims of pain, disparagement, usury, and exploitation (Isa 58:6f.). This proclamation is effective because it is the work of the Spirit of God.

Therefore, the work of Jesus can only signify rejoicing for the most exploited and undertrodden. Jesus' mission is to do away with what embitters the lives of the poor and the blind, who are condemned to a state of misery and disparagement (Mark 10:46ff.; John 9:1ff.), the lives of the prisoners who did not repay their debts with their onerous interest, the lives of the prisoners of war and those enslaved by the impossibility of paying off debts that the level of interest had rendered exorbitant.

·······

Many people admit that Jesus restored sight to the blind — not only in a metaphorical sense — and that he saved people from disparagement; but they will not admit that he got prisoners out of jail or that he alleviated the needs of the poor. At most, they accept as *isolated* incidents the multiplication of the bread, the healing of hemorrhages, the defense of his disciples who, because of hunger,

---

5. See Sean Freyne, *Galilee, Jesus and the Gospels* (Philadelphia: Fortress; Dublin: Gill and Macmillan, 1988), 160.

gleaned heads of grain on the Sabbath, the healing of the man with a withered hand, the woman bent over, and the man with dropsy. The same is true for the purification of the leper, the resurrection of the only son of the widow of Nain, and the healing of the paralytic brought in on a stretcher. They also admit the fact that when Jesus was rejected as a poor man in Nazareth, he was unable to perform any miracle there.

But can so many instances be isolated measures? What about Jesus' attitude to the weak (Mark 9:34–36)? And Jesus' own sense of greatness and vision of authority (Mark 10:42–45; Luke 22:24–27)? Above all, one should bear in mind Jesus' attitude about money and other material goods. For Jesus, the earth is God's gift, a sign of God's providence (Luke 12:22ff.). Material goods are certainly the object of petitionary prayer, but they are requested *for everyone;* neither luxury nor the accumulation of capital is requested, much less for a single person. Requested is rather *daily bread* (11:3) for everyone.

The detachment of Jesus regarding material goods is total (Luke 9:57–58), since the highest good for Jesus is the reign of God and God's justice (12:31). For Jesus, the person who thinks only about accumulating goods is an idiot and is impoverished before God (12:13–21). Material goods do not exist in order to be hoarded, but in order to be shared with those who cannot return the favor, that is, with the poor, the blind, the sick, and the crippled, in other words, with those excluded by the cream of society as useless and a nuisance, due to their lack of power (14:12–14; 18:22). Only thus will material goods cease to be perishable (12:33–34).

Invited to the banquet of God's reign are those who cannot contribute anything (Luke 14:21). At the same time, the God of Jesus has an anti-utilitarian economic vision. Jesus endows with honor and spares no expense on the person who is dead while alive and who has lost all honor (15:11–32). According to Jesus, money is to be spent on the one who suffers (10:25–37; 11:41). Otherwise, money is an insurmountable obstacle to entering the reign of God (18:24–25). In this experience of faith, there is no place for usury or any other type of exploitation or oppression. In this type of life, whatever causes hunger or imprisonment for the person in need is done away with.

This mission, which offers rejoicing and liberation to the poor, is considered by Jesus to be the fulfillment of a great hope (Luke 4:21): the realization of the agreeable year of the Lord, or the Jubilee, which neither the Old Testament nor intertestamental literature nor any secular source describes as having been put into practice. These were laws that concerned the whole country. Their purpose was to enable the poor person, crushed by debt, to recover economic independence and not to fall back into the circle of indebtedness.[6]

Various books of the Bible deal with the Jubilee year: for example, Lev 25:8–17; Deut 15:1–18; Jer 34:8–22; Isa 61:1–2, cited by Jesus in his appearance at Nazareth. The reason for this ideal law was to accept God as king in *all* spheres of life and, therefore, as someone who opposes *everything* that squashes and chains his children. It is a confession of faith in God the king who cares for those whom no one else cares for and who gives to those from whom the false owners of the land take everything (Ps 113:7; 140:12; 145:8–21; 146:5–10; Luke 1:52–53). It is *not* a question of defending *the goodness of the poor and the oppressed, but rather of accepting the fidelity and justice of God.* With Jesus, the moment has arrived in which this ideal becomes reality. In fact, we can see clearly in the teaching and work of Jesus what the project of God is and what this offers to the poor, who are the majority of the earth's inhabitants.

·······

At this point, it seems to me more than evident that the project of the International Monetary Fund (IMF) and other sources of economic power are the polar opposite of the vision of God and of Jesus, God's definitive word, as Luke gives it to us. As a Christian, therefore, I must oppose the project of the IMF with all my strength, all my mind, and all my heart.

II

Jesus' vision is shared by a Greek-speaking community prior to Matthew and Luke, for both gospels transmit to us in almost the

---

6. See Sharon H. Ringe, *Jesus, Liberation and the Biblical Jubilee* (Philadelphia: Fortress, 1985), 27f.

same words the question of the Baptist, the reply of Jesus, and the beatitude related to the reply (Matt 11:3–6; Luke 7:19b, 22, 23). Most likely, these words were uttered neither by John nor by Jesus, but by one of the first Greek-speaking communities.

The question of the Baptist does not correspond to John's vision of an imminent judgment in which Yahweh himself, with no need of any intermediary, will judge with all the rigor of his justice (Luke 3:7–9). Thus, "how could he arrive at the conclusion that the person he had baptized was the universal judge at the point of setting everything on fire with his justice-dealing wrath?"[7] Furthermore, "given that we are not informed how the Baptist reacted to the reply, our source makes clear that its formulation was not motived by any biographical interest."[8] On the other hand, the reply by Jesus presupposes a general acceptance that the terrible Day of the Lord "will be preceded by an initial visit of the divine emissary, partially disguised, who will be made known through his miracles."[9] Is there a historical basis for such assumptions?

The reply of Jesus in Matt 11:4–5 and Luke 7:22 is not a biographical sketch of Jesus, but rather an interpretation of his work in terms of the book of Isaiah; the work of Jesus is thereby illuminated. Jesus' works of mercy with the pagans, the poor widow, the publicans and sinners are understood in their profundity, when it is known who this compassionate one is and what is really happening with such acts.[10]

We are told that the future era of salvation has *already arrived.* Its blessings are *already* a *present* reality. The final definitive messenger of the faithful love of God and "his tender mercy" (Luke 1:78) is Jesus of Nazareth: "he has come as the embodiment of the blessings promised ... by [that] prophet."[11] As Jesus proclaimed the reign of God and did not preach himself, I cannot attribute this reply to him with a good conscience. In view here is a vision of faith that one of the first Christian communities had of Jesus.

---

7. See Dieter Zeller, *Kommentar zur Logienquelle* (Stuttgart: KBW, 1984), 39.

8. See Paul Hoffmann, *Studien zur Theologie der Logienquelle,* 3d ed. (Münster: Aschendorff, 1982), 201.

9. See Dupont, *Études,* 68.

10. See Heinz Schürmann, *Das Lukasevangelium* (Freiburg: Herder, 1969), 1:406.

11. See Joseph A. Fitzmyer, *The Gospel according to Luke* (Garden City, N.Y.: Doubleday, 1981), 1:667.

·······

"In his reply, Jesus preserves his secret by revealing it only once, and to hear that he sees in the light of prophecy brings one to knowledge."[12] It is by his deeds that Jesus is recognized as the one announced by Scripture. He restores health, the ability to earn a living, and respect to people considered a hindrance or a curse: the blind, deaf, disabled, and leprous. He even raises the dead. Nevertheless, the clear sign that the promised blessings arrive with Jesus is that good news is announced to the poor: God reigns for their benefit.

This sign, distinct from the others that are mentioned and listed last, including after the resurrection of the dead, explicitly cites Isa 61:1f. It is the clearest indication that Jesus is "the coming one" and that we do not have to wait for another.

The blind, deaf, disabled, and leprous were, as a rule, more than poor. Together with the blind and the deaf to be benefitted by the final intervention of God, the oppressed and the poor shall also rejoice, because God will have eliminated the tyranny and mendacity of the oppressors, according to Isa 28:17–22. Thus:

> the blessings accorded these sick are the pledge of a better future, [since]...the good news announced to the poor cannot be more than the notice that they will cease to be poor and to suffer poverty. Just as the blind see, the deaf hear, the dead have life, so what they need will not be lacking for the poor. They will no longer be victims of the unjust distribution of goods. This will happen in the Reign of God, which Jesus declares to be near, since poverty is an evil, and the arrival of the kingdom of God will do away with it, as with the miserable situation of the blind.[13]

In the mission of Jesus, these blessings are something very near, something already present.

·······

What God offers us in Jesus, the simple carpenter from Nazareth, according to the first Christian communities, can hardly be more

---

12. See Schürmann, *Lukasevangelium*, 411.
13. See Dupont, *Études*, 69.

opposed to what we are offered by the summit of economic power. Hunger, unemployment, malnutrition, threats to health and life are certainly *not* the signs of the arrival of the kingdom of God. Therefore, in no way can I honor this form of organizing the world economy, out of faithfulness to the primitive Christian community.

III

Neither Luke nor the communities before him shook off this disconcerting and critical vision. The only thing they did was to elaborate the message of Jesus in the light of their faith in the resurrection. In the first three beatitudes of Luke (6:20b–21), setting aside the framework added by the evangelist (6:20a) and the changes in 6:22–23, we find the central message of Jesus. In contrast with the beatitudes of the Old Testament or intertestamental literature, no condition is formulated here, and the adjective or participle are not accompanied by any qualifier.[14] The realization of the prophetic announcement in Isa 61:1–2 is proclaimed as something *extremely near;* nonetheless, "instead of announcing the good news to them," the concrete expression of the good news, namely, their destiny is used.[15] The kingdom of God is theirs.

Something truly paradoxical is proclaimed: *happy are those who live in unhappiness* — the poor, the starving, those who weep — not because they are poor, however, but rather because *very soon God will reign for their benefit* (Mark 1:15). God's future is for them. The great gift of God is for them (Luke 12:30). The great work, with which the reign of God shall be made manifest, is precisely the act of doing away with their destitution and ignominy.

The text does not say what the unhappy should do, but rather what God has decided to do in their favor. The destructive power of money will no longer rule nor any type of oppression. These will lose their vigor. God will rule in favor of the poor, giving them well-being, food, and rejoicing, thus fulfilling what was announced through the mouth of the prophet:

---

14. See E. Schweizer, "Formgeschichtliches zu den Seligpreisungen Jesu," *New Testament Studies* 19 (1973): 121–26.

15. See Dupont, *Études,* 69.

I will free my sheep from the gullet of their shepherds, that
they may not be food for them. . . . I will seek the lost sheep,
I will gather those who have gone astray, I will bind up the
injured, I will heal the sick. . . . They shall know that I am the
Lord when I break the bars of their yoke and I free them
from the power of tyrants. . . . The wild beasts shall not de-
vour them, they shall dwell secure, without sudden attacks.
. . . There shall no longer be deaths due to hunger in the land,
nor shall they have to endure the mockery of the nations. And
they shall know that I, the Lord, am their God and they are
my people. (Ezek 34:10, 16, 27–30)

The moment will soon arrive when God, "father of orphans,
defender of widows, who prepares a home for the disabled and re-
leases the prisoners to prosperity" (Ps 68:5–6 [6]), will show his
poor all his mercy (Isa 49:13). Jesus says to them as clearly as possible that God does not want the suffering of the poor and that,
consequently, it is about to be eliminated, because God has decided
to exercise his reign.

The poor are the beneficiaries of the beatitudes, not because of
their goodness, but because of the goodness that is God with them,
who "is not partial and accepts no bribe, he executes justice for
the orphan and the widow, and loves the strangers, giving them
food and clothing" (Deut 10:17–18). This is the justice of God.
Thus God reigns. Therefore, the Lord wants to eliminate whatever
humiliates and causes hunger for his children.

As a consequence, the central theme of the gospel message can
be said to be: "Happy are the poor, for the kingdom of God is
yours." It is merely a concrete way of affirming that the reign of
God is near.[16] The beatitudes are nothing other than the revelation
of the unmerited and absolutely generous justice and mercy that
characterize the reign of God. The poor will be filled, because they
shall take part in the banquet of God (Isa 25:6); and they shall
rule, because they will also enjoy the liberating work of God (Ps
126:1–2).

What Jesus promises in God's name is the suppression of the
current situation that crushes the poor. The beatitudes (Luke
6:20b–21) are a prophetic proclamation. They are absolute and

---

16. Ibid.

are valid for all those who in the current order come last. The paradoxical logic of the beatitudes, however, only convinces the person who recognizes the intention of Jesus, which he expresses in the proclamation of the nearness of God's kingdom.[17]

It is worth stating that the best commentary on the beatitudes is Jesus himself: his treatment of the castaways, the impure, sinners, the sick who cannot even express themselves, the starving throng, the crippled and other disdained sick, who did not even ask him and were healed, even on the Sabbath. With the feast that he demands or offers for those who lack everything; with his parables about the scandalous mercy of God that explode all logic and calculation; with his respect for and identification with the weakest; with his sense of greatness, his understanding of authority, his consideration for women, his limitless rejoicing; with his whole life, Jesus, the parable of God's love, reveals the limitlessness and generosity of the justice and love of God as king and father.

At the risk of redundancy, it is obvious that if I believe in Jesus' proclamation of the reign of God, there is no way I can accept the reign of that devouring idol which is money, the cause of the genocide called the foreign debt.

IV

After all of the above, it seems that no other conclusion can logically be drawn but the total opposition between God's reign and the reign of money. Nevertheless, we enter here into one of the major mysteries of iniquity present in all branches of multidivided Christianity.

Despite the fact that we accept Jesus as the definitive Word of God, despite the fact that Jesus spoke with sufficient clarity for whoever wishes to understand him, and despite the fact that Jesus himself gives us this conclusion, in all times and every manifestation of Christianity, we have complicated these eminently clear words and the transparent life experience of Jesus. Is this not the sin against the Spirit (Mark 3:29)? Is it not the case that many of us who call ourselves followers of Jesus keep alive the bloody opposi-

---

17. See Helmut Merklein, *Die Gottesherrschaft als Handlungsprinzip: Untersuchung zur Ethik Jesu*, 2d ed. (Würzburg: Echter, 1981), 53.

tion of those responsible for his assassination (Mark 8:17–21)? For this reason, it becomes almost impossible to study dispassionately the *logion* of Jesus transmitted in Luke 16:13 and Matt 6:24.

········

The *logion* in Luke 16:13/Matt 6:24 is made up of a proverb, an explanation, and an application to the audience. In this saying, "rare or unusual words and constructions are used in relation to the rest of the New Testament."[18] Concretely, *mamona* — besides the present *logion* — is found only in Luke 16:9, 11. The two versions of Matthew and Luke, apart from the mention of *oiketes* in Luke, coincide in practically every way. They come, therefore, from a source prior to these writings, although without any reference to the circumstances in which the *logion* was first uttered.

········

In question is not simply the opposition between "God" and "money," but rather the opposition between to "serve God" and to "serve money." In the phrases making up the explanation, we have a chiasmus:

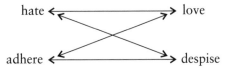

In the end, *what is at stake* is an affective disposition: it is *love,* the affectionate adherence to someone. It is not only a question of fulfilling an obligation, but rather of giving one's heart to someone through one's deeds. It is a call to make a *decision without compromise.* The opposition is absolute: either one serves God or one serves *mamona.* If one is not serving God, one is serving *mamona.* There is no sphere (of life) free from lordship.[19]

Neither in the Hebrew Bible nor in the New Testament, apart from the exceptions already referred to, do we find the word *mamona.* However, it is found in Sir 31:8: "Blessed is the man who

---

18. See Dupont, *Études,* 553.

19. See Hans Weder, *Die "Rede der Reden": Eine Auslegung der Bergpredigt heute* (Zürich: Theologischer, 1985), 202.

keeps himself blameless and is not perverted by *mamona*." This is an Aramaic word, taken from the Hebrew, which means "that in which one puts trust."[20]

Paul had written: either God or sin (Rom 6:19–23). In this *logion*, the alternative is more concrete: either God or *mamona*. The latter "has an almost demonic power; it is powerful enough to compete with God over lordship."[21] They are two realities completely opposed to one another. *Mamona* appears as a personified power contrary to God. It is an idol in direct opposition to God. It sets itself rotundly against the reign of God. It is the very opposite of God.

There is no place for self-deception. The true owner of the person who attaches him- or herself to money is this enslaving demoniacal power. "At stake here is faithfulness to God or to idolatry."[22] God's lordship is denied if one serves *mamona*, wealth accumulated or squandered without consideration for the poor (Luke 12:13–21; 16:19–31), the fruit of exploitation (20:47) or of rapacity (11:37), unshared with those in need (18:22–23, 24–25), the cause of power that excludes and marginalizes (14:21).

If one serves money, one loves it, one adheres to it, and consequently one cannot "love God with all one's heart, with all one's soul, with all one's strength, and with all one's mind" (Luke 10:27). For the same reason, one does not live a life of faith in the one God. By having two gods, I demote God to the status of an idol. If I serve money, I am its slave and I cannot serve God. If I serve God, "I am not a slave, because God makes me his child."[23] The slavery to money "perverts to the point of listening neither to Moses nor to the prophets. Abraham himself testifies to it — Luke 16:31."[24]

This is the great sin. This is the true and radical opposition to the reign of God and its justice. This is not only atheism; it is antiatheism, and of the worst sort.

20. See Fitzmyer, *Luke,* 1109.

21. See Halvor Moxnes, *The Economy of the Kingdom: Social Conflict and Economic Relations in Luke's Gospel* (Philadelphia: Fortress, 1988), 143.

22. See J. Mateos and F. Camacho, *El evangelio de Mateo* (Madrid: Cristiandad, 1981), 73.

23. See Weder, *"Rede der Reden,"* 203.

24. See Freyne, *Galilee, Jesus and the Gospels,* 101.

It is all too clear: our faith in God is a pure farce if we put ourselves at the service of its greatest enemy. There is no way to come to a compromise. Either we love God or we serve *mamona,* that terrible idol diametrically opposed to the reign of God, protector of the poor.

········

The application of this *logion* of Jesus to our own situation is abundantly clear. It is more than obvious. Question: Who, then, should pay the foreign debt? Answer: Those who caused it and have taken advantage of it. A study of the pericope about the tax for Caesar (Mark 12:13–17) would be illuminating in this regard, because in question is not one's duty to any state, but to the imperial power. It turns out, however, that I was asked to write an article and not a book.

4

The Judgment of God on the Multinationals

Revelation 18

DAGOBERTO RAMÍREZ FERNÁNDEZ

....

The Current Situation

The majority of Third World countries presently live under the imposition, from business and the World Bank, of a neoliberal capitalist economic model. As far as we can understand, the economic policy dictated by the countries of the North leaves the profits of the system in the hands of the large multinational corporations. For their part, the Third World countries have been conditioned to produce only single products or to provide raw materials and to be a lesser form of subsidiary industry that complements the larger form of industry.

With the passage of time, the application of this economic model has left the countries of the Third World with the weight of a tremendous foreign debt that has become impossible to repay. Many studies have been done on the origins and injustice of this debt. These studies have warranted the consideration of the churches as well.[1] Until now, there are no general solutions. On the

---

1. We refer especially to certain works that have recently appeared that demonstrate the concern of the churches regarding this theme. See, e.g., Lynne Jones, ed., *The Debt Crisis: A Call to Action and Solidarity,* Debt Resource Material 1 (Geneva: Commission on the Churches' Participation in Development/World Council of Churches, 1988); idem, *Taking a Stand: Highlights from the Ecumenical Hearing,* Debt Resource Material 2 (Geneva: Commission on the Churches' Participation in Development/World Council of Churches, 1989). See also F. J.

contrary, every solution is complicated by the fact that this debt is only an expression of the larger international financial crisis.

Nevertheless, what makes this situation all the more serious and unjust is the fact that its burden falls mainly on the poor countries, who have had nothing to say about this economic project, but suffer its effect in the deterioration of the quality of life of their peoples. The effect on these peoples' lives is enormous: lack of work, low salaries, minimal buying power by the middle and lower social sectors. As a consequence, we have serious problems of nutrition, education, and health services in these same sectors.

On the other hand and in inverse proportion, the upper social sectors, identified with the indicated economic model, have seen their profits increase in ways previously unknown until now. As can easily be demonstrated, the separation between the two sectors grows ever greater — clear evidence of the injustice that results from the application of this economic policy.

How to solve the crisis is difficult and worrisome, also for those countries where the situation originated.[2] We are neither able nor interested to discuss this matter from a political-economic angle. Rather, we are interested in analyzing the conditions under which the church of Jesus Christ can and ought to say and do something in defense of the life of subjugated peoples, especially in those sectors that are being primarily affected by the crisis. Many social sectors, political and union groups, and human rights organizations have raised their voices to demand justice. The church has not been absent from this protest, denouncing the injustice of the system, the artificial nature of the debt, the material impossibility of paying it off, and its disastrous effects on the life and quality of life of the majority of each country's population.

All these social, political, and union sectors in their desire to denounce the injustice of the system have not been heard. On the contrary, most of the time they have not even been tolerated; instead, they have been labeled as ideological enemies and as un-

---

Hinkelammert, *La deuda externa de América Latina: El automatismo de la deuda externa* (San José, Costa Rica: DEI, 1988); idem, *La fe de Abraham y el Edipo occidental* (San José, Costa Rica: DEI, 1989); Robert L. Ayres, *Banking on the Poor: The World Bank and World Poverty* (Cambridge, Mass.: MIT, 1983).

2. See *Documento de Santa Fe: Fundamentos de una nueva política exterior de perspectiva* (May 1980); *Documento de Santa Fe II: Una estrategia para América Latina en los noventa.*

patriotic by their respective governments. They have been met with violence, repression, jail, torture, exile, and even death.

The church ought to participate in this process of struggle, insofar as it wishes to be an incarnation of the love and justice of God among human beings. As already said, the church has not remained apart from this situation and in many cases has made its own voice heard. Nevertheless, this prophetic voice — let us confess it — has not been representative of the whole church. Sectors exist within the church that are ensnared by the system, if not dedicated to it (at least structurally). Thus the weight and cost of complaining has fallen on those ecclesial sectors more dedicated to the poor.

The price paid by these Christians and Christian communities faithful to the gospel has been the accusation, ideological suspicion, censure, and silence of their spokespersons. On the other hand, by supposedly defending the orthodoxy of the faith, we help to consolidate and to accommodate the ecclesial structures, so that they are in harmony and work together with the entire economic system to which we have referred. Important studies exist that examine this problem.[3]

With regard particularly to the situation of oppression in Spanish and Portuguese America, we ought to pay homage to all those Christians who have offered up their lives for the cause of the justice of the kingdom. The individual cases are too numerous to mention; at least, they are already very well known. The blood of many Christians — laypersons, priests, pastors, and bishops — has been poured out in this struggle, alongside many social, political, and union leaders. All of them have fallen victims to an unjust and idolatrous economic system that sacrifices so many lives every day.

It is against the background of this contemporary situation that we propose to examine the Scriptures. Our reading of the sacred text is centered in the message of the book of Revelation, particularly chapter 18. Two elements constitute the backdrop of our reading. First, our intention is to show how the political situation and, specifically, the economic situation of the Roman empire constitutes the social foundation on which the theological mes-

---

3. See Ana María Ezcurra, *Iglesia y transición democrática: Ofensiva del neoconservadurismo católico en América Latina* (Buenos Aires: Puntosur, 1988); idem, *Intervención en América Latina: Los conflictos de baja intensidad* (Buenos Aires: IDEAS, 1988).

sage of chapter 18 is developed. And second, on the basis of this social situation, we look to discover the conditions under which the Christian community develops a message that constitutes a prophetic witness that transcends history.

The message of the book of Revelation is a call to Christians to persevere and to be faithful in a situation of persecution. This persecution developed in very concrete circumstances. The Roman empire was progressively established, beginning in the first century before Christ, as a political-military system that took into its hands the control of economic and social power throughout the vast territory in which its rule was planted. In this slow political-military advance, it subjugated many nations, peoples, and small local kingdoms that were unable militarily to resist the advance of Rome's armies. Consequently, these had to submit to Rome's political power and become incorporated into the social and economic system that was imposed on them after defeat.

On the other hand, those that rebelled suffered persecution and death. The text of Revelation is written out of the experience of those sectors that resisted the power of the Roman empire. This was not a military resistance. Rather, we can say that it was a political-religious resistance by those converts to the Christian faith who, rooted in Jewish monotheism, did not bend the knee before the pretensions to divinization that the empire wished to impose. It is the response of those who gave their life before submitting to idolatrous power. The text of Revelation is thus the witness of those persecuted Christian communities that dared to denounce this power and to resist it through disobedience and in faithfulness to their Lord.

We have wanted to analyze chapter 18 of the book of Revelation, because to some degree, in our opinion, the characteristics of the reigning political power and the expression of the economic project that sustained it are reflected in this chapter. It was a system that, adorned with "religious" characteristics and based on the supposedly divine status of the emperor, was sacralized and demanded the submission of all subjects in the empire.

An analysis of this text may shed some light for us on the situation of underdevelopment in countries of the Third World. It is also possible that it will illuminate our experience of a believing people who, while persecuted for their faith in Jesus Christ, are motivated not to submit to the political and economic domination of an imperial power.

Exegesis

In studying the text that occupies us here, we follow the division of the text of Revelation used in previous studies.[4] According to this division, chapter 18 occurs in the fourth sequence of seven (14:6–19:8) under the general theme of eschatological combat. This combat will have its climax in the fifth sequence of seven, with the theme of the final victory of God over the forces of evil and the glorification of the martyrs. Both sections — (1) the eschatological combat and the persecution and martyrdom of the saints, and (2) the final victory of God and his angels — are related to one another.

Because of this observation, one should read chapter 18 with an optimistic spirit (see, e.g., Rev 1:8 and 22:7). The final victory is already secure (19:9–22:5), but not before passing through the martyrdom of the lamb and his followers. It is not a sacrifice in vain or a useless death, but the prophetic ministry of the messianic community that confronts its mission in the midst of the oppressive powers of this world with faith and hope.

In fact, the emphasis in chapter 18 is placed on the prophetic denunciation by the community of the earthly powers opposed to God. The world of human beings in Rev 14:6–19:8 is characterized as a situation of permanent conflict, in which there is oppression, persecution, and martyrdom for the faithful. A vision is offered in which history is subject to the power of forces that oppose God and his project of salvation. Nonetheless, in the following section (19:9–22:5), there is a desire to say that this world of conflict and suffering will see the glory and final triumph of God and the glorification and vindication of the saintly martyrs.

The section that begins in Rev 14:6 offers us, first, the proclamation of God's imminent judgment and the song of triumph of the community of the saved (chapter 14). Chapter 15 continues the vision with the faithful who sing the song of Moses and the

---

4. See Dagoberto Ramírez Fernández, "La idolatría del poder: La iglesia confesante en Apocalipsis 13," *RIBLA* 4 (1989): 109–26.

lamb. Then the angels (chapter 16) receive the cups of God's wrath and pour them out, thereby symbolizing the calamities that will fall on the followers of the beast. Everything here makes us recall the plagues of Egypt. Now there is a desire to announce the calamities that will come over the earth in the last times or the eschaton.

We shall pause a little longer in chapter 17, given that it constitutes the prelude to chapter 18. Both chapters are unified through 19:18 in terms of sense and literary structure. We have the following:

Theme: The Fall of Babylon. Seven Visions (17:1–19:8)

a. 1) 17:1–6a   The great whore. Imperial political system;
     2) 17:6b–18   The beast. The political power and its allies;
b. 3) 18:1–3   The angel announces the fall of Babylon;
     4) 18:4–20   Exaltation and lament over the fall of Babylon (Rome);
     5) 18:21–24   Final destruction and song of the saints;
c. 6) 19:1–5   Hymn of thanksgiving to God;
     7) 19:6–8   Wedding hymn of the lamb and his bride.

The sequence of ideas to be developed can be seen with a certain clarity, as can their relation to and progression from one another. First, Babylon is presented as a literary symbol of the Roman imperial power: a total, all-encompassing political system with allies that aid it, participate in its policies, and benefit from them (though later, at its fall, they will have to abandon it). This expression of absolute power signifies persecution and death for the faithful who oppose it, but who will finally conquer (17:14).

The second step (chapter 18) describes the structure and characteristic features of the economic power. The economic system that the political power has restored is now denounced. It is an economic-commercial project with subsidiary associates that collaborate with the central power, are in solidarity with it, support it, and also profit from it. Nonetheless, just as they share in the benefits of this imperial political arrangement, they shall also fall together with it at the time of judgment. This economic-commercial alliance, as in chapter 17, also signifies persecution, misery, and death for the faithful.

The third step (or act) is the final triumph of God and his holy martyrs (chapter 19), who sing a song of triumph and thanksgiving at the consummation of the eschaton and the end of the fall of the political-economic power.

In chapter 17, the political power is characterized as the great whore (*tes pornes tes megales,* v. 1b). This description is made manifest in the type of relations that she maintains with other powers, where nothing else matters but the accumulation of power. In this process of accumulating political power, she persecutes those who oppose her imperial pretensions, namely, the saints (v. 6) and the lamb (v. 14). The text finally announces her future ruin (vv. 16ff.) due to God's judgment.

On the basis of these antecedents in the overall discourse of Revelation, it is now possible to read chapter 18. We have the following arrangement of the chapter within the preceding framework:

1. vv. 1–3 Theophany   a. an angel from heaven
2. vv. 4–20 Theophany   b. a voice from heaven
3. vv. 21–24 Theophany   c. an angel with power

The theme is the fall of Babylon, i.e., Rome, the great whore of chapter 17, made effective now. The fall is explained in detail. In part 1, vv. 1–3, an angel descends from heaven and predicts the fall of Babylon. Although a future event, it is presented as an event that has already occurred ("has fallen," *epesen* [second aorist]).

In part 2, vv. 4–20, we have the second angelic theophany. This time, it is a voice from heaven that addresses the earth with a message directed at "my people" (*laos mou*). In this message, the people are encouraged to leave the great city in order not to be destroyed in its ruin.

Alliances are described that constitute the economic power. Nonetheless, this economic power has weak and unstable foundations, given that it is built only on the interest of each of the allies in obtaining the best for themselves. All this creates a situation that merits the judgment of God, insofar as the good of humanity as a whole is not pursued, but rather only the good of certain individual groups to the exclusion of others.

In prophetic style, the fall of the empire is announced, when its economic power will be undermined and hence its alliances destroyed. There are three woes in the discourse that proclaim this fall (vv. 10, 16, 19). The second theophany ends with a call by the holy apostles and prophets to rejoice at the fall of the imperial power and the triumph of divine justice.

In part 3, vv. 21–24, we have the third theophany. An angel with symbolic gestures describes the destruction of the imperial power and all the signs that will accompany this fall. The theological argument is explained one more time which justifies this fall: it is the judgment of God against an economic-political system that, through its very existence, not only sacrifices humanity, but furthermore brings to completion the persecution of the prophets and saints of the people of God.

The entire chapter betrays, through its composition, the use of prophetic literature. Specifically, the style of Isaiah 13 and 21:1–10, Ezekiel 26–28, and Jeremiah 50–51 is employed. In Old Testament prophecy, we have a historical background that is useful for assessing the meaning of Revelation 18. For example, First Isaiah (1–39) was redacted after the exile in times of Persian domination, when Babylon had already fallen under their dominion. The same thing happens in Second Jeremiah. As for Ezekiel (26–28), the collection of oracles against Tyre is used, which in the sixth century had become a great naval commercial power throughout the Mediterranean. This prophetic literature helps the redactor of Revelation 18 to speak of "Babylon" and refer to Rome, since both became political-military imperial powers and had great economic power.

Using all this Old Testament material, the prophetic discourse of Revelation is developed in terms of the literary genre of apocalypse. In the apocalyptic genre, one speaks with symbols that represent real historical situations. These symbols transmit a prophetic message of denunciation that, fittingly decoded by its readers, has the power of announcing God's judgment and bringing encouragement and hope for the prophets, at the same time that it demands their response of faith.

What does this discourse mean? What message did it wish to communicate to the Christians of its time? What can it say to us today? The message has three parts. First, it denounces the oppressive political power. Second, it denounces the economic power on which the political power is based. Third, it adds to these themes (at the level of social discourse) the theological theme of the denunciation of the persecution and martyrdom of the faithful and the announcement of God's judgment.

This first overview of the meaning of the text makes clear the importance of the economic fetish in denouncing the imperial power. Without leaving aside other elements that may emerge while reading the text more closely, it is important in the exegesis to highlight the denunciation of the economic power.

First Theophany, vv. 1–3:
The Announcement by a Heavenly Angel

These verses say:

> [1]After this I saw another angel coming down from heaven, having great authority; and the earth was made bright with his glory.

> [2]And he called out with a mighty voice, "Fallen, fallen is Babylon the great! It has become a dwelling place of demons, a haunt of every foul spirit, a haunt of every foul bird and every foul and hateful beast;

> [3]for all the nations have drunk from the wine of her impure passion, the kings of the earth have committed fornication with her, and the merchants of the earth have grown rich with the wealth of her unchecked luxury." (Rev 18:1–3)

In vv. 1–2a, the editor begins the prophetic discourse with a theophany. The angel from heaven is a synonym for God, who reveals himself to show his power (*exousia*) and glory (*doxe*). The dualism that characterizes apocalyptic discourse is perceptible. This scene takes place in heaven (from God) toward the earth (a message to human beings).

Next, there is the prophetic oracle. In vv. 2b–3, Babylon the great is Rome, whose ruin as an imperial power is announced. Even though this statement is a prophetic pronouncement, it is striking that it is expressed in the past tense (*epesen*: aorist). It is a prophecy *ex eventu* that wants to represent an event in the text as it will later be expressed in the eschaton. The prophet speaks from the perspective of the future and dramatizes the event. Literary parallels are found in Isa 21:1–10, especially v. 9b: "Fallen, fallen is Babylon; and all the statues of her gods he has shattered against the ground" (see also Jer 9:10; Isa 13:21ff.; 34:11–14; Bar 4:35). It also appears as the literary genre of lament in Amos 5:2; Lam 2:21; Jer 50:2b.

The reasons for the fall of Babylon, i.e., Rome, are listed. At stake is essentially her power, which is explicable insofar as she has succeeded in incorporating other lesser states into her political structure. These subsidiary powers are mentioned in v. 3: "all the nations" (*panta ta ethne*); "the kings of the earth" (*hoi basileis tes ges*); and, finally, "the merchants of the earth" (*hoi emporoi tes ges*).

In Isa 13:19, Babylon is called "the flower of the kingdoms." Many small city-states had been politically incorporated into the imperial power through commercial alliances. The same thing occurs in the Roman period. The morality of these alliances is characterized with expressions such as "dwelling place of demons" (*katoiketerion daimonion*), "haunt of every foul spirit" (*phylake pantos pneumatos akathartou*), "haunt of every foul bird" (*orneou akathartou*) and "foul beast" (*theriou akathartou*).

This is thus not an alliance of equals. The place (Babylon) is described as a place where there is corruption. Nations, kings, and merchants have participated in every type of commercial transaction and economic agreement, characterized in the text as drinking from the "wine of her impure passion" (*porneia*). Furthermore, they have participated in the licentious life of one who has great wealth, "luxury and unchecked sensuality" (*tou strenous autes eploutesan*). In this place, corruption is sheltered, practiced, and made possible.

The commercial activity displayed here unremedially implicates nations, kings, and merchants. They cannot escape the commitment that this type of alliance signifies; these cities and states are lesser partners in the empire and their activity is subsidiary and dependent with respect to the central power.

We know that from its beginning (first century B.C.E.) throughout its domain, the Roman empire adopted a policy of domination called the *pax romana* or *pax augusta*. According to this system, a policy was applied of common well-being for all the peoples who had been subjected to the empire through war. Every city or state could take part in the "security" and protection that the empire provided by paying the tribute demanded by the empire. The empire guaranteed, certainly through the high tribute that it collected in order to support the system, the existence of roads as a means of expeditious communication and kept them free of banditry. It also oversaw the minting of money, free trade, culture, etc.

In this way, the empire managed to consolidate and amplify its power through alliances with Hellenistic cities along the entire coast of the Aegean Sea, especially Greece and Asia Minor. The central axis of political-economic domination rested on this policy of alliances. In order to guarantee the system's stability, the imperial government placed war veterans as governors in the colonies and thus made political domination possible through military as well as economic means.[5]

This system progressively allowed for Rome's entry into every local government. Even when these governments maintained a certain autonomy, for example, in the judicial system, one still had to appeal to Rome. The system created a network of dependent relationships between the empire, whose head was in Rome, and the colonies and lesser states that had been subjected militarily.

This dependency extended to the political, social, economic, and military life of the peoples. In most cases, the alliances were made between the empire and these peoples' upper classes, who normally did not resist and were not allies of military resistance to foreign domination. On the contrary, their preference was to negotiate with the empire and to establish commercial relations with it.

In this fashion, the local aristocracies increased their own wealth and internal hegemony at the cost of having to accept and, in the worst case, to participate in the repression imposed on the lower classes, who were the ones that supported the heavy tax burden with their work. Many persons of the lower classes ended up losing their lands and even their families; because of unpayable debts, they were subject to slavery. In not a few cases, they lost their lives

---

5. See John G. Gager, *Kingdom and Community: The Social World of Early Christianity* (Englewood Cliffs, N.J.: Prentice-Hall, 1975). The author refers to the order of "knights," who at the same time that they were the capitalists, businessmen, and industrialists, had the additional responsibility, delegated by Rome, to watch out for the economic interests of the empire in the colonies. As is obvious, this supervision extended to the political-ideological level, given that they were supposed to be attentive to whatever movement or uprising might disturb the stability of the system.

when faced with the desperate situation of having forcibly to resist the extraction of tribute and the dispossession of their goods.

In these verses, then, we have a moral judgment on an economic-political system that "seduced," that is, attracted, incorporated, and obliged many lesser states throughout the Mediterranean basin. An all-encompassing, monopolizing economic and political project was established that made Rome rich and powerful, but also gave other lesser states and colonies a share in this wealth.

The voice of the angel from heaven constitutes the prophetic discourse developed out of the situation of the community of holy believing martyrs who put their complaint in God's mouth. This prophetic indictment has again three dimensions: political, economic, and religious. The enemy of the persecuted community is the Roman empire as hegemonic political power. The imperial system imposes its economic project and manages the network of commercial relations throughout the entire empire. The third enemy of the community to be denounced is the imperial cult.

The Roman empire, using its accumulated political power and seeking to maintain its rule, e.g., under Domitian, demanded the payment of tribute with great severity. This demand was much more heavily stressed regarding the Jews, due to the antipathy that Domitian held for them. Because of the monotheistic character of their religion, the Jews did not accept the payment of tribute to a human power with pretensions to divinity. This was understood as rebellion and "atheism" against the empire.

The Jews suffered strong punishment and persecution because of this. The same thing happened to the Christian community. The prophetic witness of the book of Revelation belongs to a community that rejected the pretensions to divinity of the empire and the emperor. They only recognized Jesus Christ as *kyrios* and had to suffer persecution because of this.

Second Theophany, vv. 4–20: A Voice from Heaven

This part reads:

> [4]Then I heard another voice from heaven saying, "Come out of her, my people, lest you take part in her sins, lest you share in her plagues;

[5]for her sins are heaped high as heaven, and God has remembered her iniquities.

[6]Render to her as she herself has rendered, and repay her double for her deeds; mix a double draught for her in the cup she mixed.

[7]As she glorified herself and played the wanton one, so give her a like measure of torment and mourning. Since in her heart she says, 'A queen I sit, I am no widow, mourning I shall never see,'

[8]so shall her plagues come in a single day, pestilence and mourning and famine, and she shall be burned with fire; for mighty is the Lord God who judges her."

[9]And the kings of the earth, who committed fornication and were wanton with her, will weep and wail over her when they see the smoke of her burning;

[10]they will stand far off in fear of her torment and say, "Alas! alas! Babylon, you great city, you mighty city! In one hour has your judgment come."

[11]And the merchants of the earth weep and mourn for her, since no one buys their cargo any more,

[12]cargo of gold, silver, jewels and pearls, fine linen, purple, silk and scarlet, all kinds of scented wood, all articles of ivory, all articles of costly wood, bronze, iron, and marble,

[13]cinnamon, spice, incense, myrrh, frankincense, wine, oil, fine flour and wheat, cattle and sheep, horses and chariots, and slaves, that is, human souls.

[14]"The fruit for which your soul longed has gone from you, and all your dainties and your splendor are lost to you, never to be found again!"

[15]The merchants of these wares, who gained wealth from her, will stand far off, in fear of her torment, weeping and mourning aloud,

[16]"Alas, alas, for the great city that was clothed in fine linen, in purple and scarlet, bedecked with gold, with jewels, and with pearls!

[17]In one hour all this wealth has been laid waste." And all shipmasters and seafaring men, sailors and all whose trade is on the sea, stood far off

[18]and cried out as they saw the smoke of her burning, "What city was like the great city?"

[19]And they threw dust on their heads, as they wept and mourned, crying out, "Alas, alas, for the great city where all who had ships at sea grew rich by her wealth! In one hour she has been laid waste."

[20]Rejoice over her, O heaven, O saints and apostles and prophets, for God has given judgment for you against her!

(Rev 18:4–20)

In v. 4a, we have the editorial introduction whereby the visionary gives us the second part of his prophetic oracle indicting the imperial power. In the first oracle, it was an angel who descended from heaven toward the earth to announce God's judgment. This time, it is a voice that speaks directly from heaven without descending. It is the voice of God that speaks, directing itself to the people. A change has occurred from an oracle of judgment to one of exhortation. In vv. 4b–8, this exhortation of God is directed at his people (my people: *ho laos mou*), i.e., the community of the saints, apostles, and prophets (v. 20). This exhortation has three basic elements.

First, there is a call to the people to leave the city. There is a similar call in Jer 50:8ff., where the people are invited to emigrate from Babylon. We also have something similar in Jer 51:6, 49–50. In Jer 50:16, those who work in agriculture are exhorted to abandon Babylon and to return each one to his own people (also in Isa 13:14).

In the book of Revelation, this offer should be interpreted as an invitation not only to gain geographic distance but, moreover, to separate oneself and not to become mixed up in the economic politics that supported the Roman empire. To become involved in this project, despite the economic gains to be made, or because of them, is to fall into sin and to make oneself subject to the judgment of God, a judgment that should fall only on the imperial power (v. 20).

We should note the theological reading of the economic factor in the text when this factor is classified as sin and subject to God's judgment. Such an economy is sinful insofar as it brings with it extreme poverty for many and, furthermore, means persecution and death for the community of the faithful. The sin, characterized as such, rises to heaven (v. 5), i.e., it has not gone unnoticed by God nor is it something in which the Lord has no interest. On the contrary, it constitutes the essence of a sinful situation that ought to be punished. God is very mindful of it; he neither overlooks nor forgets it (v. 5: *emnemoneusen*), insofar as it is an expression of the injustice between humans (*adikemata*) that must be remedied.

Second, the other action to which the people are called is to pay back the evil and suffering that this system has caused them. To pay it double for its deeds, to prepare for it the cup, are expressions of the *lex talionis* (e.g., in Jer 50:29; 51:34–40). In Isa 14:8, retribution is expressed in terms of reversed situations. From greater sin, a greater distance should be taken. Sin becomes greater when it endeavors to exhibit absolute power and authority without recognizing any other type of superior power.

The expression "sit as queen" refers to this, namely, without knowing solitude and need (widowhood), without suffering (weeping). One can read in Jer 51:5 of widowhood as solitude and need (see, moreover, Isa 47:8–11). Something similar is said in the Sibylline Oracles (5.168–71) referring to Rome. At issue is the sin of pride and arrogance that comes from the knowledge that one has total economic and political power.

Finally, the exhortation to the people to leave the city ends with an appeal to the just judgment of God. This is done in the purest apocalyptic style: to burn in fire under the superior power. In this case, it is the power of God the Lord (*kyrios* or *theos*) that is meant, who imposes his definitive form of justice in the eschaton.

Verses 9–20 continue the prophetic discourse. Their literary style reminds us again of the prophetic oracles of the Old Testament. Together, these verses form a discourse of indictment against the exercise of economic power and how this power is expressed, in the present case through commerce. Again, we have the economic factor as the basic element constituting the sin of imperial power and deserving God's judgment. There are three political-economic sectors involved: "the kings of the earth" (v. 9: *hoi basileis tes ges*), "the merchants of the earth" (v. 11: *hoi emporoi tes ges*), and the shipmasters (*kybernetes* and *ho epi topon pleon*), those who work in the sea (v. 17).

The entire discourse indicting the economic power of the empire is now directed at the allies and lesser consortiums found dispersed along all its borders (the expression "of the earth" [*tes ges*] refers to this). As in Isa 14:18, the expression "kings of the nations" refers to the small satellite countries or city-states that were dominated politically and economically (see vv. 3 and 9). Also in Ezek 26:16–18 and 27:9b, mention is made of the "princes of the sea" as those governing the islands and cities that traded with Tyre.

It is worthwhile stopping to analyze the different articles or merchandise that are mentioned. Beyond illustrating the great scope of contemporary commerce, the same articles also constitute a valuable piece of historical evidence about its character. A similar list to the one in vv. 11–13 appears in Ezek 27:12ff., where commerce with Tarshish is mentioned.

A series of products is enumerated that were sold throughout the known world and mainly concentrated in the ports of Asia. There are precious stones, luxury objects, spices, and perfumes. All these elements are evidence of the sumptuousness and opulence of the upper classes of Roman society. This fact is already indicative of a strong social stratification, whereby certain sectors of the aristocracy concentrated the major part of the economic power in their hands, a situation that allowed them to live an easy and licentious life.

A series of metals is also mentioned (gold, bronze, iron), as well as woods, marble, etc. The existence of and traffic in metals shows us the degree to which metallurgy or working with metals had advanced. These were already strategic elements, given that one could thereby produce weapons for war, although tools were also produced for artisans and cultivation of the land. To have a monopoly on these metals would be a constitutive sign of economic power. Likewise, their commercialization allowed one to obtain a high percentage of profit.

At a third level is the commerce with food: wine, oil, flour, wheat, sheep, etc. This is another dimension of economic and commercial power. Whoever has these products can obtain a certain profit; the one, however, who acts as the intermediary in their commercialization obtains the greater profit without having to produce them.

Cultivated land in many parts had been expropriated through the dispossession constituted by the high tribute exacted from those who held the land. When poor peasants lost their land, it passed into the hands of the landowners, who accumulated it and made it produce at little cost, using cheap manual labor obtained from the same peasants who had lost their land. These impoverished peasants were forced to become employees in order to pay off their debts and try to survive. The accumulation of food products is a monopolistic activity that allows one to determine the level of the prices and produces, when properly commercialized, enormous wealth.

Finally, but not less important, is the business of slaves. Slavery constituted the most important economic activity from the first century B.C.E. until the second century C.E.[6] In the Roman social order, slaves constituted the lowest class on the social scale. The slave trade reached such a point that the Roman economy depended in large measure on its existence. The majority of the slaves in the empire came from Syria and Asia Minor; they also came from Greece, Judea, Africa, and the western provinces. Josephus (*bell.* 6.420) says that around 97,000 Jews were made slaves by Titus in the taking of Jerusalem in 70 C.E. Many of these were sent to work in Egypt (*bell.* 6.418).

The reference to the system of slavery in v. 13 can be understood by analyzing three expressions in vv. 13b and 14. In the first place, we have the simple slaves (*somata*) used for field work and domestic service in aristocratic houses. Another class of slaves corresponds to the expression *psychas anthropon* (see Ezek 27:13). These are probably slaves of a higher social or cultural condition like pedagogues, writers, artists, etc., who were used for the education of the children of aristocratic families. A third category of slave is those whose shining bodies, well-formed and

---

6. See Gager, *Kingdom and Community*, 91–111.

well-nourished, covered with resplendent ornaments, were used in the circus, in theatrical productions at the imperial court, and in brothels.

The enumeration of all these elements, constitutive of the economy and commerce of the time, allows us to deduce the different social groups that together made up Roman society in all the territory of the empire. In the same way, it allows us to infer how this wealth was accumulated and distributed and who were its beneficiaries. First, therefore, by analyzing the economic lexemes in the text, we can extend our reasoning and draw conclusions about production, the accumulation of wealth and its distribution. Second, we can infer the make-up of the social classes and groups that this economic system generated. Finally, we can make reference to the social practice of each one of these groups. It is evident in the text from which social sector the indictment comes and against whom the judgment is directed. In the face of this situation of injustice, an appeal is made to the justice of God.

The entire prophetic denunciation is also expressed in this section in terms of lamentation in order to highlight the total destruction of the imperial power and all those who have benefitted from it. The song is interwoven with three woes (*threnos* in Greek, from the Hebrew *quinoth*), a literary resource very typical of prophetic literature and taken over by the New Testament (see, e.g., Ezek 24:6ff.; 26:17ff.; Isa 5:8; Jer 22:13; 50:2b; Amos 5:16; Matt 11:21; Luke 6:24).

[10]"Alas! alas! Babylon, you great city [*he megale*], you mighty city [*ischyra*]!
In one hour has your judgment come (*krisis*)."

[16f]"Alas, alas, for the great city [*he megale*] that was clothed in fine linen, in purple and scarlet, bedecked with gold, with jewels, and with pearls!
In one hour all this wealth has been laid waste."

[19]"Alas, alas, for the great city [*he megale*] where all who had ships at sea grew rich by her wealth!
In one hour she has been laid waste."

The first woe refers to the judgment of the political power. The power structure that the Roman empire has become is denounced as well as its subjugation of many nations. Together with this indictment, the imminent eschatological judgment of God on this absolute power is announced.

In the second woe, the economic rule by means of which the empire sustains itself, as well as the luxury and ostentation that accompany it, are denounced. The lament ends with the imminent judgment that will accompany its destruction.

The whole section (vv. 4–20) concludes with a song of consolation to the faithful: "Rejoice, heaven" (a variant adds: "over her," to highlight the reversal of situations produced with the consummation of God's judgment).[7] There is joy in heaven, which is accompanied later by joy on earth. The holy apostles and prophets deserve special mention. The reason for this total joy is "because God has judged [ekrinen] your case [krima] with her." Finally, with the eschatological judgment, divine justice is reestablished. This justice has two dimensions: first, the condemnation of the unjust, the imperial Roman power; and, second, the vindication of the just.

Third Theophany, vv. 21–24: An Angel with Power

²¹Then a mighty angel took up a stone like a great millstone and threw it into the sea, saying, "So shall Babylon the great city be thrown down with violence, and be found no more;

²²and the sound of harpers and minstrels, of flute players and trumpeters, shall be heard in you no more; and a craftsman of any craft shall be found in you no more; and the sound of the millstone shall be heard in you no more;

²³and the light of a lamp shall shine in you no more; and the voice of bridegroom and bride shall be heard in you no more;

---

7. The theme of reversed social situations is typical in prophetic and sapiential literature as a clear expression of the radical character that the justice of God acquires: see, e.g., 1 Sam 2:7; 2 Sam 22:28; Sir 10:14; Job 12:17–25; Ezek 21:31. In the New Testament, it appears especially in the synoptic gospels; see, e.g., Mark 9:35; 10:31, 44; Matt 23:12; Luke 2:14; further, A. Gelin, *Les pauvres que Dieu aime* (Paris: Cerf, 1968). This author proposes that the theme of reversed situations as an expression of God's justice would have arisen out of circles of the "poor of Yahweh." See also E. Hamel, "El Magnificat y la inversión de las situaciones," *Selecciones de Teología* 79 (1981): 231ff.; G. Ruiz, "El Magnificat: Dios está por los que pierden," *Selecciones de Teología* 79 (1981): 228ff.

for your merchants were the great men of the earth, and all nations were deceived by your sorcery.

²⁴And in her was found the blood of prophets and of saints, and of all who have been slain on earth." (Rev 18:21–24)

This discourse of prophetic indictment of the imperial power ends with a third theophany. This time, it is a powerful (*ischyros*) angel. We should note that in v. 10b, the term "powerful" was applied to "Babylon" (Rome), symbol of temporal power. Power is now transferred to the one who truly possesses it, namely, God.

Once more the fall of Rome is repeated in order to say what shall no longer be found in her. For this, the theme of the destruction of Babylon and of how she is thrown into the Euphrates in Jer 51:63 has been used as a literary resource. (The image of the millstone as a symbol of justice is also found in Ezek 26:12 and in Matt 18:6 and parallels.) There shall be no more rejoicing, festivals or merriment in her territory (v. 22a). Neither shall there be work or industry (*technites, techne:* v. 22b).

The decline of the economic project is predicted. The consequences of this crisis will fall on the world of work and will mean the end of all technological progress. This decline also includes the crisis that will affect the countryside and its production. The "sound of the mill" (*phone mylou*) refers to the production of cereals. The empire took pride in being the big producer and distributor of these things (see vv. 11–13).

Darkness will cover the great expanse of the empire (v. 23a). This expression appears in Jer 25:10. In similar terms, the prophet announces the nature of Babylon's fall. There too will there be neither joy nor rejoicing.

The consequences of this political and economic disaster will equally affect the structures of society (v. 23b). The disintegration of the family is foreseen. The same is true in Jer 7:34; 16:9; and 25:10.[8]

Finally, the primary cause of this slaughter is indicated. It is an economic factor (v. 23b). The large maritime businesses, charged with transporting the production of the whole Mediter-

---

8. See this element in the apocalyptic discourses of the synoptic gospels, e.g., Mark 13:2; Matt 10:21.

ranean basin, will enter into crisis, because there will no longer
be anything to transport, given that there will no longer be any
production.

This crisis of the economic project is classified as *pharmakeia*,
which can be translated as sorcery, magic, or enchantment. The
economic fetish, insofar as it is the object of idolatrous worship,
has captivated the nations and the kings of the earth. The "holy
apostles and prophets" (vv. 20 and 24) did not fall under this spell
and therefore suffered persecution and death. For this reason, the
ruin of the economic system belongs to God's eschatological judgment. In the midst of this system, the blood of innocent persons
has been poured out; prophets and saints were sacrificed (*esphag-
menoi*). Reference is clearly made to their murder by Domitian
at the end of the first century C.E. This persecution was directed
against all those who dared to reject the imperial cult.

Synthesis

The structure of chapter 18 offers us, in synthesis, the following
elements for its interpretation:

A. *First theophany:* judgment of hegemonic political power consolidated through economic alliances

   v. 1. Theophany: an angel with power
   v. 2. Babylon the great has fallen! (political power)
   v. 3. Nations, kings, and merchants (political-economic al-
         liance)

B. *Second theophany:* exhortation to faithfulness and denouncing of sin

   v. 4. Another voice from heaven; call to holy people
   vv. 5–8. Judgment of God: the people should separate them-
         selves from every form of sin in the empire
   vv. 9–20. Indictment of idolatrous economic power that cor-
         rupts and makes a sacrifice of the people

         – announcement of its imminent fall
         – joy in heaven and rejoicing on earth
         – the justice of God imposed in the eschatological
           judgment

C. *Third theophany:* eschatological judgment and revindication of the faithful

v. 21. A powerful angel in a symbolic gesture makes known the fall of the imperial power

vv. 22–23. Consequences of the destruction of the political-economic power

v. 24. Denouncing of power and its culpability in the sacrifice of the prophets and saints

The text moves between denouncing economic sin, the announcement of divine judgment, and the vindication of the faithful. Sin is clearly stated in three dimensions: political, economic, and religious. These three elements circulate in the reading of the text, and offer important elements for its interpretation.

Hermeneutic

In concluding the exegetical part of this essay, we can say that the text offers us at least three levels on which to read it: first, on a political level; second, on an economic level; and third, on a religious level. It is worthwhile briefly analyzing these three levels to see how they relate to one another in such a way that their meaning may also be significant for us today.

For the meaning-effects of the text, it is important to keep the sociohistorical aspect separate from the literary. The text as literature comes from a historical situation. Once transformed into a written text, however, it gains independence from the original historical situation and can be extended, in this case, to the contemporary situation that we want to illuminate.

With regard to the sociohistorical situation, it is clear from the data we can obtain that the text is a prophetic oracle of the apocalyptic genre written from the perspective of oppression-persecution. Christian communities at the end of the first century c.e. are in view, communities which, in their missionary dispersion, had to struggle against the hegemonic pretensions of the Roman empire.

We know that the Roman empire had a project of political-military domination, which, in turn, was supported by an economic project. This meant bringing into submission many small cities, states, and colonies all along the empire's borders, in Asia Minor and around the Mediterranean basin. This project of domination, in its search for social legitimation, developed an ideology of domination that assumed religious characteristics. Known as the divinization of the emperor, Caesar was to be acknowledged as lord (*kyrios*), given that he represented the divinity. Divinized were both his person and the empire's project of domination that he embodied.

The whole imperial system was considered divine, that is, beloved by the gods, and all had to submit to it. To reject Caesar as lord was to exclude oneself from the empire and its system. It was to put oneself outside the law. Such was the situation of the Christian communities. They rejected the pretension to divinity that Caesar and the empire had, given that they only acknowledged Jesus Christ as Lord (*kyrios*). This put them outside imperial legality. They were persecuted, tortured, and martyred. Their resistance constituted a threat to the imperial system; therefore, they had to submit or to disappear. This is a synthesis of the sociohistorical elements that underlie the text and its context.

In analyzing the linguistic codes of the text, the theme of the economy dominates. Lexemes with economic significance abound: merchants, merchandise, to buy, to sell, to become rich, wealth, ships, a large list of metals, precious stones, etc. All speak to us of the world of the economy, commerce, production and distribution, those who sell, those who buy, work (slaves, artisans, occupations), etc. These elements circulate throughout the text to explain that the prophetic indictment is basically directed at an economic project of domination that exploits some and enriches others.

If it is indeed certain that the economic aspect dominates the text, the political aspect is also present and closely linked to the former. One cannot be understood without the other. At the beginning of this essay, we noted that the indictment of the political power is strongly present in chapter 17. Nonetheless, it also appears here as part of the economic project.

The symbols of political power are, first, the symbol of "Babylon." Babylon as a symbol of hegemonic or political-military power is at the center of this political reading. Subordinate to this power are the other dependent powers described as "the nations" and "the kings of the earth." These represent the city-states and colonies implicated in the larger political-economic network of the empire.

Together with these expressions occurs the phrase "the merchants of the earth." Thus it becomes clear how the political power and the economic power relate to one another. The project of domination is based upon an economic project of production, exploitation, and commercialization. On the basis of this economic project, the political-military rule of the dominant system is consolidated.

We can now incorporate the theological elements that correspond to an ecclesiological reading of the text. We noted that the text constitutes a prophetic oracle indicting a political-economic system that compels, destroys, and leads to death. It not only wipes out those whom it exploits, but at the same time brings with it the destruction of the system itself.

The speaker in the text speaks from the perspective of God in favor of the community of the holy martyrs who are persecuted by the system. Faithfulness to Jesus Christ the Lord becomes a mode of resistance to domination. The response of the community is not the proposal of a new political or economic model; this is not its function. Rather, its function is prophetic indictment to alert the reader to the dangers that such a system creates.

The community's rejection of the imposition of the imperial political-economic model is done out of a life of faith and militant obedience. Faith, then, is a mode of theological-liberating resistance to the imposition of an ideology of domination, which had been disguised as supposed economic prosperity and political stability. The consequence of this resistance is persecution and the accusation of atheism in the face of the system's pretensions to divinity. The idolatrous cult that the system wants to impose is rejected.

Finally, the text declares the vindication of the faithful as an expression of God's justice in the eschaton. The martyrdom of the community is, of course, not to be understood in the Stoic sense. Rather, the community's suffering and martyrdom signify judgment on the oppressor. It is a militant resistance, because it actively denounces the oppressor. The persecution and death of the innocent make evident the sin of the unjust system that crucifies the exploited. In so doing, the system bears with it its own judgment.

The prophetic discourse of the text calls the community to resist domination. Three elements constitute the essence of this active resistance: to separate oneself, to denounce, and to announce. The ethic of resistance speaks of separating oneself from the sin of an economic system that seduces and awakens greed and the ambition for power in many persons. It is a power that prostitutes, corrupts, and leads to the practice of a licentious life by some, and means extreme poverty and death for others. At issue is a system to be denounced as contrary to God's justice.

The Christian community cannot render idolatrous worship to a system that sacrifices, bewitches, and condemns to perdition those whom it exploits in order to acquire wealth; and that, moreover, destroys those who are supposed to be its beneficiaries. In synthesis, at stake is the need to separate oneself from the system and to denounce the injustice of its proposals and the falsehood and guile at the bottom of its offer of security, peace, and progress. By denouncing this economic model as sinful, the judgment of God is proclaimed that will finally destroy such an unjust system.

The community's response proposed in the text is an ethic of active prophetic resistance. As is typical in apocalyptic literature, a solution to the problem is expected at the final eschaton. Only then will God's justice be fully manifest. In the meantime, it is necessary to resist as indicated: by separating oneself, denouncing, and proclaiming.

The announcement of the fall of the system of domination is made, in the language of the text, from the perspective of its consummation. The system's fall is depicted from the point of view of the eschaton, as something that has already occurred ("has fallen," "your judgment came," "her wealth has been consumed," "has been made desolate," "God has done justice," etc.).

It could be that the proposal of the text to the community of the faithful has some relevance for the prophetic role of the church in our time. In every age, the community of the faithful is called to separate itself from any political-economic system that does not have the well-being of all humanity as its ultimate goal. This is the purpose of the kingdom of God: peace, justice, and well-being for all men and women. It is the function of the church as the community of Jesus Christ to denounce the hidden intentions of any system that seeks total hegemony through the imposition of an economic system that assumes idolatrous characteristics. It belongs to the essence of the church to announce the judgment of God on sin: the gospel of the final and vindicating justice of God for God's people who serve with faithfulness and the definitive *shalom* for all humanity.

5

·······

"Do Not Extend Your Hand against the Child"

Observations on Genesis 21 and 22

MILTON SCHWANTES

··

Genesis 21 and 22 in Their Literary Context

These chapters are certainly well integrated into their literary context. Different parts of the text allow this to be seen with clarity. I shall refer to some of the evidence. The first verses (Gen 21:1–7) are clearly related to what precedes them. Their proper function becomes one of establishing this connection with the previous chapters. In this way, v. 1 is explicitly directed at chapters 17 and 18. Verse 4 connects with 17:12. Even vv. 6–7, which develop their own material, are related to what precedes them, since they point to, among other texts, 17:24 and 18:12.

Gen 21:22–34 is also clearly related to the surrounding chapters. The encounter of Abimelech and Abraham is a clear continuation of chapter 20. It also anticipates the subject matter of 26:18–35.

Finally, I draw attention to Gen 22:20–24. These genealogies prepare for subsequent scenes. For example, the figure of Rebekah (22:23) is introduced through them. In themselves, they form the bridge with 11:27–32.

We could make other similar observations to demonstrate how much chapters 21–22 are coordinated with their literary context. It would be enough to recall that Gen 21:8–21 is practically a parallel of chapter 16. In fact, Genesis 21 and 22 are inserted into their present context. This can be established even at the level of small details; it also becomes apparent in certain formulations. I think, for example, of 21:12f., which has to be read in line with 17:18–20, and of 22:18, which adapts and reedits 12:3.

The fact that chapters 21–22 are so clearly connected with their current literary context can be explained in different ways. We could attribute it, for example, to literary sources or prior documents. We could derive the connection from redactors, arguing, for example, in terms of different sources: J(ahwist), E(lohist), P(riestly writing). One could also — and this seems to me the most probable perspective — point to the work of the final composers or redactors of the text.[1] In any case, certain parts of chapter 21–22 require their literary context in order to be understood. They are especially dependent on the chapters that precede them, beginning with chapter 12, in order to be adequately situated.

Although we state, with emphasis, the fact of this interconnection between chapters 21–22 and their literary context, the matter is not thereby concluded, because our chapters also establish their own frame of reference. They contain a number of materials that are specific to them and that do not come from their literary context.

First, it is noteworthy that precisely at the end of chapter 22, the beginning is picked up again: "*Also* Milcah gave birth to children for Nahor" (22:20). This note clearly refers back to 21:1–7 and finishes what began there. These chapters (21–22) have their own specificity. They form an independent block of material. Thus, while it is true that allusions to what precedes and follows them are not missing, as already seen, the same chapters do not cease to go their own way.

This can be seen in Gen 21:1–7: verses that precisely try to pick up previous passages again. Consider v. 1. It has its own accents that distinguish it from the previous chapters to which it points. Verse 1 wants to emphasize that what was said beforehand has been accomplished (see also v. 2), a theme, moreover, that we also

---

1. See Eberhard Blum, *Die Komposition der Vätergeschichte,* Wissenschaftliche Monographien zum Alten und Neuen Testament (Neukirchen-Vluyn: Neukirchener, 1984), esp. 271–458.

know from other Old Testament texts.[2] And it is precisely this theme of announcement and fulfillment, which in v. 1 almost has the function of a title, that reappears in different parts of chapters 21–22. We find it, for example, in 21:8–21 in the divine word of vv. 12f. ("I will also make a great nation from the son of the maid"), repeated in v. 18 ("I will make of him a great people"). We find it again in 22:1–19, where the first verse already informs the reader that what follows is a test ("God put Abraham to the test").

Even in Gen 21:22–34, we find this keynote. There it is stated through the sign of the seven sheep: the well of Beersheba really belongs to Abraham. What it was has been fulfilled! Thus it can be said that in chapters 21–22, one, in fact, wants to show that what is announced (vv. 1–2!) has been fulfilled. This emphasis gives our chapters their own shape.

Two scenes mark these two chapters: the expulsion of Hagar (21:8–21) and the sacrifice or burnt offering of Isaac (22:1–19). These two scenes complement one another. This can be seen quite well at their high points, in the description of the divine action. I am referring principally to 21:17–19 and 22:11f., 14. In both cases, God acts through the "angel": in 21:17 via his "hearing," and in 22:14 via his "seeing."

The "hearing" and "seeing" of God are complementary. They form a unit. Insofar, therefore, as we recognize that God's interventions are certainly central in Genesis 21–22, we can also state that it is necessary to read the different scenes in them as part of a single unit: the "hearing" (21:8–21) and the "seeing" (22:1–19) of the angel of God are complementary. In this fashion, we observe once again that Genesis 21–22 constitute a particular composition with its own peculiar emphases.

But regarding the literary context to which, as we have seen, our chapters relate, there are delimitations. In Genesis 19, a large literary unit draws to a close, centered principally on Abraham and Lot (Genesis 13–14+18–19). In these chapters, one observes an interest in establishing social differentiations: Lot draws near to the cities, and there succumbs; Abraham, on the contrary, remains faithful to

---

2. See Gerhard von Rad, "La teología deuteronomística de la historia de los libros de los reyes," *Biblioteca de Estudios Bíblicos* 3 (1976): 177–89.

the semi-nomadic way of life and is exalted by the texts because of his sense of justice. By the end of Genesis 19 (see vv. 30–38) this theme is finished.

In chapter 20, something new begins. For this reason, it is not by accident that at the beginning of chapter 21 a subject matter is taken up again that immediately precedes the histories of Abraham and Lot, namely, the oppression of women in Gen 12:10–20. And, indeed, the subject matter of Genesis 20 is close to that of 12:10–20. In both cases, the question is not the tension between the semi-nomadic way of life (Abraham) and urban life (Lot) but intrafamilial relations, which are also the focus of attention in chapter 16. Hence starting in chapter 20, family histories predominate.

In this setting, Genesis 21–22 have a special place, insofar as their subject matter is directed at the question of the child. This makes them different from chapters 20 and 23, where the issue, aside from the fact that it does not revolve around the question of children, is still fixed on the relationship of Sarah and Abraham with foreigners: in Genesis 20, with the Philistines; in Genesis 23, with the Canaanites. In this regard, one can also perceive that chapters 21–22 are delimited with respect to their literary context.

Given all this, one can thus isolate chapters 21 and 22 and convert them into an object of independent observation, though naturally always taking into account their literary context. For this literary context is felt within these chapters, especially in Gen 21:22–34, which must practically be read as a continuation of chapter 20. With respect to their literary context, chapters 21 and 22 are therefore simultaneously delimited and correlated.

This holds true as well for the evaluation of their subject matter. But before paying attention to this, it seems proper to me that we shed light on the relation of Genesis 21–22 to their literary context from yet another perspective.

Concrete Experience

There is no way to read Genesis 21–22 that is not in the light of their literary context. After all, this is how they come to us. We only have these texts in their literary environment.

This fact can again be interpreted in a number of different ways.

On the one hand, explanations can be sought at the literary level, whether through recourse to documentary sources like the Jahwist, the Elohist, and the Priestly writing or by making full use of the possibilities of a hypothesis that takes as its point of departure the process of composition and the final redaction.[3] On the other hand, one can give greater emphasis to hermeneutical considerations that, in principle, adhere to the text in its final form.[4]

There are, moreover, good historical reasons for attributing considerable primacy to the text in its final, conclusive phase. After all, scenes and histories like the one that we are analyzing here are the work of centuries. They are the fruit of the effort of generations. This veritable stream of human beings that gave them their present form did not transmit them to us in the form of isolated scenes or individual histories, but rather as links in a greater whole, as parts of the history of a people. They are a single feature in a whole series. For this reason, also from a historical perspective, what we are told in these chapters is part of a vast assortment, a trajectory that extends to our own day. Hence it is not worthwhile atomizing.

Nevertheless, however much such a hermeneutic on the basis of the literary context is timely and necessary, it does not cease to appear problematical whenever it is used unilaterally. This is so, given that insertions due to the literary context or process of composition, when practiced in excess, tend to attribute to a particular text a specific unity or the meaning of what surrounds it. That is, they tend to say what, in any case, may already be found expressed by the literary context. The tendency is thus toward the generic, because each link in the stream becomes, as it were, a repetition of others. In this case, abstractions or idealizations can come to dominate interpretation.

The same problem could also be expressed from another point of view. Experiences such as those referred to in Genesis 21–22 integrate the life of an entire people. They possess the marks of the society in which they are embedded. Interests and social relations among the people contributed decisively to the creation of these chapters. Indeed, the experiences referred to in Genesis 21 and 22 ought perhaps to be attributed primordially to the interests of the

---

3. See above n. 2.
4. See José Severino Croatto, *Hermenéutica bíblica: para uma teoria da leitura como produção de significado* (São Leopoldo and São Paulo, 1986).

entire people. Abraham/Isaac are equivalent to an entire people! Ishmael represents a nation!

Nonetheless, in the event that we were only to consider the texts from this point of view (which certainly cannot be left unconsidered), we would tend to push their interpretation into a narrow strait. When national issues are under discussion, one generally thinks, in the end, whatever one is used to thinking. One succumbs to whatever has hegemony. "The people" think what "the people" have gotten used to thinking.

We can see this plainly in Genesis 16. There, national common sense has appropriated the text by means of vv. 9f. and 14f., profoundly transforming the sense that the text had before. In Genesis 16, the hegemonic national consensus ended up weakening the liberating sense that characterized the antecedent narrative of chapter 16 before it was appropriated by the person who included in it vv. 9f. and 14f.

It is necessary to be attentive to such "route deviations," although we cannot ignore the fact that the texts — and Genesis 16 as well! — were transmitted to us via national social relations. Indeed, we ought perhaps to acknowledge that the more we read specific texts in the light of their literary contexts, the more we incorporate into their interpretation perspectives stemming from the enveloping national society. And precisely for that reason, it seems to me very timely and significant to be attentive to certain peculiarities and characteristics of histories like those in Genesis 21 and 22, which commend an interpretation with a focus on concrete and circumscribed experiences.

Despite the fact that the literary context has clearly left its mark on Genesis 21 and 22, this does not mean that these chapters themselves constitute a unity that, from beginning to end, represents a continuous series of events. Although their contents are interrelated and the chapters are marked by the texts that surround them, the two chapters are not the fruit of a redaction that has impressed unity and coherence on them from the first to the final verse. Quite the contrary!

Without great difficulty, we can distinguish four or five smaller, specific, autonomous units. In Genesis 22, there are two such units: vv. 1–19 and vv. 20–24. They each have their own autonomy. In Genesis 21, there are two or, perhaps, three such units: vv. 22–34 and vv. 1–21 (or vv. 1–7 and vv. 8–21). No apparent connection exists between vv. 1–21 and vv. 22–34. Each one of these smaller units has its own narrative style, develops a theme very much its own, and even carries its issue to a conclusion that does not depend on the previous or subsequent scene.

This means that it is not enough simply to explain the sense and origin of Genesis 21 and 22, beginning with the final redaction or the larger literary context. It will be necessary to take into account the fact that the two chapters are made up of individual scenes: smaller units (four or five) that have their own relative life. Precisely here we need form criticism because this method helps us to perceive such smaller units and to grasp their original historical contexts. It equips us to understand the process of creation of the larger literary units beginning with the smaller units.

Later redactions, including the final redaction, did not suppress the earlier experiences. They incorporated them. Thus, they reaffirmed their validity and value. There was no creation of uniformity. Rather, there were juxtapositions and superimpositions.[5]

For example, let me refer to Gen 21:1–7, especially since these verses, without a doubt, were formulated under the influence of and with an eye toward their literary context, as can be seen in vv. 2–5. The same theme is no longer emphasized in vv. 6–7. These verses are, furthermore, not adjusted to what is said by the previous verses.

In vv. 6–7, the name of Isaac is derived from experience with the newborn. Here, the name is interpreted from the perspective of the birth, in which regard vv. 6–7 are definitely different from Gen 17:17 and 18:12 and also 21:9. Such notable differences find their best explanation when we admit that the origin of these passages is diverse: the name of Isaac is explained in different ways (17:17+18:12+21:9 x 21:6–7), because traditions of diverse origins are found reflected in these texts.

Such conclusions bring us forward. They open new doors. But they still lack a very important perspective. Our chapters refer to very concrete questions. Although it is very important to observe the structures of the language that serve as the conductors of the

---

5. For these questions, see Milton Schwantes, *A Familia de Sara e Abraão: Texto e contexto de Genesis 12–25* (Petrópolis, 1986), 11–29, 31–43.

content of these texts, be they smaller units or fuller literary compositions, this language is indubitably based on concrete historical experiences. It is not separated from reality. It does not abandon the concrete struggle for life and survival to float about on a plane of ideas and good intentions. The histories have their feet planted in concrete, real, material life.

This does not mean that in the midst of such concreteness, mutations and alterations do not occur at the center of these histories. I think, for example, of Genesis 20. The central issue of this chapter — the oppression of Sarah — suffered significant alteration. Sarah was transferred to the margins of the scene. Abraham and Abimelech come to dominate. They are the ones who speak. Sarah has been silenced. Her suffering, her oppression, tend to disappear. The problem of the king (Abimelech) increases and grows. It dominates the scene. What an alteration!

But despite this, although Sarah has been displaced as the center of attention and relegated to the margins of the scene, the history of Genesis 20, in the end, depends on the woman. It is Sarah who creates this history! Despite the fact that Abraham and Abimelech are at the center, the narrative remains concrete, as Gen 21:22–34 also testify.

Indeed, Genesis 21–22 does not abandon the level of concrete relations and experiences. The words are connected to the concrete, to small and larger hopes, principally those of ordinary people. Neither the tradition-historical process that brought them into being nor the diverse literary redactions to which they were subjected nor even the literary compositions into which they were integrated left aside such experiences, such concreteness, nor did they substitute for them concepts, ideas, reflections disconnected from reality. Their good ideas continue to have their feet planted in the soil of life.

From my point of view, it is important that we remain attentive to the evidence of such vital historicity in order not to lose its contour or centrality in theological interpretation.[6] Thus, when

---

6. The word of God "is said by specific persons, in a specific moment, in a specific context": see Hans Walter Wolff, "Der grosse Jesreeltag (Hosea 2, 1–3): Methodologische Erwägungen zur Auslegung einer alttestamentlichen Perikope," in *Theologische Bücherei* 22 (Munich, 1964): 159f. See also Carlos Mesters, "Flor sem defesa," in idem, *Flor sem defesa* (Petrópolis, 1983), 87–187.

continuing our reflection on the content of Genesis 21 and 22, we shall try to be attentive to the concrete questions, the experiences of life, brought into focus by these texts.

"Rise Up!"

Gen 21:1–21 can be taken as a single unit. Certainly, vv. 1–7 have their particularities as a bridge between the previous texts and chapters 21–22. But v. 8 ("the child grew and was weaned") is also a clear continuation of v. 2 ("Sarah conceived and gave birth to a son").

When interpreting the contents of Gen 21:1–21, certain particularities could be emphasized in which this unity, without a doubt, is also at stake. I will mention only a few: vv. 6–7 contain some interesting aspects. They have their own emphases. In these verses, the mother Sarah explains the name of her son, as much in relation to the birth (v. 6) as with reference to the father (v. 7). These understandings of the name, beyond the fact that they are more significant, stand in tension with those of vv. 3–5. The mother is the interpreter of the name of Isaac! This is in continuity with Gen 18:12–15 and points to 21:8–21, where Sarah likewise has a heightened role.

Equally significant are the contents of vv. 12–13. These verses contain an important theological interpretation. In agreement with the previous verses, Abraham was obliged to "throw out" (v. 10) his son Ishmael. This seemed to him "very painful" (v. 11). Verses 12–13 have the function of theologizing the situation. They place these doubtful and very inadequate actions within the framework of a complete divine plan. They situate them in a history of salvation, about which chapter 12 already gives testimony. God provides! This is what chapter 22 (vv. 8, 14) also will say. Chapter 24 likewise speaks of the same providence.

In Gen 21:(11)12–13, we thus meet theologians who know how to detect the ways of God in the midst of the tortuous ways of human beings. These theologians show how "God pursues his grand historical ends above the embroiled conduct of human beings."[7] This theologization, present in vv. 11–13 and in different

---

7. See Gerhard von Rad, "El libro del Génesis," in *Biblioteca de Estudios Bíblicos* 18 (1977): 286.

parts of Genesis 12–50, is, therefore, significant, despite the fact that generally it represents a late elaboration.

Besides pointing toward such content, we could also mention the narrative art of Gen 21:1–21. In the beginning, events dominate. Verse 11 already alludes to feelings, although the rest of the scene is especially marked by the actions of the expulsion: "he rose early before dawn," "took," "gave," "put," "dismissed," "she left," "wandered" (v. 14). There is much brutality: one act right after another. It is a chain of events without feeling.

Nevertheless, feeling irrupts in v. 16: "she said/thought," "raised her voice," "wept." This style of narration, placing "events" and "feelings" over against one another, is without a doubt directed at the listener and the reader. The desperate mother's tears do not cease to call to the "spectator," i.e., the reader. The person who told us this episode knew indeed how to do the job!

Such content and specific features have, no doubt, their value and importance. They illuminate details. They call attention to certain points. Nonetheless, they cannot make us forget the decisive aspects of the text. They cannot lead us away from the central questions, since that which effectively put the story in motion has still not been mentioned in the preceding observations about content.

Decisive questions are mentioned in v. 10. The slave — who does not even have a name — is segregated and expelled. The motive for this expulsion is the inheritance: "the son of that slave will not be an inheritor with my son." This is what unleashes the narrative.

To this motive should be added what is said in v. 9: "Sarah saw that the son born to Abraham of the Egyptian Hagar played with her son." The formulation of v. 9 should definitely be understood in the light of vv. 6–7: there the "playing" or the "smiling" (in Hebrew, it is the same verb) had to do with Isaac, the son of Abraham's wife. Here, on the contrary, it concerns Ishmael, the son of the slave. Ishmael "occupies" the verb (play/smile) that gave rise to the name Isaac. He becomes an inheritor (in terms of v. 10). Consequently, the problem is not the playing/smiling per se, but rather quite concretely the inheritance.

It is not helpful, therefore, to translate this "play/smile" with "make fun of" (*burlarse:* translation of Almeida) or "render ridiculous" (*ridiculizar*: Biblia Pastoral). The Hebrew term does not suggest this. When "play" is substituted by "render ridiculous," the problem tends to be displaced: the motive of the expulsion of Hagar and Ishmael would no longer be the inheritance (v. 10), but rather some foolishness between two boys (Ishmael and Isaac). This interpretation, however, does not correspond to the text.

Hagar is defeated. She is expelled from the house. This expulsion is presented as elimination and a sentence to death. She is expelled into the desert and sent to her death. She is "tossed out" and thrown away (v. 14). And she has to take her son with her (v. 15). Death and tears are the consequence.

The masters impose themselves on the life of the slave. People who are slaves, who, in any case, only "deserve to inherit" extreme poverty, can be expelled and eliminated. All that is needed is cause for suspicion such as a child's "playing" or "smile" at the wrong time. The domination of persons and their elimination are branches of the same tree. What begins as domination and exploitation ends as a grave-mound.

God, however, is different. God's ways are other. We are shown this in great detail in vv. 17–20. The events are narrated: vv. 17a+ 19–20. The words spoken by God are quoted: vv. 17b–18. In any case, the details are significant. The language is insistent. Some suspect, moreover, that these verses contain later additions. In fact, the divine words (vv. 17b–18) seem to be a subsequent effort to render more explicit the nature of the divine action (vv. 17a+19–20). Be that as it may, the narrative seeks to emphasize the work and speech of God. Without his word and action, death would have been the end of the story. Without these, one more slave, one more child, would have been eliminated because of the simple suspicion that they could become dangerous for the owner.

But God hears! This hearing is decisive. Verse 17 expresses this twice: in the narrative ("God heard her voice") and in the divine speech ("do not fear, because God heard your voice"). God hears the child who, according to the Hebrew text, did not even get to scream. The Septuagint changes the text at the end of v. 16: "the child raised his voice and wept." This change makes good sense. Nonetheless, the Hebrew text is original and older. According to this text, only the mother weeps. The child — presumably still very small — is no longer in a condition to weep. He is already dying. The one who weeps is the slave, in place of the child who is dying. And God hears, through the voice of the mother, the silence and hidden death of this expelled child. Even the people without a voice have a voice with this God! In the end, the most profound and most radical domination is the one that silences persons, the one that transforms exploitation into the "destiny desired by God," into a culture of silence.

The insistence on God's hearing becomes an allusion to the name of the child. Our story nowhere mentions the name of the little one. Nonetheless, the name resounds through the phrase "God heard," since Ishmael means precisely, "God hears/will hear" (16:11).

This hearing of God also enters into God's work. In vv. 17–20, the words of God and his action are complementary. The divine action is concrete and very specific: "Rise up!" (v. 18). He "made his eyes open" and she "gave the boy to drink" (v. 19). The divine action appears in the smallest of details. Salvation is not merely a generic affirmation. It is a drink of water! Thus, through little things and concrete and immediate gestures, "a great people" is constituted (v. 18). The God who "hears" in so specific a manner disturbs history by forcing transformations that bring to an end the domination of enslaved children and women.

This liberating experience of God is key to interpretation of our story. The "hearing" of God is the counterpoint to the command to "expel" (v. 10). Theology finds here, therefore, a decisive point of significance for overcoming oppression. God is liberation. This is how God happens.

And this recalls the Exodus. Our story, after all, provides us with another branch of the leafy tree of the Exodus, the biblical paradigm for historical experience and action.[8]

Other contents are then brought into focus in Gen 21:22–34, although they ought to be read beginning with 21:1–21 and with an eye toward chapter 22.

---

8. See José Severino Croatto, "Exodo: Uma hermenéutica da liberdade," *Libertação e Teologia* 12 (1981): 35–73.

"Since I Dug This Well"

Gen 21:22–34 does not itself continue what precedes it. These verses have their own specific focus between 21:1–21 and 22:1–24. Although they are not very connected with the units around them, the verses in 21:22–34 nonetheless certainly stand in continuity with Genesis 20. The principal personalities (Abimelech and Abraham) are the same and, more than this, 21:22–34 and chapter 20 accentuate that it is possible to live together with the Philistines.

Note as well the fact that Gen 21:22–34 (and, in my opinion, also 20:1–18) depend on chapter 26. They presuppose this chapter and quite probably belong to a very late phase in the emergence of the book of Genesis. Reflecting current research in this area,[9] I think that one can therefore begin with the following datum: 21:22–34 ought to be read in the light of chapter 26.

Once this is established, that is, once we acknowledge that Gen 21:22–34 needs to be read in correlation with chapter 26, we can turn our attention to what is specific in them. Although chapter 26 would be something like the generative matrix, our verses also reflect their own creativity.

The structure of Gen 21:22–34 is quite easy to discern. Verses 22–24 and 25–27 stand more or less parallel to one another. Initially, Abimelech addresses himself to Abraham. Afterward Abraham appeals to Abimelech. Abraham's oath (v. 24) corresponds to the covenant mentioned in v. 27. With respect to vv. 22–24, vv. 25–27 carry the matter forward. For only in these verses (25–27) is the problem effectively announced: the disagreement about the well.[10]

From my point of view, vv. 28–30 do not describe new events after the agreement mentioned in v. 27 has become effective.[11] On the contrary, vv. 28–30 detail v. 27. They constitute its specification. They relate the details of how the covenant already mentioned came to be. In other words, vv. 28–30 fit inside v. 27. The same well is the subject!

---

9. See Claus Westermann, *Genesis,* Biblischer Kommentar Altes Testament I.1 (Neukirchen-Vluyn: Neukirchener, 1979), 423f.; Blum, "Komposition," 405–19.

10. If we were to compare the unit in 21:22–34 with chapter 26 from which it is derived, we would be able to verify in detail that principally vv. 22–24 and finally the first part of this unit (21:22–24) depend on chapter 26.

11. On the other hand, v. 27 also finds itself under the narrative influence of chapter 26.

Verses 31–34 also follow a sequence with no major distur-bances. Verse 31a ("therefore that place was called Beersheba") establishes the result of the preceding scene (vv. 28–30). Thus, it is in the place that corresponds to it. Verses 31b ("since there both swore") and 32a ("they made a covenant in Beersheba") are repetitions, strictly speaking, but both are significant because one (v. 31b) recalls v. 24, and the other (v. 32a) v. 27. Thus, vv. 31b and 32a establish themselves as a sufficient enclosure for the disagreement between Abraham and Abimelech.

Verses 32b–34 bring the episode to a close. They do it in such a way that v. 32b and v. 34 contain parallel affirmations. Verse 33 is interposed between the two, insofar as its contents make sense only before v. 34. Note, moreover, that v. 32b takes up v. 22, thus giving everything a conclusion. It is not by accident that we have the con-tents of v. 34 at the end of the pericope. After all, since chapter 20 the question of living together with foreigners has been in force: "For much time Abraham dwelt in the land of the Philistines."

Thus one sees that Gen 21:22–34 indeed constitutes a unit. The verses form an organic whole. They are in continuity with chapter 20 and under the influence of chapter 26. In terms of con-tent, their main focus is the conflict about the well. This is what determines the unit, which is configured around this conflict.

In this conflict and its solution, a decisive role falls to Abraham. He knows how to direct things favorably for himself and his de-scendants (v. 23). At the right time, he knows the way to confront Abimelech. Mainly through symbolic action — the gift of seven sheep — he establishes a sign with public and unquestionable va-lidity. Thus Abraham "documented" and "sealed" the agreement: "I dug this well," that is: "I have the right to it."

On the other hand, this is one of the particular interests of Gen 21:22–34. These verses affirm and seal the right of possession to the well of Beersheba. Under "oath" these waters belong to Abra-ham (v. 31b; see v. 24). An agreement — a covenant — was made in this regard (vv. 27, 32a). This is what the tree, a tamarisk, planted by Abraham on the occasion of the episode, attests (v. 33). The sheep that Abimelech is given as a gift testify to it (vv. 27–30). They serve as "testimony that I dug this well" (v. 30).

Finally, Abraham invokes his God, Yahweh, in that place in a special way. He invoked him — possibly for the first time —

as the "God of eternity," the God from long ago. Theologically, the right to the well of Beersheba is thus affirmed with reference to "eternity," anchored in time immemorial. As can be seen, Gen 21:22–34 is very concerned with affirming and securing possession of the waters of Beersheba. This is perhaps also the motive that led to these verses' "anticipating" the story of Isaac in chapter 26, transforming it in Gen 21:22–34 into a story of Abraham.

Certainly, what matters are the waters, especially in the Negev where Beersheba is located. Nevertheless, these waters — the well — are part of something bigger. In the end, for a semi-nomadic way of life, access to a well is simultaneously access to the land and pasture. This is also at stake in our pericope: the right to use the land in which the well is located. Access to the land is guaranteed in Genesis 21 by a contract or covenant. Chapter 24 will add a tradition of land purchase. It is possible that the grave-mound represents on agricultural land (chapter 24) something similar to the well in a semi-nomadic context of pastures (chapter 21). Both constitute a right to use the surrounding land.

Abraham succeeds in guaranteeing his rights to the well. Nevertheless, though victorious in this case, he remains in the weaker position. He continues being a foreigner, as the final verse (v. 34) emphasizes. In the land of others, he is exposed to their rule. Furthermore, he is not subject to the interests of just anyone, but to the power of the monarchy itself (Abimelech) and military might (the general Phicol).

Both men find themselves far from their land of origin, namely, Philistia, testing their interests at Beersheba. Abraham, a "migrant shepherd completely weak,"[12] achieves a small victory, the right to a well, in the face of the power of the monarchy and the military. For "God is with you in all that you do" (v. 22). What is expressed here, concretely, is the wise astuteness of the weaker one in negotiating with the powerful. Our verses celebrate the little victory (a well) of a poor man (the semi-nomad Abraham).

In this regard, Gen 21:22–34 is like the unit that precedes it (21:1–21). In both instances, the life of those who are weaker is at stake: in the one case, the life of the slave and her son, in the context of familial and patriarchal structures of domination; and,

---

12. See Westermann, *Genesis,* 425.

in the other, the life of the "migrant shepherd completely weak" in the context of the oppression imposed by the state and the army. In both instances, God — *elohim,* Yahweh, the angel of God, the God of eternity — is the one who liberates, rescues and protects the threatened life. Both are fruits of the same tree of life. The differences between the two units are many, but in these decisive points they coincide: they celebrate the victory of the oppressed.

Finally, let us mention the following differences. The first pericope relates the pain of a rejected child and an expelled foreign slave. The second pericope directs our attention to a case of "right of property" or, better, the right to use a well and, obviously, the surrounding pastures in the Negev. The first certainly contains ancient traditions. The second appears to have been created in connection with another similar story (chapter 26).

Despite these differences, the two "stories" are related to one another. The redactors have not united them by chance. They have not located them by accident in the story that narrates how God "heard" Ishmael and describes how God "saw" Isaac. We shall return to this question below, but first a look at chapter 22.

"Do Not Extend Your Hand against the Child"

This "narrative full of art"[13] cannot be "reduced" to a single meaning. Its content points in different directions, precisely because it is so artistic and has been elaborated by so many generations. In Genesis 22, the knowledge of many writers and the experiences of centuries flow together. This is also one of the reasons for not dating the chapter (22) before the prophets of the eighth century.

Genesis 22 occupies a special place in the midst of chapters 12–25. In 11:30 ("Sarah was barren, she did not have children") a theme begins that is brought to completion in Genesis 22: the child was born and is preserved. The genealogical list at the end of chapter 22 (vv. 20–24) also recalls 11:27–32, creating an interesting arch that begins with 22:20–24 and extends backward (11:30) as well as naturally pointing forward.

From chapter 22 on, the principal personalities of the stories

---

13. See Hans Walter Wolff, "Zur Thematik der elohistischen Fragmente im Pentateuch," *Theologische Bücherei* 22, 2d ed. (1973): 406.

are Isaac and Rebekah. Rebekah is mentioned for the first time in Gen 22:23. Consequently, chapter 22 concludes the arch that began with 11:30 (Sarah does not have children) and starts a new one (Isaac and Rebekah). This shows that chapter 22 (together with its partner, chapter 21) plays a very important role. On that mountain, in the land of Moria, decisive things happen!

Quite varied interpretations have been attributed to chapter 22, which, no doubt, is very significant and the product of many generations. These interpretations, in fact, appear in the Hebrew text itself. It intentionally does not try to be very univocal. It opens up in different directions. It even points toward the sacrificial cult in Jerusalem.[14]

Despite this diversity of content implicit in the narrative, one cannot help but see that the sacrifice of the child is the most noteworthy theme. It is the issue that heads up the story: "Offer him [that is: the son] there as a burnt offering" (v. 2). This is the "test" (v. 1) to which Abraham is subjected. At the high point of the narrative, this "sacrifice!" is revoked: "Do nothing to him" (v. 12). A ram is sacrificed in place of the child (v. 13). Only after this can the genealogy begun in 11:27–32 be completed (22:20–24), because only now does Sarah, in fact, have a son. Genesis 22 indeed has its center of gravity in the theme of the sacrifice of the child. This is part of its concreteness.

Genesis 22 belongs to the sphere of debates about the sacrifice of human beings and children. This also makes sense when we look at the historical context in which it was formulated. It is not worthwhile situating the chapter in very ancient times before the late period of the monarchy. The theme of the sacrifice of human beings and children was debated in the eighth and seventh centuries B.C.E. Human sacrifice was increasingly and decidedly rejected.[15]

Equally significant is the fact that, precisely during this period, defense of the unprotected child was imposed. This is what we read in the stories of Elisha (2 Kings 4). I call attention to the noteworthy phrase of Isaiah: "Here we are, I and the children that the Lord gave me for signs and wonders in Israel" (Isa 8:18).

---

14. See Blum, "Komposition," 324–26.
15. I point to the indignation expressed against this practice in a passage like 2 Kgs 3:27. I recall the polemic promoted by the Deuteronomic-Deuteronomistic school (Deut 12:31; 2 Kgs 16:3; 17:17; Jer 20:5).

This Isaianic statement should be understood in the larger context of Isaiah 6–9+11. There it fulfills a special role. Likewise, it is worth recalling the end of the book of Hosea, where, in the midst of a polemic against sacrificial practices, the prophet states: "In you [that is: in God] the orphan will find mercy" (Hos 14:3). Genesis 22 belongs to this context of the defense of children and the self-conscious rejection of the sacrifice of children, sons, and, finally, human beings.[16]

The fact that this episode "in the land of Moria" (Gen 22:2) transpires at the "time" of Abraham serves precisely to reinforce the critique of human sacrifice. Our story has, then, a paradigmatic function and represents a foundational posture. From Abraham, i.e., the beginning of the trajectory of Israel, the sacrifice of human beings has been abolished! It does not exist! It cannot exist!

Many details — the artistic intricacies and fine features of chapter 22 — have as their function to reinforce this critical intentionality, namely, the rejection of child sacrifice. One of these intricacies we see already in v. 2: on the one hand, there is the demand: "sacrifice!"; on the other, the detailed description of the one who ought to be sacrificed: "your only son, whom you love." This beautiful and kind representation of the sacrifice shocks. It does not make sense to burn as a burnt offering someone who is so special: only and beloved!

After this, we have the exact and detailed description of the preparation of the sacrifice in Gen 22:9–10. This description frightens and creates terror. These verses seem to want to capture the attention of the reader-listener. They create expectation and, apart from this, frighten. Does a father thus proceed to the point of "sacrificing" and "immolating" his own son? This is brutal! Nonsense! And how strange and what a contrast is the loving and kind attitude of the father who carries in his own hands the "fire" and the "knife" — that is, the dangerous things — with which that father-made-priest prepares to "kill" and to "immolate" this son. Together, these two attitudes do not make sense. They do not go together. Either one or the other!

Finally, one must also take note of the conversation between the

---

16. See Carlos A. Dreher, "O órfão no Antigo Testamento," *Informativo CEBI-sul* 17 (1986): 26–37.

father and the son on the way to the mountain (22:7–8). In this conversation, Isaac comes out the "winner." He exposes his father.

Such artistic details and fine features have a clear and visible function: to put in question the sacrifice of children, to reveal the lie that this practice contains (22:7–8), to bring to the light of day the nonsense that such sacrifice constitutes (v. 6 in comparison with v. 10), and to denounce the brutality of this action (vv. 9–10). Our chapter is indeed an instance of art against brutality and dehumanization. It is art on behalf of what is human. It is art on behalf of life.

Nevertheless, such artistic subtleties, which already at the literary level cause indignation to well up and protest against the immolation of human beings, are founded on a theological basis. After all, sacrifice is a theological theme. It is from this angle that Genesis 22 confronts the question. From beginning to end, it is a theological narrative. It is a theological work.

In particular situations, the gods demand human sacrifices. This is even said of Yahweh (Ex 22:29; Jdg 11:30–40). Such sacrifices hypothetically would serve to assure life and to enhance it. The sacrifice of human beings promises life by making death effective. It celebrates life while causing death. The disguise is one thing; the act, its opposite.

Initially, our narrative also situates itself at this ideological level. God demands the death and sacrifice of the child (22:2). At this point, the God Yahweh is no different from so many other gods and baals. It is assumed that in the way of death, the immolation of life, one will find life.

But thereafter the decisive rupture occurs. The order ("sacrifice!" v. 2) becomes a prohibition ("do not extend your hand against the child, and do nothing to him," v. 12). This prohibition is paradigmatic and programmatic, since it is directed at Abraham, the origin of Israel. It is valid for this people from the beginning. It is valid throughout their whole trajectory.

This type of sacrifice, the immolation of human beings, is likewise abolished, insofar as a substitute is found. Verse 13 formulates this clearly: "he took the ram and offered it as a burnt offering in place of his son." The sacrifice of children ceased to exist. In other words, it became integrated into other sacrifices (which, on the other hand, does not cease to be problematic).

In this sense, Genesis 22 narrates something unique, an exemplary "episode." While narrating the sacrifice of Isaac, the chapter also deactivates this practice once and for all. Among the people of Abraham, it existed only once, and then it was not realized! The prohibition remains. The order disappears forever.

This rupture — the deactivation of the order of sacrifice — can be achieved "only" on a theological plane, since the order or demand that children be sacrificed comes from the divinity, be it one of the gods of the surrounding world (2 Kgs 3:27) or the God of Israel himself (Ex 22:29). This type of sacrifice is a divine demand. This is the cultural context of the persons who conceived Genesis 22.

In order to disarticulate, deactivate, and undo this demand and to establish a new practice, a divine counter-order is necessary, i.e., a new word of God. The solution to the question exists, therefore, on the theological plane. Genesis 22 establishes a new beginning. It creates a new custom; it stands at the beginning of a new culture. The God of life wins out over the god of death. The god who promises life while he brings about and promotes death does not cease to be an idol![17] This is the magisterial insight sponsored by our narrative.

This rupture in the conception and experience of God, who initially makes one demand ("sacrifice!" v. 2) and then states another ("do nothing to him," v. 12), is captured with much skill by the authors of our text. The reorientation is apparent even in terms of word choice. At the beginning, God (*elohim*) speaks (v. 1). Abraham still refers to this *elohim*/God when Abraham is questioned by his son: "Where is the lamb for the burnt offering?" The father replies: "God will provide" (vv. 7–8). The narrator also refers to the same *elohim*/God in the first verses of chapter 22 (vv. 1, 3, 9). Consequently, the God who demands the sacrifice of the child is *elohim*.

This changes, however, after the rupture as soon as the prohibition is proclaimed. One now begins to speak of Yahweh or the "messenger of Yahweh" (vv. 11, 14).[18] Our story is certainly not of the opinion that two different divinities are in view (the use of

---

17. See especially Franz Hinkelammert, "A fé de Abraão e o Edipo occidental," *RIBLA* 3 (1989): 49–82.

18. The mention of *elohim* in v. 12 is because of the reference to v. 2.

elohim in v. 12 precisely impedes such a conception), but rather that a new experience is happening, a new, more qualified theological perception. The God of Israel institutes a new practice in the midst of his people that originated with Abraham. Yahweh does not want the sacrifice of human beings!

It is interesting that the prohibition of human sacrifice does not find a substitute in the immolation of animals (see Ex 34:10). Abraham sacrifices the sheep, but without the "messenger of Yahweh" having demanded it explicitly. This small difference remains important, insofar as it impedes locating Genesis 22 in the vicinity of the Jerusalem temple (see above), given that v. 13 would be the appropriate place to make a satisfactory allusion to the sacrificial cult practiced in this place. Chapter 22 does not deny or exclude Jerusalem, though neither is the chapter very benevolent toward it, thus corresponding more or less to the position of the Judaean peasantry that simultaneously sympathized with and was critical of the capital city. It is, then, very probable that our text has its roots in the tradition of the people of the land of Judah.

But let us return to the theological particularities of the narrative. We just saw that the differentiated use of *elohim*/God and Yahweh is important. Even more decisive is the fact that Yahweh is qualified here in a special way: He "sees"! The entire chapter centers around this affirmation.

In Gen 22:14, we meet a formulation that seems to want to understand the whole story in terms of aetiological categories. In it, the verb "see" is used twice: the place is now called "God will provide" and "mountain where God will provide." This "see/provide" is related to the protection of the child and his "substitution" by a ram (vv. 8, 13). Abraham desired and hoped that God would come to "provide" a burnt offering (v. 8). After the "messenger/angel" has prohibited Abraham from extending his hand to the child, "he lifted his eyes and saw" a ram (v. 13). Earlier, Abraham had already lifted his eyes and seen the place from afar (v. 4).

It seems to me that even the name of the place, Moria, through assonance at the level of the Hebrew text, has to do with the "seeing" of Abraham and Yahweh. Perhaps there is also a wordplay at the level of the Hebrew text between the verbs "see" and "fear" (v. 12). In this way, Yahweh "sees," and this is the most relevant experience to which our chapter gives testimony regarding the action of God.

This theology of "seeing/providing" is certainly related to the "hearing" of God in Genesis 21. Yahweh "hears" and "sees" the suffering of the expelled and sacrificed children. When he "hears" and "sees," he overcomes the oppression and causes it to go away.

The threats to life are made to disappear, at the beginning, in a concrete manner: "Rise up!" (21:18); "Do nothing to him!" (22:12). Immediately, hopes are awakened in the direction of a new future: "I will make of him a great people" (21:18). Such a horizon was not initially present in Genesis 22. But later it was added by means of the second intervention of the "messenger of Yahweh" (vv. 15–18): "I will multiply your descendants like the stars of the heavens" (v. 17). This theology of "hearing" and "seeing," of rescue from oppression and the promise of a new horizon for the future, is the theology of the Exodus (Exodus 1–3). In its footsteps are to be found the two chapters in Genesis 21–22.

Genesis 22 is consequently a story of liberation, not oppression. It is what its title already affirms. At the very beginning of the chapter in Gen 22:1, the reader is advised that what follows is a story of testing. Abraham is put "to the test." He is subjected to "a pedagogical test." Our story, therefore, wants to present something that is not identical with what it narrates. When it speaks of Isaac and his immolation, it does not actually focus on this matter. At issue is, properly, Abraham and the test to which he is subjected.

In this sense, from the very beginning, the sacrifice itself has already been abolished. This is not what matters. This is only a part of the scene that is narrated with an eye toward the issue that really counts. "Nothing will happen to the child; thus God decided from the beginning."[19] On the basis of this premise, the trip to the place of sacrifice is rehearsed. On the basis of this premise, the "pilgrimage" takes place. It is precisely to advise the reader from the beginning that there will be no human sacrifice that things "can" be narrated in such a cruel fashion. The story "can" be so brutal and horrendous — it even provides the type of detail I pointed out above — because it already knows of the liberation that is achieved

---

19. See Westermann, *Genesis*, 442.

from the horror and brutality of child sacrifice. Thus, its origin occurs in a context of freedom.

In this way, one of the scenes underway is also presented in such a form that it begins already to deactivate the immolation of the little one. I am thinking of 22:5–8. Abraham says to his servants that he is going to "worship." He says as well: "We [!] will return together with you." This allows one already to observe that there will be no sacrifice. This is also the perspective that the story continues to assume. Thus, while underway, Abraham makes himself responsible for carrying the "fire" and the "knife" so that nothing happens to the little one. And when he is questioned by Isaac as to the animal to be sacrificed, the answer is: "God will provide."

This shows that the scenes underway already anticipate the end of the episode. They point toward it. They anticipate the prohibition: "Do not extend your hand against the child" (22:12). Abraham continues on his way toward Moria in the hope and faith that the order to "sacrifice" cannot mean what it says. He continues onward with the certainty that the God of Israel, Yahweh, wants life and not death.[20] While underway to the place of sacrifice, he is already speaking of the return of father and son (v. 5).

Finally, a word about the question of obedience, not infrequently used to interpret the chapter. Gen 22:18 makes explicit the posture of Abraham in this regard: "you obeyed my voice." In the most ancient part of the text in v. 12, the fear of God is discussed. This "fear" or "hearing"-obedience ought not to be isolated from the whole text. These statements cannot be absolutized, as though the story wanted to celebrate blind obedience. Whatever such hearing, fear, or obedience might mean, only the entire chapter can explain it. The God whom Abraham "hears" and "fears" is the God Yahweh who equally "hears" (21:17–19) and "sees" (22:8–14), who protects threatened life, and who, from the beginning of his trajectory with his people, does not want the sacrifice of human beings. This Yahweh of the poor is the God that deserves to be "feared" and "obeyed."

---

20. In this regard, see principally Hinkelammert, "A fé e o Edipo," 49–55.

6
....

"Worthless Is the Fat
of Whole Burnt Offerings"

A Critique of the Sacrifice of the Second Temple

SANDRO GALLAZZI

....

The prophets of the monarchical period were always in conflict with the cultic sacrifice of the Solomonic temple. It is sufficient to recall some classical texts:

> What does the multitude of your sacrifices matter to me? . . . I have had enough of burnt offerings . . . of fat . . . of blood. (Isa 1:11)

> Add your burnt offerings to your sacrifices! . . . For when your fathers came out of the land of Egypt, I said nothing to them about burnt offerings and sacrifices. I only commanded them: "Hear my voice!" (Jer 7:21ff.)

> Ephraim multiplied the altars for expiation; nonetheless, the altars were the cause of sin. . . . Offer sacrifices, eat the meat, but Yahweh does not accept them. (Hos 8:11–13)

> I ignore the sacrifice of your fatted animals! (Amos 5:22b)

And we could go on.

The novelty resides in the fact that in the cult of the second temple, rebuilt after the Babylonian captivity, the prophetic voice is no longer a voice of censure, but of support and stimulus. The reconstruction of the temple is done with the blessings of Haggai and Zechariah (Ezra 5:1). The realization of a happy future, a pleasing society, and peaceful coexistence is linked to the existence of the temple and the priesthood (Hag 2:1–9; Zech 3:6–10). Later, the prophet Malachi censures the inappropriate offerings for sacrifice, exhorting the people to give to God the best of what is good:

> When you offer a blind animal for sacrifice, this is evil! When you offer a lame or sick animal, is it not evil? (Mal 1:8)

What changed between the first and second temple? The Solomonic temple always served as support, defense, and ideological legitimation of the kingdom, a kingdom based on exploitation and oppression, hence the prophetic critique. After the captivity, this kingdom no longer existed (the experience of Zerubbabel was ephemeral and not properly "monarchical"). Judah was now a "province" of the Persian empire and would later be the same under Greek domination. The temple was no longer the strong support of an autonomous monarchy, but rather the only center of Jewish political, cultural, and economic identity. To strengthen the temple and its role meant guaranteeing the survival of the group as a whole; hence the support, at least initially, of the prophets.

But despite such importance and political significance, it is necessary to recall certain facts that led to a situation of abuse and oppression, one not only legitimated but also caused and provoked by the temple, a situation that would culminate in the denunciation by Jesus, who would take up again the old prophetic denunciation of Jeremiah, when he compares the temple to a den of thieves (Mark 11:17; Jer 7:11).

1. The second temple was the work of the "children of captivity," those who returned from exile and considered themselves to be the true Israel, the "remnant" purified by the testing fire (Ezra 4:1–4; 6:16, 19–21). The second temple became a source of division between those who returned from exile and those who had stayed in Judah: the "people (peoples) of the land," as they were called with disdain by the repatriates. The "people of the land" and the "children of captivity" formed two groups in conflict — serious conflict.

2. The conflict was not only "cultural," but also political and economic. The work of Nehemiah and Ezra would definitively strengthen the hand of the band of repatriates (who continued to call themselves such even after a hundred years!). The land

would be retaken legally by the true Israel, who did not mix with the other "peoples of the land." The people of the land, already mixed and impure for more than 150 years, was no longer Israel and therefore had no right to the land (Ezra 9:8–12). The friendship and coexistence with the Persian empire are definitively sealed (Ezra 7). The group of repatriates will have hegemony with the blessings of the emperor!

3. The project built by Nehemiah was an eminently "urban" project (Judah had been reduced to a little area around Jerusalem!). Jerusalem and the temple would be the center of power. The high priest and the elders (the community) would exercise this power. The land or countryside would have to sustain and maintain the city, the temple, the priests, and the men in power (Nehemiah 10). This "maintenance" would happen through the tithe, collected by force, and, above all, we suspect, through the "sacrifice for sin," about which we will speak later.

4. One thing, however, is important. The second temple shall be able to reduce the space of the prophets and to control it. The temple is the place where the "law" that Ezra brings from Babylonia with the unqualified support of the king will be promulgated (Ezra 7:11–28). The "reading," the "explanation," the "translation" take the place of the prophetic word.

The written book takes on a sacred role; in it is contained the Word. The book ought to be read, translated, and interpreted (Neh 8:1–8). The scribe, the rabbi, the teacher, the theologian take the place of the prophet! The temple is no longer rock; it will be the place of the word and its legitimate interpretation. The rest will become "apocryphal," "heretical," etc.

It was not so much the end of the monarchy that made prophecy impossible as it was the centralization of the temple and the book, which the temple appropriates. "Prophecy" will be obliged to find other ways, other channels, to manifest itself. It is our hypothesis that this way was sketched out by the "novels," by "poetry," the only space for questioning the urban project focused on the temple.

The Sacrifice of Expiation and Restitution

In order to sustain and maintain this pattern, one of the fundamental instruments employed was sacrifice, principally the sacrifice for sin and the sacrifice of restitution. These two types of sacrifice were programmatically increased and regulated by the second temple (Lev 4:5) together with the ancient sacrifices like the burnt offering, the peace or communion offering, and the offering of praise.

A Little History

It is true that we already have premonarchical indicators of the existence of the sacrifice of restitution (1 Sam 6:3, 4, 8, 17). During the monarchy as well, something similar must have existed (2 Kgs 12:17). But it was certainly linked to monetary restitution for any damage caused. (Lev 5:15f.; 21–24 also preserve this feature of "monetary" restitution for damage caused to God or to one's neighbor.) These are the only preexilic references to this type of sacrifice and were perhaps already criticized by Hosea (8:11).

In texts linked to the second temple, these expressions appear many more times (sacrifice for sin: 109 times; sacrifice of restitution: 32 times), which demonstrates that in this period, this ritual act acquired special importance. Nonetheless, it is difficult to define the historical route of this rite, even if everything suggests that the Babylonian captivity must have played a very important role in the development of this purification ritual.

Thus the last chapters of Ezekiel refer various times to the sacrifice for sin or of restitution. It must be celebrated in order to purify all Israel (45:17), to purify the temple (45:18–20), to rededicate the altar (43:19–25), in the Passover celebrations (45:22), and the feast of Tabernacles (45:25). Ezekiel begins to establish the essence of the rite. He defines the place of sacrifice (40:39), the place to eat the meat (42:13; 46:20), and the part of the sacrifice belonging to the priest (44:29). This ritual was most certainly held when the repatriates returned (Ezra 8:35). In little time, as we shall see, it permeated the entire life of the people.

The ritual of the *day of expiation* merits further comment, about which we have diverse witnesses:

- Ex 30:10 recalls the day of expiation with the rite of blood that ought to be poured out on the horns of the altar.

- Lev 23:26–32 speaks of the day of expiation without making any reference to a sacrifice of expiation (only a burnt offering is mentioned). The center of the celebration is the fast and the prohibition of work by servants.

- Num 29:7–11 recalls the rite of fasting and rest, a large celebration with burnt offerings and related oblations, and a double sacrifice of expiation.

- Leviticus 16 has the most developed and complex redaction with the sacrifice of expiation and the presence of the goat to be sent out into the desert carrying with it all the sins of the people.

It is difficult to determine the historical sequence, though it is very probable that a ritual of the common people, which had as its center the fast, was the basis of successive additional rituals culminating in the sophistication of Leviticus 19, which makes indispensable the role of the high priest, the temple curtain, and the whole apparatus of the sacred.

Characteristics of the Sacrifice for Sin

Let us look at some important aspects of the sacrifice for sin and the sacrifice of restitution, which, despite being different in their origins, end up being confused with one another and make difficult any better differentiation between the two.

LEGITIMATION OF THE SOCIAL PYRAMID. The rite celebrated for these sacrifices, as described in Leviticus 4 and 5, is very interesting for a sociological analysis. It is a sacrifice of expiation for sin. (We should not understand the word "sin" in its modern sense. Sin is a *situation of "impurity,"* regardless of the fact that it may be involuntary or unconscious.) Sin can be committed by the priest, by the (urban) community, by the head of the people, by the people of the land, by the poor, and by those without land. These are basically the "classes" that existed in postexilic Judah.

Let us look at the differences between one and the other sacrifice:

Group	Victim	Blood	Who eats
priest and urban community	bullock	behind the curtain, on the horns of the altar of incense, and at the foot of the altar of whole burnt offerings	no one
head of the countryside	he-goat	horns and foot of the altar of whole burnt offerings	priest
people of the land	ewe or sheep	horns and foot of the altar of whole burnt offerings	priest
poor	two doves	side and foot of the altar of whole burnt offerings	?
without land	4.5 liters of grade A flour	—	priest

The different victims, the different places reached by the blood, and the right to eat clearly reveal a justification of the existing social structure. In this way, the blood of the victim of the one with power arrives at the three sacred places of the temple, including the curtain, and afterward is progressively separated: the horns of the altar, the sides. In the last case, there is no longer even any blood, only a vegetable sacrifice. But the flour cannot be mixed (spoiled!) with oil as in the sacrifice of oblation; it will be stored! Every impurity implies 4.5 liters of flour — a lot of flour! Thus, the use of blood, fundamental to the meaning of expiation, is rightly what legitimates a society of domination and power. Not only does it do this; it also sacralizes that use!

The sin of the high priest is a sin that makes the entire people guilty (Lev 4:3). The high priest personifies, incorporates, and substitutes for the people as a whole: he represents and guides them at the same time. To go against this structural model is to oppose the sacred!

LEGITIMATION OF ECONOMIC CONCENTRATION. The expiation of sin is accomplished through total renunciation of the use of the victim. In the burnt offerings, then, no one ate anything of the victim, which was completely burned in a sacrifice of "soft scent" to Yahweh. The same thing happens in the sacrifice for sin of those who exercise power (Lev 4:11f., 21). In all the other cases, however, only the sinner did not eat.

At the same time, just as in the peace sacrifices, only the fat of the animal was burned. The meat belonged to the priest (Lev 7:6–10, 36), as Ezekiel already says (44:29). Furthermore, if the priest did not eat it, he would be punished (Lev 10:16–20).

Nonetheless, what interests us most is the flour: this will be stored for the sake of the priests (Lev 5:13). Seen here is a form of expropriation and taxation, masked by the universal need to feel purified. This is so, quite apart from the knowledge or consciousness of error. Sin is not the product of responsibility; it is a situation. A hemorrhage, a birth, leprosy, touching a corpse, something said while speaking just to talk: all this is motive for sacrifice, for payment (Lev 5:1–6).

LEGITIMATION OF THE IDEOLOGY OF RETRIBUTION. The life of Judah as a whole is permeated by the sacrifice for sin:

- the calendar feasts: Passover (Num 28:22; Ezek 45:22); Pentecost (Lev 23:19); Tabernacles (Num 29:12–39);

- the new moon (Num 28:15); the new year (Num 29:5); every celebration is also a celebration of expiation; above all, the *day of expiation* (Leviticus 16);

- the temple and its life: the consecration of the priests (Ex 29:14, 36; Lev 8:2, 14; 9:2f., 7f.); the purification of the temple (Ezek 45:19; 2 Chr 29:21–24); the dedication of the altar (Numbers 7; Ezek 43:19–25; Ezra 8:35);

- daily life: venereal diseases, menstruation, and hemorrhages (Lev 15:15, 30); birth (Lev 12:6, 8); leprosy (Leviticus 14); Nazarite vow (Numbers 6); contact with a corpse (Lev 5:2); and especially not denouncing the sin of others when one is notified to declare in court (Lev 5:1).

The result is a life that must be constantly purified. There is no escaping the laws, and consequently the opportunities for sin and impurity multiply. It is necessary to be purified in order not to incur punishment, damages, impoverishment. The logic is that of individual retribution. Ezekiel was the first to formulate this theology, to hearten the people and to awaken hope. Punishment would not be forever; liberation would follow conversion (Ezekiel 18).

Every sin, then, is the full responsibility of the one who commits it and therefore must be expiated. This logic allows the temple to dominate the people, especially the people of the land, who have been ignorant and impure since time immemorial — particularly the women: all women. The temple and sacrifice are the only and required modes of purification; only thus was it possible to receive from God abundance, security, and peace.

The sinner will be poor and disgraced — and the poor person is disgraced and a sinner! The possibilities for abuse are enormous, and everything indicates that many abuses did occur! The obligation to denounce one's companion has the power to split all bonds of solidarity among the "little people" who are also sinners. The neighbor, companion, relative, anyone can be or become a spy.

Consequently, a gigantic moral trap is placed before the poor. It is necessary that the poor accept being poor: they are sinners! As sinners, they must pay; it is the only way to be able to receive some benefit. If one did not receive any benefit, it is because one had sinned; again, therefore, one must pay to be purified. Thus, there is a never-ending vicious circle spinning around sacrifice, whereby the people remain and accept the domination and oppression of the temple and the priest.

The Critique of the People

Prophecy no longer has a place in this social arrangement constructed around the temple and sacrifice. Nonetheless, the people did not easily conform to such domination. The indictment of Malachi (1:8) against those who brought blind and defective animals to the altar reveals one form of reaction on the part of the people, as does the discovery by Nehemiah (13:10) that the people were not paying the tithe to his liking. In addition, the book of Proverbs censures whoever mocks the sacrifice for sin (14:4).

The people's resistance did not occur only through ritual subterfuge or by hiding things. Many writings also show that the opposition was fecund and profound. Books like Job, Jonah, Ruth, Song of Songs, and Ecclesiastes object to one or another aspect of the project of the temple.

Ana Maria Gallazzi and I have already presented part of the critique to be found in this literature from the perspective of women, who were the main victims of this system.[1] Thus, here I offer a study of Judith 8–16 in an effort to show how the theological basis and social practices of the temple are severely critiqued by the book of Judith and by the women who certainly must have helped to make this apocalyptic novel arrive in our hands.[2]

Critique of the Theology of Individual Retribution

Judith, the protagonist of the work, appears only in chapter 8 at a crucial and decisive moment. It is the thirty-fourth day of the siege of the city of Bethulia by the terrible Holofernes (7:20). The heads of the city have just finished giving God a period of five days in which to act and to fill the cisterns with water (7:30f.). The fortieth day will be decisive: the day of victory or defeat.

The decision of the heads of the city takes place in response to the people who have accused them of not making peace with Holofernes while there was still time. Now the people demand their surrender in the name "of our God...who punishes us in accordance with our sins and the errors of our fathers" (7:28). For the people, defeat is inevitable. Someone must have sinned, hence the punishment.

The heads of the city barely manage to postpone the decision. Judith intervenes at this point. Her servant is sent to call together the heads of the city. The meeting will take place in the house of Judith, or, better stated, in the tent that she has ordered to be set up on the roof. It is the space of the "house," the "tent," the space of women, where the voice of Judith will be heard: "Listen to me, heads of the inhabitants of Bethulia!" (8:11).

It is the beginning of many prophetic oracles. Prophecy now occurs in the mouth of women! It is a clear and fearless censure of the behavior of the heads of the city:

---

1. See Ana Maria and Sandro Gallazzi, "Mulher: fé na vida — 'tu és a gloria de Jerusalém! Bendita sejas tu, para sempre, junto ao Senhor, todo poderoso,'" in *A Palavra na vida* (São Leopoldo: Centro de Estudos Bíblicos, 1990), 35–36.

2. I do not wish thereby to reduce the proposals and objectives of this book, but rather merely to focus on one aspect of it and on one of the possible keys to its interpretation.

- Why do you tempt God?
- You know nothing, neither of *men* nor of God.
- God cannot be made subject to pressure. (8:11–16)

The certainty of Judith comes from the experience compressed in hundreds of prophetic pages: "Therefore, while we wait for his deliverance, let us call upon him to help us, and he will hear our voice, if it pleases him" (8:17). In this way, the heads of the city ought to have responded to the pressure of the people!

Judith, however, goes further in her reflection. It is not enough to have an attitude of trust, knowing that God will never abandon his people, except in the case of our following other gods and other projects (8:18). It is necessary to assume our responsibility, to do our part, to accept our task:

- *we will be responsible* for the profanation of the sanctuary;
- the life of our fellow citizens *depends on us;*
- the defense of the sanctuary, the temple, and the altar is *in our hands.* (8:21b–24)

For Judith, to assume a passive attitude of almost magical waiting for a miraculous intervention by God is improper, as it only affirms faith in retribution. God is gracious and sovereign. Difficulty does not mean punishment or vengeance by God. Many times it is just a test for which we ought to give thanks (8:25–27). Thus, the discourse of Judith is clear: return autonomy to God, autonomy which the temple had tied to the law and its observance, and return the responsibility for action to human beings, responsibility which the temple had emptied in a passive and almost magical attitude that was tied to the logic of retribution.

The heads of the city do not understand anything. Imbued with the mentality of retribution, they recognize the incontestable wisdom of the words of Judith, but only know how to ask that she, being full of goodness and reverence, beseech God to ... send rain! (8:28–31). Who knows? She may be heeded! Perhaps God will repay her goodness with rain!

Judith then speaks again with prophetic power: "Listen to me!"

- I am going to do something!
- I am going to go out ...

- The Lord will give aid to Israel through me!
- I am going to make it happen! (8:32ff.)

In Judith's faith, the prophetic logic capable of uniting "I will go down to liberate" with "you go to Pharaoh" from the earliest revelation of God (Ex 3:8, 10) is clearly continued. The heads of the city know nothing, they could do nothing, they remained in the door waiting to see. They can only limit themselves to prayer. The fortieth day will once more be a day of salvation: the salvation that Judith will effect and that God will effect. The two go together — indissolubly together!

Evening Prayer

Chapter 9 is the masterwork of this book. In the temple in Jerusalem the afternoon incense is being offered up. In the tent of Judith, another prayer is raised. It is the cry, out-loud, that since time immemorial has been able to call God to action.

The people's memory, the memory of women, will seek its foundation far away in the history of Dinah, daughter of Jacob, a young servant girl who suffered violence and profanation. This was indeed impurity, contamination, profanation, shame, and dishonor (9:2). The belt untied, the body undressed, and the breast profaned had the power to call forth the wrath of God.

And now history repeats itself. As with Dinah, so now the temple is going to suffer violence, be profaned, and be contaminated (9:8). The temple now as earlier the woman — what audacity! But it will be a woman who shall defend the temple from all impurity — she whom the temple burdened with sin and inferiority — because she, the woman, knows that God's name is *Lord* (*Yahweh*). She knows that God is the God who destroys wars and that his strength is not in numbers or his power among the strong. Above all, she knows that God is:

- God of the humble;
- aid of the oppressed;
- refuge of the weak;
- protector of the abandoned;
- savior of the desperate. (9:11)

This is the God of the fathers, Israel's God. It is not the God of the temple, the judge who pardons sins in exchange for blood and flour. The tent preserves the true memory of God and acts in his name. Judith does not ask for rain (Yahweh is not Baal) nor does she ask for miracles. She wants strength for her arm, astuteness for her lips, seductive words to wound and to kill, in order to strike down the arrogance of the oppressor at the hands of a widowed woman. This will indeed make the whole people — all the "tribes" — recognize that God is powerful and strong, "and that there is no other defender of the people of Israel" (9:14).

The Beauty of the Woman

Judith's weapon is her body, one prepared to manifest all its beauty. Four times in chapter 10 it is recalled that Judith was extraordinarily beautiful. She was beautiful in the eyes of the heads and elders of Bethulia, beautiful to the sentries, beautiful before those around the tent of Holofernes, and, finally, beautiful to Holofernes and all the Assyrian chiefs.

This beauty creates admiration for all the Israelites: "How can one disparage a people that has such women?" (10:19). Woman, the glory of her people! More audacity! Woman, the final victim of the temple, who could not enter the sacred precinct nor attend the celebration... woman, impure, sinner, and obliged to pay simply for the fact of having the body of a woman... woman, profaned by the temple, as Dinah was by the men of Shechem... she is beautiful! Far from being the cause of impurity, her body will be the cause of liberation and pride for Israel and of exaltation for Jerusalem (10:8).

Her body is the pleasing sacrifice offered for the life of the people, so that all might have life, including the temple — but a temple that would be "a house belonging to your children" (9:13) and not a place of power and economic concentration in the hands of a few who, in order to become rich, would not hesitate to defile the bodies of women. The lives of the high priest Joakim, of the priests, and of the heads of the city now depend upon the beautiful body of a woman! There is no other means of salvation!

The Theology of the Temple:
A Lie to Deceive Holofernes

Judith presents herself as a servant and a slave before Holofernes, who is dazzled by her beauty, and swears not to lie. Yet only deceptive words, though not suspicious to Holofernes, will issue forth from her lips. The text condenses the lie of Judith in chapter 11. But it is an especially interesting lie, since Judith does nothing more than say what the men of the temple had been saying for quite some time; perhaps for that reason, Holofernes believed her so easily:

> Long live Nebuchadnezzar, king of all the earth, and long live his power. (11:7)

The imperialism, first of the Persians and then of the Greeks, was always accepted by the temple in Jerusalem and by the Jews who were faithful and esteemed subjects of the empire. The favor of the emperor was always considered a blessing of God (Ezra 7:27f.; 9:9). Far from criticizing the despotism and oppressive cruelty of the emperors, the temple always tried to find a way to live peaceably with them. Sacrifice in honor of the emperor was customary in Jerusalem (Ezra 6:10; 1 Macc 7:33). Judith expresses the reasons for this cooperation: all power comes from God for the good of men and women: "Men and women, wild animals, cattle and the birds of the air, live for Nebuchadnezzar and his house" (Jdt 11:7).

> Our people sinned and therefore will be punished! (11:9–15)

It is the logic of retribution that is now used to deceive Holofernes. God is obliged to punish because the people sinned. What is interesting and ironic is the sin that has been committed. God is in a rage because some persons ate the part belonging to the priests: flocks, tithes of wine and oil, the first-fruits of the wheat. They ate everything that was stored in the temple (Neh 10:39f.; 12:44–47) to sustain and to enrich the dominant Zadokite priestly class, goods that came from the exploitation of the land. The people did not pay, and God punished them. The people ate, and God struck them — and, what is more, with the authorization of Jerusalem.

> You shall be the instrument of God's vengeance! (11:16–19)

God is going to use the strength of Holofernes to effect his punishment. Holofernes and Judith will perform unheard-of exploits. Holofernes will sit as "judge" and "shepherd," to care for and to guide the people. Judith, who intends to do away with the oppressor, stokes his will for power, leading him to believe that he is God's chosen one, the Messiah ("judge" and "shepherd" are eschatological and messianic terms) sent to save. Thus the devastator is transformed into a savior! How many times did the temple not make this affirmation in the face of different emperors? Alexander the Great and Antiochus III (to cite only the two most famous names) were considered by the priests to be the saviors of Israel!

Your God shall be my God! (11:20–23)

It is the height of irony. Holofernes converts. The temple and the synagogue would crisscross the world in search of proselytes. Here we have one: the greatest, the enemy. Through the words of Judith, he meets the true God: "Your God shall be my God!" as in Ruth 1:16. The difference is that Ruth (another text that is critical of the project of the temple; another text with a woman as protagonist) has life as her objective. Holofernes wants the people's destruction and ruin. Consequently, we have here the maximum expression of what has been denounced, namely, that it is possible to affirm faith in God and at the same time to want the death of the people! The same applies to the temple!

Prayer at Night

Chapter 12 prepares the climax of the story. On the one hand, there is Judith, who, though living in the enemy's camp, endeavors to observe Jewish ways and customs. She does so, moreover, in order to demonstrate coherence with the words that she has just spoken. On the other hand, there is Holofernes, who wants to take advantage of the woman so that he is not ridiculed for not having sexual relations with her. Thus there is ablution and prayer on the one hand, perturbation and intense desire on the other. On the one hand, a search for the "way to revive the sons and daughters of her people"; on the other, the will to seduce and a lot of drunkenness.

The two sides enter into conflict on the thirty-ninth day, the eve of the people's great salvation. That night Judith will not leave for prayer, but will enter into the tent of Holofernes. In front of the oppressor who has fallen down drunk in his bed, Judith lifts her supplication to the Lord of all power. It is a summary of her faith. What is going to happen will be the combined fruit of the strength of God and of Judith:

> Look favorably on what my hands are going to do.... Help your inheritance and carry out my plan.... Give me strength, Lord, God of Israel. (13:4b–7)

The Great Celebration

Judith's return is the beginning of a great celebration that dispenses with and even substitutes for the temple. "Open, open the gates!" (13:11) is the cry that signals the start of the celebration, just as in Ps 24:7, 9 or Ps 118:19: "Open for me the gate of justice, and I will enter to give thanks to God."

"The Lord our God is with us..." (13:11). It is the ancient formula of faith in the powerful protection of God, a summary of the faith of the Exodus and of the journey of the people (Gen 26:3; 28:15; Ex 3:12; Jdg 6:12). Thus starts the great celebration led by Judith. What she did to save her people gives her the right to preside and to conduct the liturgy.

When the gate is opened and the people gather around the "fire," Judith calls forth the great public act of praise: "Praise God, praise him! Praise God" (13:14). It is praise for God's mercy and for victory against the enemies "by my intermediary."

> As the Lord lives, who has protected me in the way I went, it was my face that tricked him to his destruction, and yet he committed no act of sin with me, to defile and shame me. (13:16)

The acts of Judith call forth a series of blessings. There is the people's blessing for God who defeated the enemies (13:17). There is the blessing of Uzziah:

> Blessed are you... above all women on earth! And blessed be God the Lord... because you did not hesitate to risk your life when our people was brought low. (13:18–20)

There is the blessing of Achior the Ammonite chief, who prostrates himself at the feet of Judith and proclaims: "Blessed are you in every tent of Judah! In every nation those who hear your name will be alarmed" (14:7). In all these blessings, one thing is certain: Judith will be remembered, will be exalted, will be heaped with goods, will be admired. Her name will also provoke fear because she performed the true sacrifice. She offered her life for the life of the people and at the same time sacrificed the life of Holofernes with the strength of God.

This gesture converts Achior himself who, despite being Ammonite and therefore excluded categorically from the temple (Deut 23:3f.), is circumcised and "admitted into the house of Israel" (Jdt 14:10). The barriers created by the temple fall to earth! The knowledge of God is open to all without distinction. Even an Ammonite can return to Israel through the action of Judith!

However, the most important "blessing" is placed in the mouth of the high priest, Joakim. After the definitive defeat of the enemy, Joakim and the council of elders of Jerusalem (the supreme authorities) go to the "house" of Judith. There, in this house that has been converted into a new temple, they proclaim together the blessing:

- You are the *glory* of Jerusalem!
- You are the *pride* of Israel!
- You are the *exaltation* of our people! (15:9)

Everything that was said about the high priest and the temple itself (Sir 50:5, 11) is now said about Judith. Furthermore, it is said by someone who always kept his honor for himself. And it is said about a woman! "Blessed are you eternally with the almighty Lord" (Jdt 15:10f.). The "Amen" of the people confirms it (15:10).

At the center of the celebration is neither the cult nor the temple nor sacrifice, but Judith and her liberating prowess. Things have been rearranged at the axes. First the people, then the heads of the city, and, finally, the temple recognize, affirm, and bless Judith and God, both inseparable in their search for the life of the people.

The Retaking of the Temple

After his blessing, the high priest disappears from our story. Judith and the women will conduct the feast and the procession to Jerusalem. Branches, olive crowns, and dancing all manifest the joy that results from the definitive victory:

> Judith went before all the people, leading the dance of all the women. The men of Israel accompanied her, bearing their arms with crowns and singing hymns. (15:13)

The situation has reversed itself. The woman who was always suppressed because of her situation of constant impurity is now out in front. She will "retake" the temple that had remained closed to her; she will reconquer it with the right of someone who knows who the true God is and who fights for the life of the people. Judith now has the authority to do what only the high priest was allowed to do once a year, and precisely on the day of expiation (Sir 50:20), the day of sacrifice for the sin of all Israelites: to invoke the *Name* (Jdt 16:1). She knows and proclaims that the place of God is not the temple, but rather: "He keeps his camp in the midst of the people" (16:2=2 Sam 7:6; Isa 57:15).

For this reason, a widow and a woman without children (a condition of extreme precariousness for an Israelite woman) becomes the *mother of all:* of "my" youth, of "my" children, of "my" maidservants, of "my" little ones, of "my" weak, of "my"...(16:4, 11). For this whole "house" she fought, with her beauty, with her perfume, with diadem and linen clothing, with her sandals, with all her invincible weapons as a woman; she did not hesitate to take the scimitar and cut the neck of the one who threatened the life of her people.

The conclusion, then, is clear:

- Lord, you are great and glorious....

- *All creatures serve* you....(16:13–14)

Since the time of the Exodus and the prophets, what counts as the true worship of God is serving God and doing God's will. In perfect alignment with authentic prophecy and preserved in the heart of the women of the people of the land, Judith proclaims:

> The fragrant sacrifices *are indeed a small thing;*
> the fat offered as a burnt offering *is almost nothing;*
> *who fears the Lord is great forever!* (16:16)

The temple will be retaken. Three months of feasting in the atria of the temple seal the victory. Burnt offerings and spontaneous sacrifices (missing is the sacrifice for sin) are offered by the people as a sign of thanksgiving.

The New Society

The narrative does not end here, however; it does not end in the temple, but rather in the "house," the "inheritance," the "land" (16:21), since it is there in the place of production that freedom must come. It is not enough to defeat the enemy; it is not enough to retake the temple. All that makes sense if justice and the law truly happen.

Judith gives the final and definitive example, bringing to pass the project of the *year of the Lord's favor* with regard to its most important elements:

- possession of the land (16:21);
- freedom of slaves (16:23);
- distribution of goods (16:24).

Now the sword can rest. Now nothing will cause the people to fear because our God continues to be the God who *does not want sacrifices but mercy, the knowledge of God more than whole burnt offerings* (Hos 6:6; Isa 1:10–17; 58:6f.; Amos 5:22–24; Micah 6:8; Matt 9:13).

7

The Subversive Memory of a Woman

2 Samuel 21:1–14

ALICIA WINTERS

The vigil of Rizpah in the desert beside the cadavers of her executed sons took place to protest the abuses of David's government and to demand better treatment for the survivors of the house of Saul. Thus it emphasized the spirituality of women and their participation through solidarity in the struggle for justice.

"There was hunger for three years, year after year." The Hebrew text communicates the people's increasing desperation when faced with no rain. As king, David felt himself responsible in some way to confront the situation. Therefore he turned to Yahweh and discovered that the fault lay with Saul and his family for a previous massacre of the Gibeonites, allies with whom Israel had in force a treaty of mutual defense.[1]

When the survivors of Gibeon were consulted, David learned that in their hearts there burned a desire for vengeance that did not allow for economic indemnification or reprisals against the Israelites but specifically sought the public execution of seven of Saul's descendants. As it turned out, there were still seven men who stood directly in the line of Saul. The three sons of Saul's wife Ahinoam were dead, but two sons remained that Saul had had with a concubine, Rizpah. Five grandchildren, the sons of his daughter Merab, also remained. These would serve the purposes of the Gibeonites very well, and David wasted no time in handing them

---

1. We do not know about this massacre from any other biblical text.

over so that the Gibeonites could hurl them before Yahweh off a mountain cliff.

The biblical text then runs as follows:

> Then Rizpah the daughter of Aiah took sackcloth, and spread it for herself on the rock, from the beginning of harvest until rain fell upon them from the heavens; and she did not allow the birds of the air to come upon them by day, or the beasts of the field by night. When David was told what Rizpah the daughter of Aiah, the concubine of Saul, had done, David went and took the bones of Saul and the bones of his son Jonathan from the men of Jabesh-gilead, who had stolen them from the public square of Beth-shan, where the Philistines had hanged them, on the day the Philistines killed Saul on Gilboa; and he brought up from there the bones of Saul and the bones of his son Jonathan; and they gathered the bones of those who were hanged. And they buried the bones of Saul and his son Jonathan in the land of Benjamin in Zela, in the tomb of Kish his father; and they did all that the king commanded. And after that God heeded supplications for the land. (2 Sam 21:10–14)

Commentators generally pay little attention to this part of the story. If at all, they mention it as a beautiful illustration of maternal tenderness. Even David was impressed, they say, by Rizpah's heroism and nobility of heart and consented to show his respect for the feelings of an unhappy mother by arranging for the burial of her sons. This reading is surprisingly naive, passing over the economic and political aspects of the story and the fusion of sex and politics in the person of Rizpah.

Sex and Power

The name of Rizpah first appears in the biblical text in the battle for succession to the throne of Israel that developed between Abner and Ishbosheth over sexual possession of the concubine of Saul (2 Sam 3:7–8). The exchange of women established the relations of power between men, and sleeping with the king's concubines constituted a declaration of pretension to the throne (Absalom, 2 Sam 16:20–22; Adonijah, 1 Kgs 2:13–25). When Abner asked

Ishbosheth ironically why he insulted him, calling him to account for something so despicable as a woman, he expressed, in effect, the importance that the same woman had for both men as a means of defining power. Later, when Abner finally handed over the tribes of the north to David, David also demanded the delivery of a woman to confirm the covenant: no longer a mere concubine, but Saul's own daughter.

David's domination of the other men is identified as much by his sexual as by his military conquests (Abigail and Bathsheba). The other mother in this narrative, Merab, daughter of Saul, was a sister of the woman who was handed over in the agreement with Abner. Merab had once been publicly appointed by her father to be David's wife, but the action was no more than a subterfuge. Saul demanded a military victory over the Philistines as a condition for the marriage, hoping in this way to free himself of David, who seemed to him to be more and more a rival. When David ended up triumphant, Saul reneged and gave his daughter to Adriel of Meholah, the father of five of the men executed by the Gibeonites (see 1 Sam 18:17–19). When David handed these men over to the Gibeonites, not only did he eliminate the descendants of Saul; he also eliminated the descendants of Adriel, the man who took a woman away from him.

In effect, the reference to the two women, Rizpah and Merab, as the mothers of the seven executed men is quite explicitly an allusion to the struggles for power in Israel and the fragility of the consensus on the basis of which David began his reign in the north. These two names allow us to recognize that David was not a neutral intermediary in the vengeance of the Gibeonites. Saul and Ishbosheth were dead and David occupied the throne, but the position of king was by no means secure in the face of the powerful and tenaciously independent tribes of the north. David owed his power more to the intervention of the army than to popular support, and he knew very well that an ample sector of the people were loyal to the house of Saul, above all in Benjamin, where many probably shared the idea of Shimei that David was "an assassin and a scoundrel" (2 Sam 16:7). In fact, a good part of the north would later follow Sheba the Benjaminite in open rebellion against David (2 Samuel 20).

These circumstances create suspicion as to what motivated the

Gibeonite request. It smells like a conspiracy with David to help him consolidate his power. The alliance of Israel with Gibeon also included, according to Josh 9:17, the cities of Chephirah, Beeroth, and Kiriath-jearim, all located in the same strategic valley in the land of Benjamin. There, just to the north of Jerusalem, the land sloped down markedly, offering easy access to the elevated plain from the coast and from the Jordan valley.

It is now interesting to recall that two men from Beeroth assassinated Ishbosheth, the son and successor of Saul (2 Sam 4:1–12). The men from Beeroth poorly judged the moment; if their action indeed favored David in the struggle for the throne of Israel, the delicate political situation in the north did not allow him any response other than the death penalty for the two. Nonetheless, the commitment to David is noteworthy, as is the decided intervention in the internal affairs of Israel by these cities that are carefully identified both in chapter 4 and here in chapter 21 as "not Israelite."

The extermination of the male descendants of Saul, like the assassination of Ishbosheth, came as a splendid gift to David, given that any one of the seven could have risen up as a pretender to the throne. The text indicates that, out of loyalty to his friend, David deliberately did not include the son of Jonathan among those he handed over to the Gibeonites. Nonetheless, 2 Sam 9:1–6 suggests that David first learned about the existence of Meribaal when there were no longer any other descendants of Saul, that is, after the execution of the seven. The stories of the final chapters of 2 Samuel are not arranged in chronological order, so that it is very possible that 2 Samuel 21 refers to an incident that occurred before the meeting with Meribaal described in chapter 9. In any case, even though David did not kill Jonathan's son, David had the son brought to Jerusalem where an eye could be kept on him under a sort of house arrest that was disguised as the attention to be given to a guest of honor.

Against this backdrop, there can be no doubt that the action of Rizpah in the desert had political, even subversive, implications. Her presence at the side of the dead kept their memory alive for all the Benjaminites and all Israel, putting in question the right of David to occupy the throne and his means of staying in power. In order to understand these implications, it is necessary to know both Rizpah's situation after the death of Saul as well as the burial customs of ancient Israel.

Widows and Concubines

The widow is frequently cited in the book of Psalms and in other parts of the Bible, together with the orphan and the stranger, as representative of a class of persons that had special need of Yahweh's protection. In a patriarchal society like ancient Israel, a woman's economic security depended on her connection with some male relative. She entered and became part of her husband's family when she married; if the husband died, she continued on as part of that family, subject to the authority and protection of another male of his parentage. In fact, even when she returned to live with her own father, the husband's family maintained responsibility for her.[2]

Although such a woman could have property or money in her own name, it does not seem that she would have been able to sustain herself after her husband's death. Normally, she would count on the help of her children or father-in-law; but when these men disappeared, as in the case of Rizpah, the widow would lose her place in the social structure and be left destitute.

Rizpah was a widow and probably lived with her two sons until their execution. Given that the action of David and the Gibeonites in this massacre effectively extinguished the house of Saul in Israel, no male was left who might take her side.[3] The possibility exists, therefore, that she remained in the desert after the execution, at least partly because she had nowhere else to go. If the two executed sons represented her only source of economic sustenance, her heroic vigil at the rock may have been the fruit of her desperation. Her current situation was certainly in severe contrast to the life of luxury that she would have enjoyed when she was the king's favorite.

Nevertheless, two factors in the case of Rizpah create doubt that this explanation alone is sufficient. First, Rizpah was not mar-

---

2. The widow Tamar returned to her paternal home because there was no brother of her husband available to marry her; nevertheless, when she was accused of prostitution, it was her father-in-law who ordered that she be burned (Gen 38:24).

3. If Meribaal was already with David, he was a client of the king and in no position to help Rizpah.

ried. Her social category is identified as that of "concubine," which is to be clearly distinguished from the category of wife and also from the category of prostitute. Second, Rizpah is identified as the "daughter of Aiah."

The size of the harem indicated the power of the king.[4] But not only kings had concubines. We know, for example, about the concubines of Abraham, Nahor, Jacob, Gideon, and others, because their children appear in the biblical genealogies, carefully distinguished from the children of the wife (or wives). Even a Levite had a concubine in the problematic narrative of Judges 19–21, which, despite the textual and historical difficulties, seems to provide interesting and probably trustworthy access to the structure and social relations of concubinage in Israel, as a complement to the laws on the matter in the ancient Code of the Covenant in Ex 21:1–11.

The concubine was basically a slave, a possession, an object that could be bought or sold, even by her own father (Ex 21:7). According to the law in Exodus, a male slave could be redeemed and remained free after six years of service, but a woman could not. If certain (Spanish) translations of wide circulation indeed speak of the possibility that her master could "take her for a wife" (Ex 21:8–9; see the Biblia Latinoamericana and the Reina Valera version), one must recognize that nothing in the Hebrew text suggests an intention to elevate her rank; the verb used here has the sense, "to destine, to designate," and the law seems to consider that even when the owner might take her as a concubine, she continued being a slave. It was certainly this way in the cases of Hagar, Bilhah, and Zilpah.

On the other hand, the concubine had certain rights according to this law: redemption was not automatic, as in the case of the man, but if the owner rejected the concubine, he could not sell her to foreigners (but to Israelites?) and ought to allow her redemption with money. If the owner decided that she was to be the concubine of his son, he ought to treat her as a daughter; and if he took another woman, but stayed with her, he ought not to reduce her food, clothing, or conjugal rights. If her master failed to honor his obligation to the concubine in any of these respects, the law gave

---

4. Saul had one concubine, David had ten, while Solomon had three hundred concubines in addition to all his wives.

the woman the right to abandon him without having to pay the price of redemption.

It is possible that the concubine of the Levite in Judg 19:2 made use of this right, returning to the house of her father after becoming angry with the Levite, according to the reading of the ancient versions adopted in the Jerusalem Bible. We do not know if the father of this concubine had sold her to the Levite, but it is possible (Ex 21:7). Noteworthy are the father's efforts to appease the Levite and the success that he had. The Levite came to Bethlehem, according to the text, intending to "speak to the heart" of the woman, but it seems that he spent most of his time eating and talking with her father (Judg 19:4–9). We can conclude that it was not unusual for the father of a concubine to maintain good relations with her owner.

It is now important to note the second factor, namely, that Rizpah is identified in the biblical stories as the "daughter of Aiah." The use of the patronym, relatively rare for women in the Hebrew Bible, reminds us that there is another man in the life of Rizpah, namely, her father. It is probable that the relationship between Saul and Aiah was at least as friendly as that of the Levite with the father of his concubine.

The name "Aiah" appears in 1 Chr 1:40 as one of the sons of Zibeon, chief of an Edomite clan. We know of an Edomite, Doeg, who served in the army of Saul, and it is possible that Rizpah's father was another, related to the clan of Zibeon, who found his fortune in the service of Saul of Benjamin. Saul, as king, would not marry a non-Israelite woman, but could make her his concubine.

Foreigner or not, Aiah undoubtedly received generous compensation for his daughter and a privileged position in Benjamin during the reigns of Saul and Ishbosheth. When fortune shifted and David assumed the throne, the properties of Saul were confiscated, but David would have had no reason to confiscate the property of Aiah acquired during the years when his daughter enjoyed the favor of the leading family of Israel. Thus Rizpah very likely had the option of returning to a family that was comfortably off.

According to this reading, the action of Rizpah, who stayed at the side of the corpses of her sons instead of returning to her father's house, not only represents the pain of a mother deprived of her sons or the desperation of a widow without support, but a thought-out and intentional political protest. It is possible that Rizpah's family supported her during her stay in the desert, taking her food and water and perhaps accompanying her during the night watches; but the initiative and perseverance in this regard are clearly hers.

In the meeting between Abner and Ishbosheth (2 Samuel 3), Rizpah is presented as a passive victim of rape and reduced to a thing. She is invisible, with neither voice nor vote regarding her future. The writer's interest circles wholly around the two men fighting over her. But although her words are not recorded, her actions speak loud enough.

Death and Burial

Death was the normal end of life in the earliest thinking of ancient Israel; until the last centuries before the Christian era, there was little speculation about life after death. The ancient blessings and promises show that the "multiplication of one's descendants" was the future hoped for by an Israelite (Gen 26:23). Human life was understood in social, political, and communitarian terms. Life was not simply biological life, but included all the benefits of the covenant with Yahweh: "Look, I put before you today life and happiness, death and disgrace.... I put before you life or death, blessing or curse; choose life, that you and your descendants may live" (Deut 30:15, 19).

Life was relationship with others, that is, life in community; through one's children, an individual continued to participate in the community. The possibility of being "cut off from one's people" was a fearsome threat for an Israelite (Lev 20:1–6). Not even physical death occurred in isolation; as a member of the community, the dying person was "united to his or her people" (see Gen 25:8; 35:29; 49:29; Deut 32:50) or "to the fathers" (Judg 2:10; 1 Kgs 2:10). If indeed there was a popular concept of the place of the dead ("Sheol"), the official theology of Israel did not pay any attention to it.

Israel understood necromancy and worship of the dead to be incompatible with Yahwism (Deut 26:14; Lev 19:26b, 28). Although prohibitions against such diviners (see, e.g., Lev 19:31; 20:6, 27; Deut 18:10–11) indicate that these practices persisted in certain sectors, and although we are told that Saul himself visited a woman diviner in order to consult with the dead, nothing suggests that Rizpah was a diviner or that she stayed beside the corpses as a form of communication with the dead or to worship them. In fact, 1 Sam 28:3, which states that Saul had expelled the enchanters and diviners, makes this interpretation virtually impossible.

On the other hand, a correct burial of the dead was very important in ancient Israel. The frequent references to burials in the Hebrew Bible and the thousands of tombs excavated in biblical lands testify to this importance. Rites of lamentation accompanied the burial; and in the formal lament of a death, women frequently performed a special role that seems to have implied a specialized preparation (Jer 9:17, 20; 2 Chr 35:25). Nonetheless, the lack of burial of these corpses does not allow for the possibility that Rizpah stayed beside the seven corpses as a professional mourner.

Ancient customs and laws, as well as the requirements of the climate, all point to a quick burial of the dead. Families had traditional places for their dead, and it was important for the dying person and for that person's family to know that he or she would be buried there. Various traditions exist regarding the transfer of the bones of Jacob from Egypt to be buried in a family plot in Canaan (Gen 49:29–32; 50:4–14; Ex 13:19; Josh 24:32). The collection of laws in Deuteronomy includes the stipulation that a criminal who has been hanged ought to be buried the same day as his or her execution (Deut 21:23). Obviously, however, no provision had been made for the burial of the seven inheritors of Saul executed by David and the Gibeonites, and this omission seems to be intentional.

Although many modern versions say that the seven were hanged, the verb here from the root *yq'* is not the same as the one employed in the passage from Deuteronomy, where hanging is clearly in view. In Gen 32:25, which refers to Jacob wrestling with an adversary, *yq'* signifies "to dislocate or separate (a bone)." In Ezek 23:16, the root is employed to speak of the desire that comes out of the mind of a person; and in Jer 6:8, Yahweh himself as the subject of *yq'* threatens to *separate himself* from Jerusalem. The only other use of this verb in the Bible (Num 25:4) also has to do with a ritual execution, whose purpose was to make an example of those who had directed a heretical cult in Israel; and it is specified that the action of yq' was done "in front of the sun," an emphatic term which implies that those who were executed had to remain visible, that is, unburied. The Jerusalem Bible translates yq' as "throw over a cliff." Thus the execution of the seven would have been similar to that of 2 Chr 25:12, although this passage does not employ the root yq'.

It seems, in effect, that the execution, whatever its form may have been, included the public exposure of the corpses after death as part of the punishment. Mutilation and neglect would be the final humiliation of the victims. The danger of scavenger animals and birds would be constant; and without the vigilance of Rizpah, the corpses would have rapidly disappeared.

The Israelites feared remaining unburied after death, and the threat of being consumed by scavenger animals or birds constituted a fearsome curse (1 Kgs 14:11; 16:4; 21:23–24; see Jer 8:1–2; 25:33). It was apparently the intention of the Philistines that the bodies of Saul and Jonathan suffer this humiliation when they stuck them on the city wall; although they were rescued in a heroic raid by the men of Jabesh-gilead, their bones still remained in that city on the other side of the Jordan and had not been handed over to their kin to be buried in the family tomb.

Spirituality and Solidarity

Rizpah was a survivor. Death had touched her in various ways. She had lost her husband in war, and now her sons had been killed because they represented a threat to the regime in power.[5] Enduring in the desert the odor of the bodies, thirst and fear during the cold night and under the red-hot sun, day after day and night after night, Rizpah scared off the birds and the beasts to keep alive the memory of her sons, the lineage of Saul, and everything that had happened to the house of Saul since David fixed his eyes on the throne.

Who let David know what Rizpah was doing, and what did they say to him? It could have been a Benjaminite, threatening David,

---

5. It is hardly probable that the Benjaminites swallowed the excuse of the supposed massacre of the Gibeonites as justification for this execution.

or perhaps it was one of his own councillors, advising him of the potential in the situation for disturbances.

When David learned about Rizpah's action, he evidently felt that he was the object of her protest, for he immediately went into action. He did not go to see Rizpah, which would have been the logical step, had he wished to congratulate her on the nobility of her heart. Rather, he personally went to Jabesh-gilead to ask for the bones of Saul and Jonathan in order to give them burial in their family tomb together with the bones, picked up by messengers, of those who had recently been executed.

Apparently David gave orders for a great ceremony to be held, and it could be for this occasion that he composed the elegy now found in 2 Sam 1:17–27. It seems that the original plan of the (Judean?) editor of 2 Samuel did not include this narrative about Rizpah and the bones of Saul and Jonathan. Rather, other hands (from the north?) added the story afterward, because the history of the life of Saul remained incomplete.

This burial ceremony would have signified much more than a simple rite of lamentation, given the social and political context. It would represent an effort on David's part to placate the Benjaminites and the Israelites of the north: it constituted a promise that the persecution of Saul's sympathizers would stop. We have already seen that it was probably in these circumstances that David asked if any son of the house of Saul still remained, claiming that he wanted "to treat him favorably out of love for Jonathan" (2 Sam 9:1).

2 Sam 21:1–14 can also be seen as the fruit of David's effort to justify himself in the eyes of the tribes of the north. The text seems to want to defend David by showing that the execution of the seven was not capricious or malicious, but a just restitution that the king felt obliged to demand from those who carried the guilt for violating a solemn oath sanctioned by Yahweh.

These observations confirm the suspicion that Rizpah's action was conceived and carried out as a political protest, and that it was understood in this way by its intended object, the head of the government. It was a political act but, at the same time, an act of profound spirituality. Rizpah's solidarity with these victims demonstrates the power that arises out of a commitment to others and makes God's presence manifest in the world.

Rizpah, of course, wept for her sons. But her presence beside the corpses after the massacre represented much more than a mother's pained heart; or, better stated, what a woman's pained heart truly means remains unrecognized in the context of a patriarchal world. Women survivors like Rizpah are those who remain to care for the sick and the suffering. Amid the brutal destruction of life in Latin America, they endure the disappearance of fathers, husbands, children. They witness the assassination of their loved ones by violence and by hunger. They themselves are the victims of rape, abandonment, exploitation, and extreme poverty. Nevertheless, to this day women carry on the struggle of Rizpah against assassination, violence, and death, opting for action to protect and to defend life.

Rizpah not only mourned the memory of her sons. She had the firm resolve to restore the human dignity of the seven victims that had been reviled and abandoned so that their bodies would be mutilated. Her response to a savage massacre was to affirm her own ability to continue being human in the midst of a dehumanizing situation. Surrounded by corpses, she testified to life.

This woman did not submit to the eradication that threatened the victims of the massacre. She challenged the terror of disappearance, something worse than the terror of the beasts, because she could not allow her sons to be simply wiped out as though they had never existed. She was determined to preserve their dignity, even if, in doing so, she courted death herself. In her commitment to life, Rizpah finally ceased to be a passive victim and assumed her own identity.

The execution took place at Gibeah, the capital of Saul's government. Without a doubt, the place was replete with Saul's relatives and sympathizers. Perhaps the majority of them had thought to save their own hide by expediently not seeing, not speaking, not remembering. But by insisting on the memory of her sons, Rizpah succeeded also in making herself memorable. She promoted the visibility of what had happened, so that it would not go unnoticed and become forgotten. She understood the importance of commemorating and making history visible, because she herself had been invisible.

Her sons would not return to her. But Rizpah would not cease to struggle on their behalf until they were "reunited with their people." This woman kept alive the sense of being a people at a time of uneasiness and anxiety. Furthermore, in responding to what also threatened others, she acted on behalf of all those who lacked defense in a struggle that she engaged through accompaniment, mutuality, and solidarity in order to overcome the same death.

The vigil of Rizpah would have strongly attracted the attention of the Benjaminites in the city and its surroundings, keeping hatred alive for the detested usurper. Thus her action became an indictment of the injustice and inhumanity of human being against human being. Rizpah refused to become accustomed to injustice. She would not accept it as just a fact of life.

For this very reason, her action called others together to join her in the cause of all the lives that she commemorated with her own sacrifice. She took, perhaps, the first step into that stream of resistance against the increasing tyranny of David and Solomon that would end a century later in a people's revolution and the organization of the independent state of Israel (1 Kgs 12:1–16).

According to the text, the incident with Rizpah began with a drought. The sacrifice of the seven men by the men of Gibeon was supposed to remedy the assumed cause of the resulting hunger. Nevertheless, the arrival of rain is not directly linked in the text to the sacrifice of the men, but rather to the woman's sacrifice, which is a sacrifice of another sort. In the end, the text suggests that God was satisfied only when the revindication implicit in the woman's action had received a response, namely, the revindication of justice.

8
·······

The Powerful Prayer of Lament and the Resistance of the People of God

A Particular Approach to the Book of Psalms

MARCELO DE BARROS SOUZA

···

In various regions of our continent, black cultural groups offer diverse services. Indigenous people have "shamans." Ancient traditions of popular Catholicism speak of benedictions and "powerful prayers." In the Bible, the psalms are powerful prayers for the believing community, which thereby can have recourse, with confidence and faithfulness, to the Lord God and God's covenant.

Invitation to a Prayerful Reading

In all of Latin America, for those of us who, taking as our point of departure the journey of the various base Christian communities, seek to know and to follow more closely the Word of God as lived in the faith of the people, the *Revista de Interpretación Bíblica Latinoamericana* has been a basic tool. In these communities, we find ourselves, persons of various countries and of different churches, as comrades in Bible study.

Celebrating this gift, I wish to speak here about the psalms as the power of a believing people. I invite those who are reading what I write to meditate together on the nature and intensity of the prayer contained in the many psalms of individual and collective supplication which form the majority of the biblical psalter. I propose to do this, mindful of our people's power of resistance in Latin

America and especially the many popular Christian communities that, in recent years, have rediscovered the psalms in individual prayer and corporate worship.

As happens in our base Christian communities, a good method of entering into this theme is to dialogue with the psalms in their own universe, namely, that of a loving relationship with the Lord. As we read prayerfully, we enter into the most profound spirit of the book and not just its intellectual content. Since 1962, I have had the gift of knowing the psalms as a central element of daily prayer. It was through prayer that I got to know and learned to love the psalms, and to receive strength and courage from them during life's difficult moments.

At the beginning of this meditation, what are we to pray? Since the third century C.E., many Christian communities have met daily to sing the psalms, at least in the morning, in the evening, and at midday. It is in communion with those churches that praise and beseech God in the name of Jesus that we now can recall to life the invocation of the psalms that, since antiquity in the West, begin the canonical hours. In Brazil, the popular communities sing: "Come, my Lord, come to help me, come and do not delay in aiding me" (Ps 70:2).[1]

Some Experiences on the Journey

For some years now, I have belonged to a group of pastors, liturgists, composers, women and men who have translated the psalms into Brazilian speech and melodies. In this way, we help the popular communities to use the psalms in their prayers. During this time, I have seen and studied many examples of how the psalms have helped to express the most profound prayer of believers and of how this prayer has been a means of resistance for individual persons and communities.

Some time ago now, during the military dictatorship of the 1970s, when we had not yet had this experience of the psalms translated into popular speech, the police took prisoner a friend of mine. He was a professor of history in a high school in Recife.

---

1. Here I will refer to the psalms with their Hebrew numeration as used in the vast majority of contemporary versions of the Bible.

After this experience, he told the story that when he was being tortured in order to get the names of possible comrades, at the most difficult moment, he could only remember the verses we had sung from Psalm 23 in our Saturday-night masses. By repeating this psalm, he resisted suffering he never thought that he would be able to endure and conquer.

In the desert of Northeast Brazil, a group of landless laborers conspired to occupy an uncultivated *hacienda* in 1982. They decided on two in the morning of a specific day. But without anyone knowing exactly how it happened, word seemed to have spread that there was danger of violent repression. The community became divided. Some preferred to postpone the occupation; others argued that if they were to let it go now, it was unlikely that they would have the same opportunity again. So they took a vote. The result was that they decided to enter the land.

Everyone, however, felt the fear and doubt in the air. Someone then tied two shafts of wood together to make a cross. Another person took a Bible in his hand, and another began to sing a song that they had sung the previous Sunday:

> God rises up where our enemies are;
> in his presence the iniquitous perish,
> they are like smoke that disappears,
> they exist in the flame that later goes out.[2]

While singing this psalm, the landless laborers began the adventure of the occupation; no one stayed behind. At first, there was no repression. It occurred a few days later. So the community took up the psalm again. Some members of the group had participated in a course on the struggle for land in the Bible. They had learned that, according to the Bible, when the ancient Hebrews marched to conquer the land "that the Lord had given them," they went singing this psalm (see Num 10:35). Thus the psalm became the hymn of the camp.

The psalm-translations and melodies have since spread throughout Brazil; I have heard many examples of how praying the psalms has strengthened the resistance of laborers and marginal communities. But I do not wish to turn the present conversation into a

---

2. Sung version of Ps 68:2–3.

simple telling of these histories. Instead, I propose that we see how the psalms were used by the people of Israel from the moment of their creation and throughout the history of their use in Jewish communities.

In this sense, perhaps before opening the Bible, it is worthwhile to refer to two contemporary witnesses. First, in reference to his own (Jewish) people, André Chouraqui states: "we are born with this book [of Psalms] in our guts."[3] Second, what the singing of the psalms represents for the communities of the people of the first covenant, we can sense even more strongly in this moving testimony about the Jews who were prisoners of the Nazis:

> Only fifty years ago, men and women were taken to Ausch-witz in blinded wagons to be exterminated there. But in those trains, they refused to renounce their humanity and sang through the psalms their faithfulness to God. Who of us, Jews and Christians, do not have deep pains or immense joys in the darkness of the night in a dark room or in the radiant light of midday? Before the immensity of the horizon, who is the believing person who has not sensed the need to open his psalter and to shout to God with the passionate and never surpassed words that the Bible attributes to David?[4]

The Most Ancient Histories of the Bible and Songs of War

When there are physical fights in the Far East on television or in movies, we see that when it is time to defend oneself or to attack, the fighters let loose a great scream. Like an animal roar, it has a double function. First, it frees up one's own breathing and stimulates the warriors' courage; at the same time, it frightens the enemy and instills terror. Thus, like other ancient peoples, Israel also had its war cries (see Num 10:9; 1 Sam 17:52).

In antiquity, it was common for people to think that such a word, shouted in combat or sung in war, had more force than

---

3. See André Chouraqui in the preface to *Le Cantique des Cantiques: Suivi des Psaumes* (Paris: Presses Universitaires de France, 1970). He takes up this preface again in his 1990 translation of the psalms (Paris: Desclée de Brouwer).

4. See Collette Kessier, "Les psaumes dans la liturgie juive," *Lumière et Vie* 202 (1991): 13f.

others. For example, the most powerful and important songs and shouts were kept in secret. In various biblical psalms, there are allusions to the "cry" (*teru'ah*), a more or less magical war shout that became the "Hurrah!" of victory and, at the same time, a shout of praise to Yahweh. The God of the Hebrews was considered the Conqueror. We read, for example: "Come, let us praise the Lord with rejoicing, let us shout [*nariy'ah*] to the rock of our salvation, let us come before him with acts of thanksgiving, let us acclaim [*nariya'*] him" (Ps 95:1–2). We find this same shout to God the Conqueror that went from battleground to worship service in Ps 47:2; 60:10; 65:14; 66:1; 81:2; 98:4, 6; 100:1, and in various other biblical texts.

I went through the Bible, looking for psalms that were used in struggles and situations of resistance by communities and friends of God. Generally, the exegetical studies confirm that the oldest biblical texts that we know are songs of praise to God and of thanksgiving for victory in wars of liberation and for the resistance of the people against their enemies. Most of these psalms are attributed to women prophets and leaders of the people.

One of the oldest is the song of Deborah (Judg 5:1–31). According to the Jerusalem Bible, this song was composed a little after the events that it relates: the victory of the people liberated by Deborah and Barak from the Canaanites. The song celebrates the faith that it is the Lord himself who fights against the enemies of his people (vv. 20, 21, 23).

Another similar song that became even more important historically is the song of Moses and Miriam after the crossing of the Red Sea (Exodus 15). It is the first song of the Old Testament that the Christian communities used as a psalm (see Rev 15:3). We might also recall the song of Hannah in 1 Sam 2:1–10, a psalm-type composition from the time of the monarchy that expresses the hope of the poor.

Someone will say, perhaps, that the examples I have given are songs for victories already obtained more than they are songs of resistance. That is true, but these songs rightly served as a foundational experience so that in other moments and situations of danger the people might cite them to ask the Lord to repeat, in that new moment, the saving intervention that he first had made during the Exodus and at the time of the conquest of the land. Thus a psalm like Psalm 86 — a supplication for God's protection, perhaps composed before the Maccabean war — picks up the language of the song of the Exodus:

> Among the gods, there is no other like You;
> nothing that can equal your works. (Ex 15:11; Ps 86:8)

Another example is Psalm 74, a collective lamentation after the destruction of the temple. In this lament, in order to bring forth a complaint to the Lord for having rejected the people "who were the flock of his pasture," the psalm refers to the song of the Exodus:

> Remember your assembly that you acquired from the beginning, the tribe that you redeemed as your inheritance. (Ps 74:2; Ex 15:17)

Now an experience we all have working with base Christian communities is that one of the most common ways the people have to give themselves strength in their struggles is to sing as though victory were already secure. Even when experiencing failure and difficulty, the communities sing and shout: "The people united will never be defeated." It is an act of faith.

In the Bible, we find the same sensibility of the poor. Certainly in the Bible, the people of God go beyond the stubborn persistence of Brazilian poet Thiago de Mello, who wrote: "It is dark, but I sing." In the book of psalms, we find terrible situations. Luther wrote:

> Where could one find words of affliction more lamentable and anxious than those which are found in the psalms of lamentation? There [you] will be able to read in the heart of all the saints ... how everything turns dark before the terrible wrath of God.[5]

Meanwhile, the psalm-community always seems to say to us: "It is dark and, precisely for that reason, I sing." If you find this an exaggeration, look at the many psalms of supplication and lament. The situation described is one of anxiety, suffering, and oppression, but the community that sings bases its lament or its shouting on the confidence of salvation that the Lord gives.

---

5. See Martin Luther, "Preface to the Psalter" (1531), as cited by G. Ravasi, *Il Book of Psalms* (Bologna: EDB, 1986), 1:49.

"Sadness Has No End,
but Happiness Does..."[6]

Thus sang Vinícius de Moraes in the Brazilian popular music of the 1960s. The impression, however, that suffering is a bigger part of life than the bits of happiness that life brings was already felt by oppressed people in biblical times. We find the memory and expressions of this experience in the book of Lamentations, for example, or Ecclesiastes (Qoheleth) or Job or other books that reflect the sufferings of Israel, primarily from the fifth century B.C.E. on. But it is in the book of Psalms where these laments acquire the greater force of prayer and receive the strength of hope. Here the lamentation that defines the tone of half of the 150 psalms in the Bible assumes the character of supplication and of such a loving hope that the lament becomes resistance and a path to victory.

When we first began working with base Christian communities, some colleagues involved in the process questioned the use of a number of proposed psalms because of the melody. The melody seemed to them too sad, and the rhythm did not help the communities to dance and to celebrate while singing, as is customary in the *encuentros de caminada*. Personally, I was worried about this, and on various occasions I agreed with the criticism.

It was necessary, however, to learn to appreciate the ways of the poor themselves, who are able to play and to celebrate also with pain. In speaking with various persons of the communities, I found that the songs they knew best by heart and repeated in their prayers were: "From the depths of my sorrow, I call to You, Lord, hear my prayer" (Psalm 130); and "I lift up my eyes to the hills, asking who will help me" (Psalm 121). The first of these is sung in a way that mixes the "depth of the abyss" in the refrain with a more animated style in the verses. In the Center-East of Brazil, Psalm 121 is sung with a melody from the well-known blessing of the pilgrims of the Divine Eternal Father.

The popular refrain states: "Whoever sings, frightens their evils away." In Brazil, we could collect many songs of the oppressed who frighten their evils away by singing. Some years ago, Clementina de Jesús made a record with the songs of slaves (DiscoBan).

---

6. "La tristeza no tiene fin, la felicidad sí...."

Studies have been done of the songs of coffee-cutters in the south of Bahía, and of those who plant cacao, and of the eulogies (*loas*) of the blacks east of Minas. Even in the marketplace and commercial venues, almost all of the music from the rural areas, despite the fact that it is sometimes machista or expresses social prejudice, laughs at life's suffering, and despite the pain transforms sorrow into songs of human communion. This corresponds to a very specific way of praying. In order to enter into the same spirit, it is worthwhile trying to understand better how the biblical psalms embody this way of praying.

"The Heart Has Reasons That Reason Does Not Know"[7]

This popular proverb[8] comes to mind when I think of the diverse interpretations with which exegetes have tried to understand the psalms. I do not know if any other book of the Bible exists in which exegetes have analyzed and deduced such different things without any definitive conclusion being reached.

There are certainly studies that have been almost unanimously accepted. The form-critical school and the contribution of Hermann Gunkel at the beginning of this century, for example, help us to understand the psalms by grouping them into diverse families or literary genres. Even if one gives up the pretension of an exact classification, one may still succeed in further unifying research into the literary sources and the historical "roots" of the psalms.

The discoveries about the origin and life context of many psalms are common knowledge today. No one now thinks that the majority of the psalms are by David. Psalms have been discovered that derive from ancient Canaanite or Egyptian hymns (e.g., Psalms 19A, 29, 104).

Despite the fact that some things remain open, there is a certain consensus that the life context of most of the psalms was worship, specifically, postexilic worship in the restored temple and in the synagogues. It was a time when the Jews were politically dependent on the Persian empire. Their only true autonomy was religious,

---

7. "El corazón tiene razones, que la razón desconoce."
8. The saying is, of course, one of Pascal's *Pensées*. But it appears to have become also part of popular culture in Brazil [trans.].

hence their identity as the people of God was heavily dependent on worship. Thus, the religious and cultural resistance of Israel was organized around the temple and the priests.

As many people already lived in the diaspora outside the country, the local assembly of each city, later called a synagogue, grouped communities around a scribe or rabbi: someone essentially equivalent, in this regard, to our "pastoral agent" or committed lay persons who teach the Bible and coordinate the worship of the Word of God. In the synagogue, animal sacrifice was not permitted as it was in the temple at Jerusalem. Hence it was in the local communities and synagogues that the psalms assumed ever greater importance. Without the ancient sacrifices, the singing of the psalms came to represent the offering of the assembly; through the words of the psalm, the covenant with the Lord God was thus renewed.[9]

The worship in the temple or the use of the psalms in the synagogues was apparently no different from the prayers of Israel's neighboring peoples and other religions in the ancient Near East. If we read the majority of the psalms, we find their contents to be similar to those of many other religions. In most of these other religions, ritual prayer always had three basic elements: petition, praise, and promise (oath) or, frequently, oracles, when people came to consult the pythonesses or priests. These elements are found to various degrees in the prayers of ancient Egypt, in Assyria and Babylon, in the religion of Persia, and, afterward, in Greco-Roman religions.

If we look closely at the psalms, however, we find that these common religious elements have been assimilated insofar as they are able to express or confirm the covenant of the Lord with his people. This relationship between the psalms and the covenant is so strong that a few years ago some authors thought that various psalms originated in solemn rituals devoted to renewal of the covenant. Thus, A. Weiser supposed that in Israel there was in biblical times an annual festival of the covenant. Another scholar, Sigmund Mowinkel, placed the psalms in the context of an annual enthronement festival of Yahweh as King. These

---

9. See Jacques Vermeylen, "Ou en est l'exegèse de psautier?" *Lumière et Vie* 202 (1991): 83.

theses were hotly debated, but never became more than hypotheses. The Bible makes no allusion to these festivals. Without going to such extremes, M. Mannati classifies psalms like Psalm 50 or Psalm 78 and fourteen other psalms as a "ritual psalm of the covenant."[10]

In any case, it is important always to bear in mind that the prayer of the people of God always occurred at three levels: (1) in the family circle; (2) in the local community — whether it was a sanctuary of the interior in preexilic times or, later, the synagogue; and (3) in the temple and national festivals. We can readily recognize those prayers and hymns in the psalter whose origin reflects predominantly a family mentality or the worship of a small northern sanctuary or, quite clearly, the liturgy for the festival of the dedication of the temple.

By virtue of their style and the social context that the texts in general presuppose, it seems that the psalms of individual supplication — our main focus here — had their origin in the prayer and devotions of the "people of the land" in the sanctuaries of the interior; later, they were taken up by the synagogue.[11] This fact is not to be explained through mere logic. The opposite could have occurred, namely, keeping worship at a greater distance from the suffering of the people, which was, in fact, what happened with the temple. These contradictions, however, or dialectical movements are better understood with the heart than through reason.

Thus, by turning over the words of the psalms with affection and by putting myself in step with the movement of contemplation and its relationship with the Lord, I perceive the suffering and resistance of the poorest people who, from a position of religious marginalization, succeeded in making their word be understood as the word of God and the official expression of the cult of the covenant. I believe deeply that the history of this evolution of the psalms is really related to the way in which, at each stage of the history, the communities of the people of God celebrated the covenant.

---

10. See M. Mannati, *Les Psaumes* (Paris: Desclée de Brouwer, 1966), 1:39.
11. See E. Gorstenberger, *Salmos I* (Sinodal, 1982), 42–45.

The Proper Force of a Supplication
Made in the Intimacy of the Covenant

The point is not now to describe the evolution of the theology of the covenant in the Old Testament. In the beginning, the *berith* was a military or strategic agreement between tribes and clans and was, for Israel, a covenant made in Yahweh, that is, in his name. Yahweh was held as guarantor, but the covenant was not seen so much in this light as it was perceived to be a direct relationship with the Lord.

The theology of the covenant is postexilic and late, as we here assume. Whoever prays and ponders the psalms, however, will find in them many of the movements of offering and of the sacrifice of praise and thanksgiving or supplication based on the confidence that is the result of a personal relationship with the Lord. Thus we could say that the people of God first prayed and lived the spirituality or *mística* of the covenant and only after a considerable amount of time thought about it and expressed it rationally.

This dimension of the psalms also constitutes a significant subversion of the vision of God developed thus far in Judaism. In order to see this better, it is enough to recall how a prayer would sound in which the person praying said: "I calmed and quieted my desires, like a child suckled in the arms of its mother" (Ps 131:2). Implicitly, it is plainly understood that the arms of God are meant. Moreover, let us recall the psalms in which the psalmist asks to see the face of God (see, e.g., Ps 27:8–9). Through the psalms, a new understanding emerged of the relation of Israel to the Lord.

In a certain sense, this is a universal path. Saint Basil said: "Just as we are baptized, thus ought we to pray."[12] In the same vein, Saint Augustine taught: "Tell me how you pray and I will tell you how you ought to believe." This is what we say in liberation theology when we state that Latin American theological thought is first of all a spirituality and only later a theology.

I think, for example, of popular religion in Brazil. Many times, the formulation of belief is unclear or contains concepts that we

---

12. See Basil of Caesarea, *Liber de spiritu sancto,* 69–70 (J.-P. Migne, *Patrologia graeca,* 32:193A).

would consider less than biblical. When we see, however, the signs, gestures, and symbols of the people as words of prayer, we discover the same dimension of a loving relationship with the Lord that the Bible calls covenant.

To understand and to pray the psalms as a word of covenant renewal helped me better to understand what characterizes a psalm as prayer and even to see the difference between a psalm and any other biblical song or poem. The distinction between a biblical song and a psalm did not exist in the first stages of biblical history until the time when the psalter was fixed (third–second century B.C.E.). A psalm was simply a song accompanied by a musical instrument called the "psalter." Later, little by little, the musical instrument came to designate the type of song.

Even today, people generally use the tambourine or the accordion for more animated music and use other stringed instruments to accompany more nostalgic or solemn occasions. If we were to review the Hebrew titles of the psalms, we would not be able to determine a single style, content, or perspective that determines when a poem, even when it is included in the psalter, receives the title of psalm. In the psalter there are fifty-seven psalms that have the title *mizmor* (psalm). Among them, there are penitential songs for liturgical processions such as Psalm 15 and Psalm 24. There are others that receive the double title of psalm and song (Psalm 65 and 68). It is obvious, however, that most of these psalms are individual supplications. The person praying in them describes a situation that is anxiety-producing for him or her, and then with confidence addresses the Lord directly (see, e.g., Psalms 1, 3, 4, 5, 6, 12, 13, 22, 51, etc.).

There are many psalms in this *quina* (lament) style that at first glance, as I have already mentioned, seem to be a type of prayer through which, until today, the poor in different religions ask God for protection. By looking at these psalms in a more profound way, however, we may observe that the dominant note is not really one of complaint or lament. It is, rather, the confident certainty that the situation, however bad it may be, can be changed and that the person always has recourse to a weapon, namely, the Lord's promise that he will be faithful to his covenant.

It was precisely in commenting on the psalms that Saint Augustine said the following:

We can count on the Lord as the most faithful of debtors. We cannot give or lend him anything and we have him as our debtor. How? On what basis? Why? Due to his promise. We are faithful to God, if we believe in the promise. God is faithful, because he keeps his promise with us. We cannot pray, "Give us what we lent you," but we can always ask, "Give us what you promised."[13]

Celebrating the Covenant in the Midst of Conflict

When we see a well-established religious community praying or singing most of the psalms in the Bible, we do not realize the incredible situations that these psalms originally described. In Brazil, many people know an adaptation of Psalm 139 much liked by charismatic-type movements: "You know me when I'm seated; you know me when I'm standing up." The people sing enthusiastically: "Wherever I go, wherever I flee," but they sing as if the psalm discussed the religious-emotional conflict of the unconverted individual versus a pious life. But as Father Ivo Storniollo well wrote, Psalm 139, like many other psalms of the persecuted poor, describes the reality of a persecuted person who has been unjustly accused and on whom the death sentence can still be pronounced. For this reason, the poor person goes to the temple of the Lord to implore the Lord's aid and to ask for his salvific intervention. Thus the psalm says: "Lord, you investigate and search me out" (a much stronger expression than "you know me").[14] When praying this prayer, the psalmist is complaining and not praising God for always being with him.

The Jewish tradition attributes Psalm 3 to David when he fled from his son Absalom. The reality described, however, is that of a military blockade: the enemies rightly base their sense of strength on the fact that "God is never going to save him" (v. 3). Nonetheless, the persecuted poor person confidently shouts: "Rise up, Yahweh; save me, my God. From you comes salvation and blessing for your people" (vv. 8–9).

---

13. See Saint Augustine, *Enarrationes in psalmos.*
14. "Tu me investigas y me penetras."

Psalms 6 and 38 and various others reveal a very sick person, surely leprous, who is thought to be a sinner and has been condemned by the community. These psalms, which are joined together in the Christian tradition as penitential, ask the Lord for healing and pardon: "Return, Lord, free me, save me by your love" (Ps 6:5 [4]). "Come rapidly to aid me, my Lord, my salvation" (Ps 38:23).

In this shout by the psalms for salvation can be seen both an attitude of confidence and a reaction of resistance by the poor. Various verses contain a curse or malediction. The psalm says: "Leave me alone, all evil-doers." The original text says: *po'ley 'awen*, those who bring to pass what is in vain. According to some scholars, there were persons who prepared maledictions against the poor or wounded them with the word. Psalm 59 contains an anti-malediction (vv. 13ff.).

There are psalms whose origin was the prayer of a poor man, surely a laborer, who shouted in a sanctuary of the interior: "Raise up, Lord, . . . your hand, do not forget the poor" (Ps 10:12). There are other psalms in which the oppressed people lament: "You handed us over like sheep for the slaughter, you scattered us among the nations" (Ps 44:12). There are psalms of pilgrims who came from the temple to repay promises and others in which the triumphs of kings are remembered.

The expression or word that appears in all these psalms is the term "to save." The verb, which comes from the Hebrew root *yš',* appears, with its variants, in the book of Psalms more than in any other biblical writing. For example, of all the other books of the Bible, the book of Judges is the one that uses this expression most, employing it 21 times. In the book of Psalms, however, the verb appears 326 times.

Perhaps it is worthwhile looking at how this term "to save" appears in Spanish (Portuguese) in our different translations of the Bible. For example, in Psalm 98 a number of our Bibles have the translation: "su diestra le trajo a la victoria," the Lord made his victory known. It is an unfortunate translation; the correct expression would be "his salvation," that is, the action of God who is faithful to the covenant, who comes to liberate, and in this sense who gives us victory.

But salvation has a more profound meaning. To save means

more than to aid or to help. In any religion or ordinary human relationship, any person can shout for "help" or can ask for help from another person or, in the case of prayer, from God. But only someone involved in the relationship of the covenant can call for salvation and shout, "Save me." When a psalm says, "You are the God of my salvation," we cannot simply translate it: "God of my aid."

"Salvation" and "savior" are two terms in the psalms that designate the proper mode of being of the Lord our God:

You are my savior and my God. (Ps 41:7)

You are the God of my salvation. (Ps 25:5)

The Lord is the saving rock, the fortress of salvation. (Ps 31:3)

God gives our salvation, for the glory of his name. (Ps 78:9)

We do not need to go into the terms of rescue and the role of the Lord as defender of the people (*go'el*) in order to see that, in the psalms of supplication, salvation is also the crown of everything more specific and proper that we can ask for from the Lord:

Restore to me the joy of your salvation. (Ps 51:14)

I trust in your mercy, that my heart can rejoice with your salvation. (Ps 13:6[5])

I sigh for your salvation, and your law is my delight. (Ps 119:117)

It is certainly not by accident that one of the best-known psalms most loved by our people is Psalm 91 (90). We frequently find this psalm written on the walls of houses. Our communities sing it, using the beautiful version of Reginaldo Velloso, rightly taking as the refrain the last verse of the psalm: "When you call, I will respond; in affliction, I will be with him, I will liberate, I will glorify, I will show him my salvation." It seems that in the beginning the words of this psalm referred to the situation of a persecuted pilgrim who took refuge in the temple and consulted with the Lord about his fate. The Lord responded with this promise of salvation. Later, but still in the Old Testament, the people of God interpreted these words as referring to the Messiah, whence, according to Matt 4:1–11 and Luke 4:1–13, Satan uses a verse of this psalm to tempt Jesus to use his religious power for his own benefit. In every instance, at issue is the concept of salvation that is basic to this psalm and to all the psalms.

Biblical salvation is the relationship of life and protection given by the Lord and rightly joined to the title of King that is given to Yahweh, whereby he commits himself to save his people. In this sense, he is the "rock of our salvation" (Ps 95:1; 89:27, 29). "You are my King and my God, who decided the salvation of Jacob" (Ps 44:5). Supplication can thus be supported with praise.

There are also psalms that begin with praise and then give way to lamentation and supplication. It is the same movement of trust: the certainty that the Lord is faithful and fulfills for us what he has promised. This makes it possible that the shout of supplication for salvation may already be joined with thanksgiving (Ps 22:23; 40; and others). Furthermore, it is also what we see Jesus experience in terms of prayer. He gave thanks to the Father in front of Lazarus's tomb when Lazarus was still in there, dead. Already before Jesus saw that his prayer had been answered, he gave thanks: "I give you thanks, Father, because you always hear me" (see John 11:41).

This is the root of the resistance and the power to struggle of the persons who pray the psalms. The psalms express our pain, our fragility, our anxieties, and our fears. In addition, they bring with them the power of God's covenant, who is the defender of the small and the liberator of oppressed persons. For this reason, the people of the communities increasingly identify with the psalms. Saint Augustine says: "If the psalm asks, ask with it; if the psalm groans, groan as well; if it hopes, hope deeply; and if it expresses fear, let this fear rise up in you. All these things written there are mirrors of ourselves. It is the Spirit Itself that prays in you."[15]

Let Us Bless the Lord

In various Western liturgical rites from ancient times, the person who leads a service or sings ends by saying as an invitation: "Let us bless the Lord." At first glance, it may seem strange that this invitation is made at the end of the worship service and not at the beginning. But expressed here is the desire that the community,

---

15. See Saint Augustine, *Enarrationes in psalmos* 30.3.1 (Latin).

having heard the Word of the Lord and having received the power that comes from prayer, return to the commitments of everyday life and transform each moment of the day and night into a continuous benediction of the Lord.

This liturgical custom comes to mind as I end this meditation on the psalms as the believer's strong prayer of resistance. You surely know or have already heard about certain prayers which, in certain contexts of Brazilian popular religion, are thought to be strong prayers. Years ago, the groups that combined the traditions of Roman Catholicism with the ancient customs of *feticheras* spoke of the "magical power" of the prayer of Saint Cyprian or the so-called "prayer of the black goat," which contained, in the midst of its words, what they called the "backward creed" or negation of the creed. These prayers are considered "strong" because they deal with secret powers.

For the ancient Christians, the creed had a special value. So, too, today. One day I was celebrating the Sunday Eucharist in a chapel in a popular district. After communion, a man entered the church and without anyone expecting it, shot at another man three times and came toward the altar, shooting in the air. I tried to calm the people down and to see what might be done. An old woman beside me said, "Father, begin to pray aloud the creed of God the Father." I immediately obeyed her and saw that everyone in the church had then followed me. Little by little, we controlled the panic that had been created.

This notion of strong prayer can be magical; in this sense, it is pagan. But it also has a human aspect that is quite comprehensible. In personal relationships, when we know someone well, we know the best way to approach that person and how to get what we want from them. It is as though each person had a weak spot and, in affective relationships, people learn how to work with this.

It may seem strange, but our God has a weak spot, and the person who believes can always defeat him, like Jacob defeated the angel when he asked for a blessing (see Genesis 32). It is in this sense that the psalms are our strong prayer. They celebrate the Lord's promise and invoke the covenant of love that he has made with us.

In the tradition of popular Catholicism, the psalms have not been known as strong prayers. Only in recent years, with the experience of the base Christian communities and the fact that the Bible has become more accessible to the people, has this love of the psalms flourished once again. The person who joins together faith and the people's life and struggle likes the psalms more and more and always prays them. Without knowing the Bible and without joining faith together with the struggle for justice, the people cannot like the psalms.

In the first centuries of the church, it was also this way. Saint Basil of Caesarea tells the story in one of his letters that anyone who passed through the city in the middle of the day heard workers and laborers singing the psalms while they worked. A saint of the same period (fourth century c.e.), Abba Philemon, said:

> I can guarantee you: God impressed in my poor heart the power of the psalms as happened to David. Without the sweetness of the psalms, I could not live. The psalms contain all the Sacred Scriptures.[16]

In any of life's circumstances, even in the midst of the worst conflicts, we must fight today and conquer our land or our right to work and justice. Just as the people of the Bible, we too can take advantage today of the treasure of the psalms and in them sing the covenant of the Lord God, who attends to our supplication "because his mercy is eternal" (see Psalm 136).

---

16. See *The Philokalia,* ed. and trans. G. E. H. Palmer, Philip Sherrard, and Kallistos Ware (London and Boston: Faber and Faber, 1981), 2:347.

9

Matthew

Good News for the Persecuted Poor

CARLOS BRAVO GALLARDO

The gospel narratives as such have been edited intentionally with a structure. They are not a simple conjunction of loose memories lacking purpose. Intentionality is revealed particularly in their structure, which is the author's most characteristic work. To have an interpretative key that permits us to know the structure of the gospel will therefore grant us access to the deepest part of its message and the author's intention.

In this essay I offer a comprehensive key to the interpretation of the gospel of Matthew, proposed as a hypothesis,[1] which I will

---

1. The following is a basic bibliography on the theme: R. Aguirre, *La Iglesia de Antioquía de Siria* (Paris: Desclée de Brouwer, 1988); Pierre Bonnard, *El Evangelio de San Mateo* (Madrid: Cristiandad, 1983); Raymond E. Brown and John P. Meier, *Antioch and Rome: New Testament Cradles of Catholic Christianity* (New York: Paulist, 1983); Beryl David Cohen, *Men at the Crossroads* (South Brunswick, N.J.: Yoseloff, 1970); Shaye J. D. Cohen, *From the Maccabees to the Mishnah* (Philadelphia: Westminster, 1987); Dan Cohen-Sherbok, *The Jewish Heritage* (Oxford and New York: Blackwell, 1988); W. D. Davies, *El sermón de la montaña* (Madrid: Cristiandad, 1975), 104–12; Jacques Dupont, *Las bienaventuranzas,* Cuadernos Bíblicos (Verbo Divino); idem, *Les Béatitudes: Études bibliques,* 2 vols. (Paris, 1969); Sean Freyne, *Galilee, Jesus and the Gospels: Literary Approaches and Historical Investigations* (Philadelphia: Fortress, 1988); Lucas Hendricus Grollenberg, *Visión nueva de la Biblia* (Herder, 1972), 437–41; J. D. Kingsbury, *Matthew as Story* (Philadelphia: Fortress, 1988); Roger Le Deaut, "La vida y el pensamiento judío después del año 70," in George-Grelot, *Introducción crítica al Nuevo Testamento* (Herder, 1982), 1:227–36; J. Mateos and F. Camacho, *El Evangelio de Mateo* (Madrid: Cristiandad, 1981); Warren Matthews, *Abraham Was Their Father* (Macon, Ga.: Mercer University Press, 1981); Louis Monloubou, *El Evangelio de Mateo* (Sal Terrae); Jacob Neusner, *Judaism in the Beginning of Christianity* (Philadelphia: Fortress, 1984); idem, *A Life of Rabban Yohanan ben Zakkai* (Leiden:

formulate in the following fashion: the gospel of Matthew is addressed to a community of poor people who are persecuted and living through a profound crisis of identity in relation to their Jewish past as a consequence of a controversial relationship with the synagogue, which itself is undergoing a restructuring process in connection with Rabbi Yohanan ben Zakkai in Jamnia after the destruction of Jerusalem.[2]

For its original audience, the gospel of Matthew is a gospel of consolation, of christological revelation regarding the identity of Jesus, of ecclesiological revelation about the true Israel, and of ethical revelation about what constitutes the true justice granting access to the kingdom. In this way, the gospel of Matthew seeks to reground their hope and their ability to resist in this situation. The beatitudes are a hermeneutical key for discovering the internal structure and central thread of the gospel.

The Situation of Matthew's Church

Community in Connection with the Temple and Jewish Traditions

After Jesus' death and resurrection, the community of disciples in Jerusalem (later to be the Palestinian church of Syria, from which would be born the important church of Antioch) continued living

---

Brill, 1962); idem, *First-Century Judaism in Crisis: Yohanan ben Zakkai and the Renaissance of Torah* (Nashville: Abingdon, 1975); idem, *From Politics to Piety: The Emergence of Pharisaic Judaism* (Englewood Cliffs, N.J.: Prentice-Hall, 1973); idem, *Between Time and Eternity: The Essentials of Judaism* (Encino, Calif.: Dickenson, 1975); idem, *The Rabbinic Traditions about the Pharisees before 70* (Leiden: Brill, 1971); J. Andrew Overman, *Matthew's Gospel and Formative Judaism: The Social World of the Matthean Community* (Minneapolis: Fortress, 1990); Le Poittevin, *El Evangelio de San Mateo,* Cuadernos Bíblicos (Verbo Divino); J. Schmid, *El Evangelio según San Mateo* (Herder, 1967); Eduard Schweizer, *The Good News according to Matthew* (Atlanta: Knox, 1975); Graham Stanton, ed., *The Interpretation of Matthew* (Philadelphia: Fortress; London: SPCK, 1983); William G. Thompson, *Matthew's Story: Good News for Uncertain Times* (New York: Paulist, 1989); Wolfgang Trilling, *El verdadero Israel* (FAX, 1974).

2. Within this hypothesis, there is yet another question: Is there any relation between Matthew's church and the community of John? Both confront the problem of Pharisaic Judaism, whose point of departure was precisely the synagogue of Jamnia. I believe that two hypotheses can be proposed: either they are the same community that treats the problem of the law in different ways at distinct times, or they are two different communities that confronted the same problem of continuity and rupture with the law and responded in diverse fashion. I only signal here an area of investigation for further exploration.

in the holy city in contact with the temple (Acts 1:4, 12). They continued to observe the Jewish feasts (Acts 2:1) and share the conviction of belonging to the people of God, with whom they shared Jewish religious practices, though on the basis of their conviction that in Jesus the promise of God had been fulfilled.

In this community there began to occur signs and wonders that confirmed it in its faith, but few others dared to join them: it was a community that started to come under suspicion. The disciples suffered persecution at the hands of the Jewish center, due to their proclamation of what had happened in Jesus and his resurrection. But it was a minor persecution, from which they emerged strengthened and content at having suffered for the sake of Jesus.

Identity and Differences

Until this point, we have been dealing with a very homogeneous community that lacked internal differences. Differences begin to present themselves in connection with the problem of identity. Who is the community of salvation? This was a problem because in the community there were Jews from Palestine (Galilee and Judea) and the Diaspora (Cyprus, Asia Minor, Greece, and even Rome). These converted Jews, who would be called "Hellenists," had a more open mind-set and would be key to opening up this still Jewish church. The solution to the increasingly strong tensions was to give the Hellenists their own organization.[3]

Steven was the head of the group of "Hellenists." He understood the source of the conflict that Jesus suffered with the priests because of his own critical position vis-à-vis the temple and the Jewish cult. Accused of blasphemy "against Moses and against God," Steven was stoned around the year 35–36 C.E. (Acts 7). The true persecution unto death was unleashed not so much against the Jews who had converted to Christianity but against the "Hellenists," that is, those of the Jewish race but of Greek culture who, coming from the Diaspora, discovered in the faith in Jesus a greater coherence with their wider way of living the Jewish faith.[4] The persecuted Christians fled and were dispersed throughout Samaria, while Saul the zealous Pharisee continued merciless against them.

---

3. See Aguirre, *Iglesia de Antioquía*, 23.
4. Ibid.

The Universality of the Mission Is Born from Persecution

What happened to Saul does not concern us directly. Let us follow the path of the persecuted. Returning to the Diaspora, they continued preaching wherever they went, although only to Jews (Acts 11:19), because they still had a nationalist vision of salvation. Some of them, however, born in Cyprus and Cirene, broke with this narrow vision and because they were sensitive to the situation of their friends and relatives in the Diaspora, "upon arriving at Antioch began to speak also to the Greeks, announcing to them the Lord Jesus" (Acts 11:20). It is probable that without them the church of Jerusalem would have remained in its narrow vision of salvation reduced to the Israel of which they considered themselves the definitive seed, center of the eschatological pilgrimage of all peoples, but without the dimension of universal mission.[5]

This opening-up of the message to the pagans surprised the church in Jerusalem. Luke gives us a benevolent picture of the Jewish-Christian opposition, but it is probable that the sending of Barnabas was not initially so peaceful an act (see Acts 11:22ff.), judging by the incomprehension that existed after the conversion of other pagans (Acts 10: Peter and Cornelius) and by the problems that Paul had with the Judaizers coming from Jerusalem, including Peter and his posture before James, head of the church in Jerusalem and rigid defender of the Jewish version of Christianity (see Gal 2:11–21). This line was the dominant one in the church at Jerusalem.

Opposition to the Enculturation of the Faith

A double problem exists here. First, there is the inclusion of pagans in the people of God, which ignores the demands of the law of Moses and foregoes the privilege of the people of Israel. Second, there is the reformulation of the faith in Greek categories (Jesus is presented as Kyrios and not so much as Messiah or Son of Man; the kingdom of God is also of secondary importance).[6]

In the face of resistance to the enculturation of the faith, which made it difficult for those who came from the Greco-Roman world to belong to the community of Jesus' followers, the Council of

---

5. Ibid., 30–32.
6. Ibid., 24.

Jerusalem (year 4) offered a solution that sounds a little like a concession made under pressure from Barnabas and Paul (see Acts 15).[7] But all this polemic did not modify the attitude of the Jewish-Christians, who continued to consider themselves Jews and inheritors of the promises; many of them, moreover, troubled the Pauline communities with these demands. Paul severely warned some early Christians against these Judaizers, whom he called "false brothers who infiltrated in order to spy on our freedom — which we have thanks to Jesus Christ — in order to enslave us" (Gal 2:4).

For Paul, it was not only a question of enculturation; the position of the Judaizers had denied Jesus his status as savior (Gal 2:21). The law had been the nursemaid; once the Messiah came, the nursemaid no longer played a role (Gal 3:23–29). In Galatians 5, Paul sets forth his position rather brutally: "If you let yourselves be circumcised, Christ will no longer serve you for anything... those who seek justification by the law have broken with the Messiah and fallen into disfavor.... As Christians, it is all the same to be circumcised or not; what counts is a faith manifest in love."

Distance from Warring Nationalism

During the 40s of the first century C.E., there appears to have been a messianic outbreak (see Acts 5:36) that was violently repressed by the Romans.[8] Cuspius Fadus took prisoner the sons of Judas, head of the Zealots, and ordered them to be crucified.[9] Provocations by the Romans caused the resistance of the Jews to become even more intense: one soldier, for example, provoked the pilgrims at Passover with obscene gestures;[10] another ripped and burned a volume of the Torah.[11] Caligula, who considered himself God, demanded to be worshiped as such, and ordered his image to be set

---

7. It is not clear which of the two versions is the historical one: the more demanding and Jewish version in Acts 15:23–29 or the version in Gal 2:9f., which presupposes the triumph of the more open position of Paul and Barnabas. But it makes one assume a tightening and loosening that probably was not easy.
8. See A. Paul, "La destrucción del templo judío y sus consecuencias," in George-Grelot, *Introducción crítica,* 219. In view is Theudas. See Leipoldt-Grundmann, *El mundo del Nuevo Testamento,* 1:182.
9. Leipoldt-Grundmann, *El mundo del Nuevo Testamento,* 1:182.
10. See Josephus, *bell.* 2.12.1, 224.
11. See Paul, "La destrucción del templo."

up in the temple. But before this order could be executed, Caligula was assassinated in January of 41.[12] Pontius Pilate had earlier introduced some shields with pagan images into the temple and used the temple's money for construction of an aqueduct.[13]

Thus a Jewish nationalism began to ferment that would reach its peak in the 60s. Jewish Christians started to suffer pressure as much from extremists (Zealots) as from traditionalists (Pharisees). Internally, they continued to be disconcerted by the extension of the Christian faith among the pagans. The Christian community found itself in a difficult situation between the dynamic of continuity and of rupture vis-à-vis both the people of the Old Testament and the pagan world.

In 62, there was complicity between the Roman governor, Albinus, and the high priest, such that, in order to deprive the Christian community of its leadership, James, the brother of Jesus, who presided over the church of Jerusalem, was executed, perhaps together with John the son of Zebedee.[14] The Pharisees condemned this action and, at their petition, the high priest was deposed by Agrippa II.[15] Thus the Jews still did not have the attitude of profound rejection toward the Christians that they would come to hold in the 70s.

One of the reasons for later animosity against the Christians was their refusal to join in the anti-Roman activity led by the Zealots. The Zealots considered armed resistance against Rome to be a demand of the Jewish faith, which would later spill over into the Jewish war. The Christians withdrew to Pella in Transjordan.[16] An important group of Pharisees, united around Yohanan ben Zakkai, also opposed the war, because they considered useless any resistance that would seriously compromise the destiny of Israel.[17] This was seen by many as evidence of a lack of solidarity with the national destiny of Israel, and influenced the distancing that occurred

---

12. See Leipoldt-Grundmann, *El mundo del Nuevo Testamento,* 1:181.

13. Ibid., 1:179f.

14. Ibid., 1:183.

15. This shows the closeness that would have existed between the Christian community and the Jews. See ibid.

16. They did so under the guidance of a Jewish-Christian prophet, whose echoes are perhaps still present in the apocalyptic discourse of Mark 13:14ff. See ibid., 1:185.

17. Ibid.

between the Jews and Jewish Christians, among whom probably stood Malcus, a converted scribe.[18]

Reconstruction of the Jewish People around the Law

The destruction of Jerusalem and the temple in 70 C.E. at the hands of Titus was a blow to the faith of both the Jews and the Jewish-Christians. But the Jewish capacity for resistance quickly reorganized around the Pharisees, who then would be the element of cohesion among those who saw in the return to the law the condition for divine pardon and future liberation. A few years later, possibly between 75 and 80, Yohanan ben Zakkai, chief of those who had opposed armed resistance to Rome and who had fled from Jerusalem during the hostilities of 66–70, undertook the huge task of reorganizing the Jews in terms of the synagogue. Jamnia sought to be the beginning of the end of the sectarianism whose diversity had so disturbed the people.

The so-called "Council of Jamnia" (ca. 90 C.E.) represents the most significant event in this process. It signified the establishment of the Rabbinate as the normative body for Judaism. A reasonable hypothesis is that various Jews, including Yohanan ben Zakkai, had settled in Jamnia during or after the siege of Jerusalem. After 70, a rabbinical school was established in Jamnia, with the authorization of Rome, in order to unify fragmented Judaism, thereby forging a coalition.[19] The legendary symbol of Jamnia thus marked the beginning of the task of the social reconstruction of Judaism after the destruction of Jerusalem.

The coalition was supposed to look at the definition, establishment, and legitimation of the Jewish way of life. It established a center for the study of the law and created a Sanhedrin that defined the canon of the Jewish Scriptures; it thereby made Judaism a religion of the law, which was the only thing the Jews had left. *"With the temple in ruins, the priesthood suspended, the ancient institutions in ruins, it was up to the learned Pharisees, specialists in the Torah, to assume responsibility for the destiny of the people."* [20]

---

18. See Bonnard, *Mateo,* 319.

19. "Do not make separate factions, but only one group all together" (Sifre Deut 96).

20. See George-Grelot, *Introducción crítica,* 228.

Who could teach, judge, interpret, and sit in the Sanhedrin was defined; from now on, they would be called "Rabbis."

The Christians returned from Pella, probably entering into contact with the Jewish synagogue, and installed themselves again in what remained of the city whose destruction put their faith to the test as members of the people of God. It is difficult to reconstruct what happened during these obscure years.

During this period of emergency, when basic demands required closing ranks, the need to determine criteria for belonging to the people of God imposed itself. Among other things, the prayers were standardized, including the *birkat-haminim,* a malediction against heretics and Nazarenes, that is, the Syrian-Palestinian church (see Acts 24:5, where the Pharisees refer to the Jewish-Christians as the "sect of the Nazarenes").[21] The Christians had to choose either to be integrated into the synagogue or to abandon it definitively and begin a process of consolidation with a different identity.

An Excommunicated Community without Identity

This excommunication was a blow to the Jewish-Christians' self-understanding of their identity and sense of belonging. They were now thrown out of the synagogues and officially separated from the people of the promises. A severe identity problem presented itself: Who were they? Had they lost everything, the promises, even God? Who, then, was Jesus for God? What were they? Who were the true people of God?

Furthermore, all of this carried with it another consequence. While the empire considered Judaism a *religio licita,* the Jewish-Christians remained unprotected before Rome. The persecution that had afflicted the pagan Christians in the empire could now also incorporate them.

Thus the rupture between the two confessions was consummated. The Christians ceased frequenting *their* synagogues, *their* rabbis, *their* cities. The process of full rupture, however, would be

---

21. The Palestinian recension of the Shemoneh Esreh says: "And may there not be hope for the apostles, and may the insolent kingdom be eradicated soon in our days. And may the Nazarenes and the heretics soon perish and be erased from the book of life and not be registered with the just." See Emil Schürer, *Historia del pueblo judío en tiempos de Jesús,* 2:596.

slower. The idea began to acquire acceptance that if the Christians were the *true Israel,* the mission of the Jewish people had therefore come to an end; the future now belonged to the *ekklesia,* not the *synagogue.* Therefore, the pagan world that had responded to the gospel also formed part of the true Israel; Jesus was the true Messiah.

In this situation, the gospel of Matthew has the following characteristics:

a. It is a *gospel of consolation* for the excommunicated and persecuted Jewish-Christians and their painful problem of identity and synthesis of continuity and rupture with the people of the promise, who due to their hardening have closed themselves to the good news and excluded themselves from the promise.

b. It is a *gospel of revelation:* Jesus is the true Messiah, the final Moses, the culmination of the whole Old Testament (as realization and plenitude and as correction of the law); and they are the true Israel, the true people of God in whose favor God reigns historically. It is a revelation with three dimensions: *theological, christological,* and *ecclesiological.*

c. It is a *gospel of new Christian praxis:* the consequences of this message is the operative projection of a *new justice,* one that will be greater than the justice of the scribes and Pharisees; at the same time, it is a warning to those who continue looking back with nostalgia to former practices and the Jewish past.

The Sermon on the Mount as a Key to Interpretation

The Sermon on the Mount begins with a provocative declaration by Jesus in which the essential part of the identity problem of Matthew's church is touched upon: (a) *who is God and how does God reign in their favor?* (b) *who are the poor?* and (c) *what promise is in question and how does it apply to them?*

The beatitudes have a literary structure that helps one to remember them. Furthermore, the beatitudes are structured in such a way as to place the different elements in a symmetrical relationship to one another. In terms of grammatical form, the beatitudes correspond to one another as follows: the first (a) and the last (a'), the second (b) and the penultimate (b'), the third (c) and the sixth (c'), the fourth (d) and the fifth (d').

This structure, however, does not exist merely to facilitate memory. The *chiastic* or *inclusive* structure also underscores the parallelism in the concepts. The following listing lets us study this parallelism; the terms are translated very literally:

Happy are:

a	the poor in spirit because to them belongs the kingdom of heaven	pres
b	those who suffer because they will be consoled	fut pass
c	those not violent because they will possess the earth as an inheritance	fut act
d	those who suffer hunger and thirst for justice because they will be satisfied	fut pass
d'	those who show pity because they will be pitied	fut pass
c'	those clean in heart because they will see God	fut act
b'	those who make peace because they will be called children of God	fut pass
a'	those persecuted for the sake of justice because... to them belongs the kingdom of heaven	pres

Who Is God and How Does He Reign in Their Favor?

The first and last beatitudes speak of the kingdom of heaven as something that already belongs[22] (in the present) to the group of persons typified by two characteristics that, in the concrete history of the community, are understood to refer to one another: *they are poor with regard to [kata] the spirit and persecuted as a consequence of justice*. Because persecution is something that happens historically, so too is poverty (typified for the moment as "with regard to the spirit," which we shall shortly explain). These two notes refer, then, to something historical suffered by this group of *poor and persecuted* persons.[23]

---

22. Literally, "of them" is the genitive with the verb "to be" and indicates the idea of possession or belonging to.

23. It is very probable that real poor people are historically meant and that, at another level, it is the Christians who were persecuted by the synagogue of Jamnia and constituted the Matthean community. Both terms ought to be interpreted in the same sense. If one speaks here of a real, historical, socioreligious and political persecution of a concrete group of men and women, as the community of Syro-

These persons are not promised an inversion of their situation whereby the poor would be rich and the persecuted become persecutors. It is simply declared that *for them God reigns.*[24] The other six beatitudes then clarify what it means to say that *God reigns.*

If we look at the other six statements, we find a perfect inclusive symmetry (b-c-d / d'-c'-b').[25] The promise is now made for the future, but the future passive is employed in four phrases, while in the other two, the future active. The future passive is the form used

Palestine was persecuted and marginalized by the synagogue of Jamnia (in the *Sitz im Leben* of Matthew's community), their poverty could not be of any other sort, e.g., purely internal or referring to mere intentions. To what reality, then, does the term "spirit" refer? We know that the Hebrew mind-set would have understood such a reference in a way very different from the Western world's dichotomous way of thinking. "Spirit" refers to the totality of the human being characterized by a style of existence that was guided by the spirit and not by the flesh. It has nothing, therefore, to do with a hypothetical "intentional internal detachment" from love of money, which could coexist with the possession of enormous wealth. At least, it does not seem that this could have been good news for any one in Matthew's community, which was essentially a group of persecuted poor persons. Perhaps the most complete translation of the term *ptochoi to pneumati* would have to be a gloss that contained all of the following elements: (a) the root *ptak* makes reference to the poor person's "trembling with fear" in the face of their threatened existence due to the lack of what is needed for life; (b) the full existential dimension of the term *pneuma* (spirit) which refers to the vital force and activity at the center of one's relations and actions, whence a style of existence is established and a way of being in the world and in history is begun; (c) the theocentric dimension that is implicit in the correlative Old Testament concept *anaw,* i.e., the one who is socioeconomically and religiously poor and marginalized and is conscious of his or her marginal social situation, of not counting or being worth anything in society, but of being worth something to God, in whose saving action confidence is placed. Exactly who the "poor in spirit" are is made explicit later on in Matt 6:19–34, when one speaks of the attitude, coherent with the new justice of the kingdom, that one should have vis-à-vis earthly goods; (d) the dimension of religious fidelity to God and not to money: the poor person who breaks with the god Money to accept exclusively the reign of God; (e) the fidelity that the "poor in spirit" are declared to have implies the satisfaction of existential needs, which are mentioned in the subsequent beatitudes. All this provides content for God's action in the world on their behalf: God already intervenes in history, transforming it on behalf of the poor; (f) the double dimension of the present and the future of the kingdom, which appears in the verbal forms of the text, should remain clear, including the already and the not yet, history and eschatology, task and gift.

24. The Nueva Biblia Española translates it adequately: "because they have God for king." We should understand this reign on the basis of the biblical tradition, where the king is the protector of the poor against the rich, the one who ensures respect for the rights of the widow and the orphan, the oppressed and the stranger, who guarantees a form of justice in which the weak need not fear the strong.

25. This symmetry does not appear in the version of the Jerusalem Bible, which changes the order of the second and the third beatitudes. It does not say, however, why it chooses this order instead of the one in Aland's Greek New Testament, which is the version we follow here.

by the Jews to refer to God because of the prohibition against pronouncing God's name. Matthew, who shared this Jewish mentality, has used the formula "kingdom of heaven" to avoid naming God. As a beneficiary of the Hebrew mentality, he also uses the passive form (or "divine passive").

In translating the beatitudes, therefore, "God" should be the subject of the intervening actions whereby God reigns in favor of the poor: it is God who consoles and strengths the suffering one (b), who gives the name of children to those who make peace (b'), who satisfies those who suffer hunger and thirst for justice (d) and who has mercy on those who show mercy to others (d').

Who Are the Poor?

The description of the characteristics of the poor and persecuted is also enriched. They are those who suffer, who make peace, who suffer hunger and thirst for justice, who show mercy to others.

They are "those who suffer" (*penthountes*). The term implies both pain and its exterior manifestation (see Isa 61:1). The community, dispossessed of the promise and its identity as people of God, can, with reason, see itself reflected here.

They are the nonviolent ones (*praeis;* see Ps 37:1, 7, 11), that is, the poor who, having lost their economic independence and freedom because of the greed of evil persons, cannot make their protest count in the face of the dispossession occurring to their land. The community of Matthew, thrown out of the synagogue, has no way to defend itself and appears to lack any right to the promised land, the guarantee of God's fidelity to them. Because they put their hope of redemption in God, the land is offered to them.[26]

These poor persons, deprived of justice, experience the same urgent need for justice as human beings do for food and water when they have hunger and thirst. In terms of the covenant, justice is indispensable for life; only justice makes plenitude possible. To those who stand at the edge of resistance because of the lack of justice, God himself "will satisfy" them, making real the new justice and new social relations.

---

26. The term *praus* reappears in Matt 11:28–30, referring to Jesus, the nonviolent one of humble heart.

These three beatitudes form an inclusive block in which suffering (affliction/hunger and thirst for justice) is related to nonviolent defenselessness that cannot make its rights count. The following three beatitudes form another coherent block: the merciful and those who make peace (actions) do so with an inner attitude, namely, purity of heart.

Other characteristics of the *poor and persecuted* come into view. They are those who act on behalf of their neighbor, motivated by mercy (*eleemones*). The term "mercy" — heart turned toward the "miserable"[27] — presumes efficacy. It is never just a merely inward sensitivity that would remain a vague sentiment of ineffective solidarity in favor of the person in misery. Mercy and fidelity are characteristics of the God who acts for the sake of his people in the Old Testament.

"Purity of heart" obviously has nothing to do with the reductionistic Western understanding of "purity" as related to "chastity." Rather, it has to do with the "innocent hands" of Ps 24:4 or Psalm 15. It presumes that one does not harbor evil intentions to unleash evil actions against one's neighbor, but has the transparency whereby one can confide in the other as the fundamental condition of access to the experience of God. This is made manifest in the person who removes the obstacles from his or her own heart.

Peace is the result of justice and law, of a right relationship with God, with others, with the world, and with oneself. This is God's project, who desires that human history be configured in accordance with this plan. God "calls"[28] (= makes) his children those who work to realize this project of justice in social relations. This is what makes one like God: to act for the sake of human beings out of love.

Those who live for the sake of the new justice of the kingdom will be persecuted as a consequence. The present perfect indicates a reality that has happened in the past and whose effects endure: *dediogmenoi* = those who have been and continue to be persecuted. The passive voice of this form has, as agent-subject, a society organized around exclusive self-affirmation, one centered in power,

---

27. Translator's note: In Spanish, mercy is *misericordia;* "miserable" or poor is *miser.*

28. To give a name is equivalent to entrusting a mission or causing to be in a specified manner.

the making of demands and imposition, that is, practices opposed to those of the beatitudes. To experience the happiness of the kingdom of God and God's justice implies, therefore, and bears in its train the assumption of poverty and persecution, not because of a necessity imposed by God but because of the logic imposed by the same history of oppression of human beings by human beings.

What Promises Are in Question?

Finally, we have two phrases in the active voice, whose subject is the people, namely, the poor and persecuted. They will possess the earth as an inheritance (c) and will see God (c'). The parallel is noteworthy between two things that would seem to be poles apart — as distant as "from heaven to earth." But Jesus declares that possessing the land as an inheritance (the promise that always guided the hope of Israel) and seeing God (the fullness of life, unattainable for human beings, because no one can see God without dying) are equivalent. Israel's possession of the land was a condition for "seeing" God because in the very possession of the land as land it experienced the fidelity of Yahweh to the promise; in a foreign land, on the other hand, access to life proved as difficult for Israel as access to God. Israel never knew how "to sing to God in a foreign land."

The *poor and persecuted,* therefore, not only should not feel themselves put in question through being poor and persecuted, but ought to find in their poverty and persecution the reason for consolation: this is the assurance of belonging to the kingdom.

The Beatitudes: Gospel of Revelation

Up until this point, the text has spoken in the third person plural: "they." The ninth "beatitude" summarizes the message and concretizes it by referring it to the community of disciples: "you." Furthermore, in the living context of the text, which was the persecution suffered by the Christians through the synagogue that had been reorganized in Jamnia, they are given a hermeneutical key for understanding this persecution and discovering the profound identity that exists between *them* and the prophets: "thus *they* treated the prophets before *you.*"

The phrase *en tois ouranois* (you will have a great reward "in heaven") does not refer to the "other life" or "other history" but, as a circumlocution for God, means that God translates into human history God's own manner of being in heaven; God rules on earth in favor of the persecuted and represents their reward. The New Spanish Bible appropriately translates the phrase: "God will give you a great reward." The sign of belonging to God and to God's kingdom and the prophetic dimension of discipleship is thus the persecution that the disciple suffers.

To those who are *poor and persecuted,* therefore, discipleship is being revealed: who God is and how God acts in their favor, who they are, why they are persecuted, and what their destiny is *both today and in the future.* At the same time, it is revealed that they are the true people of God, the people of the covenant, precisely because they follow Jesus, the one persecuted by the synagogue, the one crucified by the political and religious powers and the one resurrected by God.

The Beatitudes: Gospel of the New Christian Praxis

The entire text concludes with two other declarations about the status of the disciple: *as a group, you are all salt,* symbol of the covenant in the Old Testament (see Lev 2:13; Num 18:19). It is an eschatological declaration: you are the salt (of the covenant), the true Israel, no longer the old one. You guarantee the covenant of God with humanity. But if you do not fulfill your role of making the new justice possible, then you will not serve for anything in terms of the covenant.

The second symbol is one of *light.* In the Old Testament, the glory of God was understood as light. No longer is it in the temple or the old Israel, but in the disciples and their works (as described in Matthew 5 and 7–9) that this light is to be seen. Something like this cannot be hidden. The importance of works for Matthew is unquestionable and definitive. In the opposition between orthodoxy and orthopraxis, one is inclined toward the second term as a criterion for recognizing the true Israel.

In opposing the Christian practice to the previous practice of the scribes and Pharisees, which now is no longer in force, the *persecuted poor* are told, after defining their role in planning the law: "Truly I say to you that if your justice is not greater than that of the scribes and Pharisees, you will not enter into the kingdom of heaven" (Matt 5:20). The old justice is insufficient in this time of the kingdom, that is, in this time of reordering relationship with God, with men and women, with the world, and with oneself. It is the time of new relations and a new justice.

Jesus does not annul what there was in the Old Testament law of access to God, but surpasses it in a radical way. The text of the Sermon on the Mount refers, first, to the interpretation of the law on which the scribes based their understanding of justice, and then to the works of piety that constituted the justice of the Pharisees. Because Jesus is more than Moses, Jesus declares that one should interpret the law from the point of view of the radicalness of the future and not the literalness of the past. To this end, Jesus declares, beginning in Matt 5:21, "you have heard it said... but I say to you..." in order to open up new ways of radical justice. Later, Jesus will criticize the piety of the Pharisees, as much for their works as for their spirit: for this reason, he criticizes their manner of prayer, of fasting, and of giving alms. One must do these things out of a new spirit that breaks with the past tied to the letter and dares new unthinkable things such as calling God by his own name: Abba.

The Hope of the Church of the Poor

At present, the poor people of God, the church of the poor, is suffering through a situation similar to that of Matthew's church. Meant by the church of the poor are those communities that, in terms of economics, receive only bad news. On them falls the heaviest weight of the foreign debt, inflation, and the diminished buying power of their daily wage. Their children's future is limited to unemployment or underemployment, marginal housing, and lack of medicine and other essential services, which leaves them unprotected and with a reduced life expectancy.

The earth, God's inheritance for all God's children, is, for the poor, an unreachable dream; even if they succeed in getting some land, it will be inadequate to sustain them, either because of its size or lack of productivity. The opportunities supposed to be provided by an education are a chimera: perhaps a few years of elementary education, which will not equip them with better skills to face the challenges of the world of work.

In the political sphere, they are a people without the ability to make decisions about their own future. Deceived through demagoguery and manipulated by bureaucracies, they are victims of the oppression by the powerful that Jesus already denounced. They are victims of the repressive violence of governments that, in their effort to sustain the privileges of a few, suppress popular discontent through the police and the army. They are victims of the violence of those who get rich through death, whether they be arms-traffickers or drug-traffickers, and also of the violence of those who seek to change this situation through armed resistance. They are also the victims of the violence that is generated among themselves by the unbearable situation of the slums.

Within the church itself, they come last. The attention paid to these people by pastors of the official church is minimal. Because they live in places far from the religious centers with deficient roads and other means of communication, it is impossible for the poor to have access to the Bread that the Father wished to give us Christians. It also makes access to the Word difficult, which remains still unknown to most of us in Latin America.

If native groups or Afro-Americans are considered, the difficulty becomes even greater by virtue of the cultural distance and lack of enculturation of the message of the kingdom in their own cultures (earlier thought to be inferior or unworthy to express the profound Christian mysteries), not to mention the poor experience of evangelization practiced during the last five hundred years and the resistance to it created by the violence of the imposition with which, many times, the gospel of grace and love was supposed to be implanted.

After five hundred years of ecclesial life on this continent, one still finds no autochthonous church with its own face. One still finds, moreover, incomprehension and abandonment by some of the pastors of this church, and even the opposition of ecclesiastical powers to ministers who have identified themselves with the life and suffering of the church of the poor.

In this one-way world configured as such after the triumph of capitalism, the poor have no place. For the world of the market, there exist only consumers and those who provide it with a labor force. The poor are "dysfunctional," because the only thing that they generate is demands, irritations, discontent, and a bad example. They are the "no-bodies."

To these people, the power of this world says: "You are nothing. The reign of life is not for you." Relegated to the margins of humanity, they eventually ask themselves, "Where is my God? What has happened to the promises? Is the kingdom also just a chimera?"

To these people, the gospel of Matthew says: "I congratulate you, persecuted poor, because God continues to keep his decision to reign on your behalf." The beatitudes *console* these poor (a material poverty pertaining to a marginalized and persecuted people, but assumed through faithfulness to the justice of the kingdom for which Jesus was also persecuted). This consolation is based on the *revelation* that not only are these persons not excluded from the promise (of the land and the kingdom of the Father), but that they are actually the nucleus of the true people of God, believers in Jesus, the true Messiah, the new Moses, God-with-us, the revealer of the Father and his project of the kingdom, which *belongs to them* by virtue of the free and willing decision of the Father precisely because they are poor and persecuted.

This is not a gospel that foments passive hope: such would be pure ideology, the kind that has been criticized as an evasion of the pain of existence and the harshness of life. Rather, it is an impulse to become agents of the kingdom. Those who heed it will be the salt of the new covenant and the light of the glory of God for the world insofar as they construct a new world of social relations through *a new praxis of justice:* a praxis that consists in the reordering of relationships with God, with men and women, with the world, and with oneself. In this way, the message of Matthew regrounds hope and the ability to resist in this situation.

The foundation of a spirituality of resistance for the poor and oppressed people of Latin America does not consist of a slogan imposed from without, but rather is the revelation of the more profound reality that exists in their own being and vocation. The church of the poor is the true church of Jesus, constituted by the people who are poor and the pastors who have identified with their fate. God and God's kingdom are their inheritance, the property that they already own.

This is not a form of revelation that leads to *gnosis* or an enclosed world of esoteric knowledge, but to an experience. It is a form of revelation whose realization is not promised only for "the next life," but one that already begins to manifest itself in history, for which it shows new possibilities and to whose transformation it is committed. This revelation establishes an identity within whose sure definition and irrevocable certainties a sectarian spirituality is nonetheless not generated, but rather seeks to speak with the whole world and to "make them disciples" who realize what Jesus taught us while living the new justice.

The true people of God excludes no one. It includes everyone, but places conditions. These conditions are those that the same God had already imposed in the prophetic poem:

Then the wolf shall live with the lamb
and the leopard shall lie down with the kid,
the lion and the bull-calf will graze together, shepherded by a
    child;
the cow shall pasture with the bear, their young shall live
    together,
the lion will eat straw like the ox. . . .
They shall not hurt or destroy in all my holy mountain,
for the land will be full of the knowledge of the Lord.

                                            (Isa 11:6–9)

Not any wolf will live with the lamb, only the one that gives up eating lamb. The lion that enters this new world will be the one that agrees to eat straw like the ox. It is a world constructed in terms of "the least of these." This is the kingdom that has been promised to the persecuted poor. And it ought to be constructed in this world, so that the history of salvation might be — or begin to be — salvation in history. The powerful who do not agree to order their lives in keeping with the life of "the least of these" and do not consider the needs of their smaller brothers and sisters will distance themselves to such a degree from God that, in the end, he will not recognize anything of his own in them.

Therefore, *when the son of man comes in the fulness of his glory, they will gather together before him all* the peoples of the earth. He will separate one from the other, as a shepherd

separates the sheep from the goats.... Then the king will say
to those on his right: "Come, blessed of my Father; inherit the
kingdom prepared for you since the creation of the world. Because I was hungry and you gave me something to eat, I was
thirsty and you gave me something to drink...." Then the
just will reply to him: "Lord, when did we see you hungry
and give you something to eat, or thirsty and give you something to drink?..." And the king will answer them: "I assure
you: every time that you did so to one of these small brothers
and sisters of mine, you did it to me...." And he will say to
those on the left: "Depart from me, you damned... because I
was hungry and you gave me nothing to eat, I was thirsty and
you gave me nothing to drink, I was a stranger and you did
not take me in, I was naked and you did not dress me, sick
and in jail and you did not visit me...." These will also reply:
"Lord, when did we see you hungry or thirsty or a stranger
or naked or sick or in jail and we did not help you?" And
he will answer them: "I assure you that every time that you
neglected to do this to one of these small ones, you neglected
to do it to me." (Matt 25:31–45).

Since then, the good news given to the poor is that God identifies with the future of those who suffer, that he takes them up as
his own, that they are God, his body and living presence able to be
questioned in human history. This is the ultimate foundation of the
identity of the church of the poor, that which constitutes its most
profound consolation and the certainty of its hope: that God has
identified himself with the poor, assuming as his own their cause
and destiny, from the moment in which he made himself one of us,
poor among the poor, Jesus of Nazareth, confirmed by the Father
as Lord and Judge of history.

"Wait for the Day of God's Coming and Do What You Can to Hasten It..." (2 Pet 3:12)

The Non-Pauline Letters as Resistance Literature

RAÚL HUMBERTO LUGO RODRÍGUEZ[1]

·····································

I want to show that the non-Pauline letters — especially James, 1 and 2 Peter, and Jude — can be read as "resistance literature" or literature that produces hope in difficult times. After looking at the genre of exhortation, or paraenesis, I will then study in detail two specific examples: 1 Pet 2:13–17, which treats the relation between Christians and the political authorities; and 2 Peter 3, which concerns the role of utopia in Christian hope. The conclusions should be of interest to our communities that must try to survive when neoliberalism is gaining strength.

Current Status of the Study of the Non-Pauline Letters

When we review the Second Testament, we find a section traditionally labeled "letters" that is located between the book of Acts and Revelation. A first classification of this material makes Saint Paul the author of some of these writings. The *corpus paulinum,* as this collection of letters attributed to Paul is called, has been intensely

---

1. To Father Leonardo Boff, O.F.M., as simple company in solidarity during these moments of crisis for hope.

studied over the years. Alongside these letters, however, the other letters have tended to remain eclipsed. In most commentaries, the latter are presented with the title "the other letters," perhaps because the only thing that they seem to have in common is precisely their non-Pauline character.

Excluding the letter to the Hebrews, which is a theological sermon about the priesthood of Christ, and the letters of John, inserted for study in the collection of Johannine writings, we are left with four writings that more or less have common characteristics. They reflect an important stage in the life of the early Christian communities and offer us a panorama of the different problems that these communities were facing and the enriched and diversified Christian praxis of the first centuries c.e.

Nonetheless, these letters are precisely those that, in the collection of the Second Testament, constitute the most forgotten section for exegetical study and reflection. A sort of "inferiority complex" in the face of the Pauline letters has brought about a lamentable neglect in the investigation of these little gems of early apostolic tradition.

Modern European and North American Scholarship

It is only in the last three decades that there has begun to be increased interest shown by scholars in this part of the Bible, especially the letter of James and 1 Peter.[2] Recently, sociolinguistic studies have considered certain aspects of the letter of James in detail. Clarifying the life context of the social group that stands behind the letter has been extremely useful for those who seek a hermeneutic capable of relating the life of the reader to the experience that has been concretized in the apostolic writing.[3] This same tendency has caused the social-ethical aspects of the letter to be underscored.[4]

---

2. Forthcoming is an article of mine entitled "La Primera Carta de San Pedro en los estudios actuales," in the journal *Efemérides Mexicana* of the Universidad Pontificia de México. We have taken some elements from it for the present work.

3. The most widely available example of this approach is *La carta de Santiago: Lectura sociolingüística,* Cuadernos Bíblicos 65 (Estella: Verbo Divino, 1989).

4. See L. F. Rivera, "Sobre el socialismo de Santiago," *Revista Bíblica* 34 (1972): 3–9; R. S. Bressan, "Culto y compromiso social en Santiago," *Revista Bíblica* 34 (1972): 21–32; L. Alonso Schökel, "Culto y justicia en St 1,26–27," *Bíblica* 56 (1975): 537–44.

1 Peter has also received special attention from different scholars in recent years. The contribution of the sociological reading by J. H. Elliott distinguishes itself with singular brilliance.[5] 2 Peter and Jude have not had the same luck: there are very few modern studies of these letters, though it seems that the use of Jewish apocryphal literature in these writings might allow for some interesting interpretations, especially now that midrashic studies have begun to receive citizenship papers in modern biblical exegesis.

Latin American Scholarship

In Latin American exegesis, studies of the Pauline letters have multiplied,[6] while the non-Pauline letters have hardly been touched by biblical specialists. Apart from the contribution of Elsa Tamez to the study of James,[7] I know of no works especially dedicated to the non-Pauline letters. It is a shame, because the vitality of the communities that stand behind these letters and the diverse problems that they had to face would be a good point of departure for a hermeneutic looking to illuminate the journey of the poorest of the poor on our continent.

It is, therefore, precisely from such a perspective that the present essay has been written. In this essay, we want to show how the paraenesis, or exhortation, proper to the non-Pauline letters is an element that can produce hope during these difficult times for our ecclesial communities when neoliberalism is gaining ground, even within the boundaries of the church.

---

5. See J. H. Elliott, "Ministry and Church Order in the New Testament," *Catholic Biblical Quarterly* 32 (1970): 367–91; idem, *A Home for the Homeless: A Sociological Exegesis of 1 Peter* (Philadelphia: Fortress, 1981); idem, "The Rehabilitation of an Exegetical Stepchild: 1 Peter in Recent Research," in Charles Talbert, ed., *Perspectives on First Peter* (Decatur, Ga.: Mercer University Press, 1986).

6. Suffice it to mention, in the Protestant camp, Elsa Tamez, *Contra toda condena: la justificación por la fe desde los excluidos* (San José, Costa Rica: DEI, 1991). From the Catholic point of view, see J. L. Segundo, *El hombre de hoy ante Jesús de Nazaret*, vol. 2.1 (Madrid: Cristiandad, 1985), esp. the section "La cristología humanista de Pablo." See also the magnificent commentary on the Pauline concepts of "flesh" and "spirit" in the work of Gustavo Gutiérrez, *Beber en su propio pozo* (Lima: CEP, 1983).

7. See Elsa Tamez, *Santiago: lectura latinoamericana de la epístola* (San José, Costa Rica: DEI, 1985).

Paraenesis as Resistance Literature

The Nature of Paraenesis

The literary genre of the non-Pauline letters can be called epistolary only with some difficulty. Their content is rather that of exhortation, or paraenesis, in the style of the Greek diatribe or Jewish moral catechesis. When we speak of paraenesis, we are referring to "passages in which the exhortative tone that is proper to practical moral teaching predominates."[8] There are certain characteristic verbs, stereotypical expressions, linguistic crutches, etc. that give singularity to this literary genre and make its identification possible.

As a genre, paraenesis does not provide a grandiose collection of doctrines, but rather offers a series of recommendations or counsel that was directed at Christians and was surely understood to be a consequence of the doctrines that were preached. Sometimes, the genre utilizes homiletical procedures to fulfill its exhortative function, but always for the purpose of discovering the tight connection between the central affirmations of the faith and the concrete daily life of those to whom it is directed. In this sense, paraenetic literature is a privileged occasion for recognizing that the origins of the Christian life are found not in a rehearsal of doctrine or truths that one must believe, but in practicing a life that coheres with the explicit offering made of one's whole life to Jesus Christ in baptism.

Paraenesis is certainly not a Christian invention. It has been amply demonstrated that there are very close connections between the Christian exhortation of the non-Pauline letters and Hellenistic *Haustafeln*,[9] as well as the exhortative literature of Judaism.[10] Nonetheless, it is precisely the combination of such diverse elements (Old Testament citations, material of Palestinian and Hellenistic backgrounds, etc.) that makes Christian paraenesis a singular phenomenon.

---

8. See L. Alonso Schökel and Flor Serrano, *Diccionario de terminología bíblica* (Madrid: Cristiandad, 1979), 57.

9. Thus the familiar catalogues of duties are called in German exegesis: a type of list of the obligations of every good citizen, which were spread around by the philosophers, especially the Stoics. We find something similar in certain Pauline letters and in 1 Pet 2:11–3:22.

10. For the origin of paraenesis, see E. Lohse, "Paränese und Kerygma im 1. Petrusbrief," *Zeitschrift für die neutestamentliche Wissenschaft* 45 (1954): 68–89. This article still preserves all of its validity.

This combination of elements has its most peculiar touch in the so-called "christologization" of such paraenesis. The counsel in the letters of the Second Testament always has a christological foundation, whether it be extremely brief as in 1 Pet 2:13 where submission to the authorities has as its motivation the "day of the Lord," or large and extensive as in 1 Pet 2:18–25 where the attitude of slaves to their non-Christian owners is based on the attitude of the suffering Christ, whose pains are explained from a catechetical perspective. Thus, paraenesis becomes, for the early Christian community, another means of transmitting the kerygma.[11]

As already mentioned, paraenetic literature is thus a witness to the relationship between theory and practice in early Christian communities; hence the contingent character of these writings, since new problems demanded new and creative responses from each community. Christian doctrine, in turn, is itself enriched from the difficulties that the community experiences, since these difficulties cause new aspects of the message of Christ to be reflected on and/or given emphasis.

Recently there has been a lot of discussion about the provenance of Christian paraenesis, especially the exhortative form of the catalogues of duties. Although some scholars still speak of the influence of Paul on James and Peter, more recent work in this regard recognizes a common catechetical-paraenetic tradition in early Christian proclamation.[12] This means that, just as there was a catechetical collection that took shape around the truths of the faith, beginning with the formulations that little by little came to constitute the *regula fidei,* the common situation of early Christians facing pagan contexts likewise gave rise to a second catechetical collection regarding the norms of conduct needed to respond to concrete problems. This second catechetical collection, which we might call the community's "practical creed" (with the contingency discussed above), can be found in its basic outline in what we now call "paraenetic literature."

---

11. See ibid., 87.

12. See, e.g., Raymond Brown, "Synoptic Parallels in the Epistles and Form-History," *New Testament Studies* 10 (1964): 27–84; E. Best, "1 Peter and the Gospel Tradition," *New Testament Studies* 16 (1969–70): 95–113.

Paraenesis and the Living Situation of the Communities

An important aspect of the paraenesis of the non-Pauline letters is that they make clear the life situation through which the community was passing. Reading them, one can deduce the most pressing problems for these communities. One of the foremost of these problems is the felt necessity of the community that each Christian be equal to the "decent" citizenry of the time in order to allow for the diffusion of the gospel without delay.

This means that Christians had to exert themselves in order to live the novelty of Jesus' message in such a way that, at the same time and without betraying the gospel, they could serve as an example for the men and women of their time. For the Christians, especially those who lived in the Jewish diaspora, this was supposed to guarantee their Christian identity in the midst of society, but at the same time it meant assuming and Christianizing the more genuine values of the human community in which they lived with others. The challenge, then, was to be different without being stand-offish.

Another important element was the renewal of the rupture with the synagogue and the proximity of the persecution that the Roman empire would unleash against early Christian communities. Although we cannot be certain that any passage of the non-Pauline letters is to be situated in a context of violent persecution, it is certain that these communities manifest an evident preoccupation in the face of a model of social life that was hostile to them and a rejection that placed each community in grave danger of social isolation.

This situation, made clear in many passages of the letters to which we are referring, caused very serious problems for early Christian communities: what to do in order to distinguish oneself from the groups that, supported by a specific ideology, fomented anarchy or rebellion; how to show that the subversive force of the Christian life does not necessarily reside in confronting the authorities just because they are authorities, but rather believing in the possibility of ferment from within the social structures, in such a way that there is more and more space for the personal and social novelty that the kingdom came to bring.

Another consequence was the disheartedness and sadness that

seemed forcibly to spread through the ranks of the followers of Jesus Christ. What could be done in order to encourage, console, and help those who felt alone when they faced a power apparently stronger that their own? How could the hope-giving message of the gospel be made known in the midst of conflicts that did nothing but remove hope from the heart of the believers? How should one confront pagan criticism without the whole community feeling undermined or diminished? The apostolic paraenesis tries to reply to all of this.

"Submit to Authority…": An Example from 1 Peter

The Complex Relations between Christians and the Political Authorities

The first text to be looked at more closely from the perspective of paraenetic literature as resistance literature is 1 Pet 2:13–17, which confronts one of the most pressing problems for Christians who lived in non-Palestinian circles in the midst of a social context with a very pronounced state ideology: the problem of the relationship between believers and the civil or political authorities.[13] Beginning with this text and its Pauline parallels,[14] we shall try to imagine the questions that the Christians would have asked themselves in this regard, giving rise to the paraenesis that we are now analyzing.

Should the Christians, reborn to liberty through baptism, submit to the civil authorities? Did the fact that they were now citizens of heaven exempt them from all responsibility to society and the established powers? Is it permitted for Christians to participate in violent revolutionary movements? Up to what point should the diffusion of the gospel make the Christian adapt him- or herself to the values of the world, as long as the gospel continues to be announced without danger or fear?

The author of 1 Peter tries to respond to these and other questions when illustrating in his catalogue of duties what ought to be the "good work" that characterizes the Christians. In so doing,

---

13. I have treated this text in detail in R. Lugo Rodríguez, "El verbo *hypotassein* y la parénesis social de 1 Ped 2, 11–17," *Efemérides Mexicana* 9 (1991): 57–70. Here we mention only some of the conclusions.

14. The same theme is treated in Rom 13:1–7; 1 Tim 2:1–4; Tit 3:1–2.

the same writer confronts the problem of the relationship between Christians and the civil authorities in 1 Pet 2:13–17.

A Triple Argument

In order to situate this paraenetic text (1 Pet 2:13–17) in what we are calling "resistance literature," we are served by three conclusions. Before accepting or rejecting the different accusations that have been made against this text, namely, that its content is "reactionary," we must pay close attention to three elements that contribute to a more complete understanding of the text.

1. The verb *hypotasso,* translated into English by the verb "submit" (Spanish: *someterse*), gives the impression of blind conformity and passivity. Nonetheless, the Greek verb alludes to a voluntary submission[15] and is related in its use to the idea of *order.* The invitation to submit corresponds to the ethical ideal of the Hellenistic world in which "everyone should be in his place in accordance with the role that God has established for him."[16] The same verb, therefore, *cannot be interpreted as blind conformity* at the risk of missing the mind-set of the author; it has, as its opposite, not to "rebel against," but to "stand apart from." The verb *hypotasso* is thus an invitation to participate, to occupy one's own place, not blindly to submit to anything or anyone.

2. This interpretation is supported by the description of the ideal role of the authorities in 1 Pet 2:13b–14. From this, one can deduce "legitimately that *hypotassein* is requested to those authorities (*anthropine ktisei*) who know what their duty is and fulfill it."[17] Although this justification by 1 Peter is bound up with the state ideology of the time (the governor as distributor of individual justice), it could be extended in our day to include those characteristics that are presently ascribed to an exemplary governor, e.g., unreserved respect for human rights.

3. Finally, a piece of textual data that corroborates the intuition that here we have a text of resistance is the mention of freedom in 1 Pet 2:16. We cannot explain how *hypotasso* could mean blind submission, if the author immediately invites the reader

---

15. See G. Kittel and G. Friedrich, eds., *Theologisches Wörterbuch zum Neuen Testament* (Stuttgart: Kohlhammer, 1969), 8:40–41 (*hypotasso*).

16. See R. Fabris, *Lettera de Giacomo e 1a. di Pietro* (Bologna: EDB, 1980), 209.

17. See Lugo Rodríguez, "El verbo *hypotassein*," 64.

to be free in the face of all power and affirms that we are only "slaves of God." The apparent contradiction between "submit" and "be free" indicates that the author is speaking about the position of Christians before the state and authorities that has nothing to do with blind obedience or submissively accepted oppression, but rather with loyal and critical participation, simultaneously respectful, free, and demanding.

These three elements are enough to demonstrate that the paraenesis of 1 Peter, at least in 1 Pet 2:13–17, is in line with the literature of resistance because it is conceived "as an aid to Christians in safeguarding their identity in the midst of a world opposed to the values of the gospel."[18]

"The Principle of Hope": An Example from 2 Peter

Posing the Problem

As already stated, 2 Peter is one of the least studied letters of the Second Testament. This is a shame, because the letter contains — beyond the problem of false teachers, where evident contact exists with the letter of Jude — the priceless witness to one of the conflicts that presented itself to Christians of the second generation, namely, the problem of the delay of the parousia.

To the situation of social pressure, alluded to in 1 Peter, had been added the conflict represented by the fall of Jerusalem without the promise of the second coming of the Teacher being fulfilled. This situation, doubtless the cause of some confusion or at least of inner disheartedness for some members of the community, got worse when the opponents of the Christian project, whom Peter describes as "people who live in accordance with their own evil desires," began to make fun of the hope fed by the preaching of the apostles and the promise of the Lord. This crisis of hope is addressed by the paraenetic text in 2 Peter 3.

The opponents' objection is found in 2 Pet 3:4. It refers to the promises made by Jesus Christ himself regarding his second coming (Matt 10:23; 24:29). The sayings of Jesus about his future coming surely circulated in the Christian community from early on. A first fanatical interpretation created a certain tension, about which

---

18. Ibid., 61.

Paul speaks to us in 1 and 2 Thessalonians. Now the community needed to advance a little more in the long and complex evolution of eschatological hope in order to direct its attention to a more profound — we might say "qualitative" — hope. 2 Peter is the clearest expression of an acute phase in this change of consciousness.

"Hasten the Arrival ... ": Utopia and Resistance

The author of 2 Peter, in order to inspire the resistance of the community in the face of the danger of losing hope, does not accentuate the second coming of Christ, but rather displays a fundamental truth that his adversaries do not seem to recognize, namely, that God is the one who drives history; God began it, God sustains it with God's word, and God will bring it to a definite conclusion.

Although 2 Pet 3:5–7 reveals to us a cosmological conception that is quite confused, in which the author makes allusion either to the stories of Genesis or to diffuse mythological legends or to originally Stoic beliefs,[19] the doctrine of the author is certainly clear: God rules over everything with God's word and directs history in order to prepare for a radical renewal of the universe.

In a second moment (2 Pet 3:8–9, 11–14) the same author gives greater precision to his proposal: God's apparent slowness to fulfill God's promise is due to the complexity of the work of salvation that is not accomplished without the collaboration of men and women and, more than anything else, is due to God's desire to save everyone. Thus the idea of the parousia and its proximity is not abandoned. There will indeed be a second coming that will bring with it the destruction of everything that is defective and wicked and, at the same time, will make possible to infinity everything that is good.

The third step of the author's reflection remains. It is precisely at this level that the text most clearly acquires the characteristics of resistance literature. In the face of emerging realities, the author's proposal is that Christians change the tenor of their hope: emphasis should be placed on an *active* waiting that contributes to the realization of that kingdom which has already begun, but is also still to come. In 2 Pet 3:11–13, the author draws a practical conclusion: active waiting signifies a life of holiness and righteousness.

---

19. See the note in the Jerusalem Bible at 2 Pet 3:10.

Christians should not conduct themselves according to their own criteria or those of the world, but should live in accordance with the commitment that binds them to God. Thus history becomes a period of grace, not a pretext for egotistically losing interest in earthly things.

There is an active participation that God expects from the just in the development of the history of salvation. For this reason, the author can state in 2 Pet 3:12 that the just should help to *hasten* the end-time. Through the mediation of a personal and social life lived in accordance with the kingdom, the time of the parousia is advanced.

At the base of the entire exhortation, as though directing the author's reflection, we find the promise of "the new heaven and the new earth." This expression, taken from Isaiah (65:17; 66:22), refers to the radical and complete messianic renovation to which history will irreversibly come. There will be perfect harmony between humans and God, among human beings themselves, and between humans and the natural world. Justice will then be the fundamental characteristic of creation. All injustice shall be definitively overcome. But it will only be possible to live in the land where justice shall rule (2 Pet 3:13) if we have known and practiced beforehand "the way of justice" (2 Pet 2:21).[20]

The way, then, to nurture community resistance is to derive from the eschatological hope, the utopian kingdom, the energy needed for our *topos,* for here and now, to use the words of the author of 2 Peter, in order to live a life that is "holy, without stain or defect, upright and righteous" (2 Pet 3:14).[21]

Guidelines for a Spirituality of Resistance

Until this point, we have been studying biblical texts. Sometimes arid and apparently out of touch with our own day and age, the paraenetic texts have shown themselves, upon closer inspection, to be indeed sources for a spirituality of resistance. In this concluding series of guidelines, we shall now try to extract the principles

---

20. See E. Cothenet, *Les épîtres de Pierre,* Cahiers Évangile 47 (Paris: du Cerf, 1984).

21. This same message was taken up by Vatican Council II in *Gaudium et Spes,* 39.

that might help us to read the apostolic paraenesis from a Latin American point of view, one that tries to view things from the perspective of the poorest of the poor, from "the underside of history," as Gustavo Gutiérrez would say.

A first element for reflection may be observed in the fact itself that the letters we have analyzed were ever written. This demonstrates that pastoral accompaniment becomes, in times of crisis and disheartedness, an indispensable resource for the people.

Exhortation is not out of fashion; it never will be. Perhaps one of the main contributions a pastor can make to the journey of a Christian community is this support, this accompaniment in solidarity, this staying close to the poorest and their struggles, to the cause of their liberation.[22] It is in this sense that the heroic example of the martyr Archbishop Oscar Romero has remained inscribed in the historical memory of the Latin American people. In promoting a spirituality of resistance for our communities, it is indispensable to highlight the pastor's function of accompaniment as distinct from the one who "works only for money and when he sees the wolf coming, leaves the sheep and flees, because he is not the shepherd and the sheep are not his" (John 10:12).

A second element for reflection stems from the nature of paraenesis itself: to desire the unity of faith and life. We can never insist too much in this regard. It is necessary that, as Latin American Christians, we increasingly take hold of the working dimension of our faith, and always remember that famous phrase of the author of another non-Pauline letter: "So it is with faith alone, that is, if it does not manifest itself *with works,* it is dead" (James 2:17).

Study of the texts of 1 and 2 Peter in particular provides us with a third element for reflection: the importance of maintaining a utopian vision. Both texts analyzed offer to the community an ideal image as an important part of the task of providing encouragement in the midst of various difficulties: in the case of the relationship between Christians and the civil authorities, by presenting the ideal image of a governor; in the case of the parousia, through the inspiration that derives from "the new heaven and the new earth where justice lives."

---

22. For what the pastor (as intellectual) can contribute to the people (as masses), see the magnificent book of J. F. Gómez Hinojosa, *Intelectuales y pueblo* (San José, Costa Rica: DEI, 1988).

This third element acquires special emphasis in the face of the current situation of liberal capitalism's ideological advance and the collapse of the regimes of the ex-Soviet bloc. The proposal of the new "modernity" is a regime of efficiency, of productivity, and of technological advance. It is the negation of other types of values like art, the dignity of the human person, the need not only to produce but also to distribute with justice, etc. But above all it is the death of dreams, the negation of ideals, the orphaning of utopian visions.

This type of mentality, with so many modes of propaganda at its service, threatens to undermine the strength of our communities in their struggle for liberation, especially since it has also infiltrated the bounds of the church itself. For this reason, it is an important and urgent task not to cease to nurture the dream of a new society where justice and equality dwell, where we all have the right to be happy and the opportunity to be brothers and sisters.

To deny this utopian vision is to kill all possibility of resistance. To announce it, on the other hand, is to deny the collapse of the kingdom and to spur on the constructive hope of Christians. Confidence that Jesus is the Lord of history, bringing it to the kingdom's final full communion, can help us to overcome the crises that derive from this new advance of conservative ideology and its apparent triumph.

A final element of reflection comes from the type of exhortation displayed in the letters studied here: resistance is achieved in simple everyday things, not in those that are extraordinary and make waves. Thus in the non-Pauline letters that we have studied, distinctive virtues of Christian heroism are not demanded; rather, positive attitudes are called for, able to confront the disheartedness caused by everyday life. This leads us to view with esteem the numerous small accomplishments of our communities: the increase in solidarity with one another, the times when the exchange of goods heralds the conquest of a new consciousness regarding material things, mutual aid and learning the art of pardoning, the small projects of community work achieved through everyone's support, the increase in respect for differences, the passion evoked in the struggle for justice, etc.

The ability to contemplate the problems that surround us and to allow ourselves to be questioned by them ought not make us lose the contemplative vision of the one who knows that God acts in what is small and in the small ones, and that history, when everything is added up, is not finally written by the powerful, but by simple poor people. I believe that these guidelines for reflection, growing out of an attentive and prayerful reading of the paraenetic texts of the non-Pauline letters, can be of enormous utility in constructing and experiencing a spirituality of resistance and for developing a theology of liberation in times of captivity.

Indexes

······································

INDEX OF ANCIENT NAMES

207

INDEX OF MODERN NAMES

INDEX OF PLACE NAMES

INDEX OF SUBJECTS